Slavery, Mobility, and Networks in Nineteenth-Century Cuba

With a focus on nineteenth-century Cuba, this volume examines understudied forms of mobility and networks that emerged during Second Slavery. After being forcibly taken across the Atlantic, enslaved Africans were moved within Cuba and sometimes sold to owners in other Caribbean islands or the U.S. South. The chapters included in this book, written by historians and literary critics, pay special attention to debates between abolitionists and proslavery ideologues, the ways in which people and ideas moved from the countryside to the city, from one Caribbean Island to the next, and from the United States or the coasts of West Africa to the sugarcane fields. They examine how enslaved persons ran away or were captured and coerced to relocate, how they mobilized information and ideas to ameliorate their situation, and how they were used to advance other people's interests. Movement, these chapters show, was regularly deployed to reinforce enslavement and the suppression of rights, while at times helping people in their struggle for freedom.

This book will be a great resource for academics, researchers, and advanced students of Latin American literature, global slavery, and postcolonial studies. The chapters were originally published in the journal *Atlantic Studies: Global Currents.*

Daylet Domínguez (PhD, Princeton University) is Associate Professor in the Department of Spanish and Portuguese at the University of California, Berkeley, USA.

Víctor Goldgel Carballo (PhD, University of California, Berkeley) is Professor in the Department of Spanish and Portuguese at the University of Wisconsin, Madison, USA.

Slavery, Mobility, and Networks in Nineteenth-Century Cuba

Edited by
Daylet Domínguez and Víctor Goldgel Carballo

LONDON AND NEW YORK

First published 2024
by Routledge
4 Park Square, Milton Park, Abingdon, Oxon OX14 4RN

and by Routledge
605 Third Avenue, New York, NY 10158

Routledge is an imprint of the Taylor & Francis Group, an informa business

British Library Cataloguing in Publication Data
A catalogue record for this book is available from the British Library

ISBN13: 978-1-032-52335-4 (hbk)
ISBN13: 978-1-032-52340-8 (pbk)
ISBN13: 978-1-003-40621-1 (ebk)

DOI: 10.4324/9781003406211

Typeset in Myriad Pro
by Newgen Publishing UK

Publisher's Note
The publisher accepts responsibility for any inconsistencies that may have arisen during the conversion of this book from journal articles to book chapters, namely the inclusion of journal terminology.

Disclaimer
Every effort has been made to contact copyright holders for their permission to reprint material in this book. The publishers would be grateful to hear from any copyright holder who is not here acknowledged and will undertake to rectify any errors or omissions in future editions of this book.

Contents

Citation Information

The chapters in this book were originally published in the journal *Atlantic Studies: Global Currents*, volume 18, issue 1 (2021). When citing this material, please use the original page numbering for each article, as follows:

Introduction

Slavery, mobility, and networks in nineteenth-century Cuba
Daylet Domínguez and Víctor Goldgel Carballo
Atlantic Studies: Global Currents, volume 18, issue 1 (2021), pp. 1–6

Chapter 1

Teresa Mina's journeys: "Slave-moving," mobility, and gender in mid-nineteenth-century Cuba
Camillia Cowling
Atlantic Studies: Global Currents, volume 18, issue 1 (2021), pp. 7–30

Chapter 2

Forty-one years a slave: Agnosia and mobility in nineteenth-century Cuba
Victor Goldgel Carballo
Atlantic Studies: Global Currents, volume 18, issue 1 (2021), pp. 31–50

Chapter 3

Slaveholders in the South: The networks of Cubans and Southerners in the age of the second slavery
Daylet Domínguez
Atlantic Studies: Global Currents, volume 18, issue 1 (2021), pp. 51–69

Chapter 4

Traveling tropes: Race, reconstruction, and "Southern" redemption in The Story of Evangelina Cisneros
Thomas Genova
Atlantic Studies: Global Currents, volume 18, issue 1 (2021), pp. 70–86

Chapter 5

The journey of Víctor Lucumí Chappotín from Saint-Domingue to Cuba: Slavery, autonomy, and property, 1797–1841
Aisnara Perera Díaz and María de los Ángeles Meriño Fuentes
Atlantic Studies: Global Currents, volume 18, issue 1 (2021), pp. 87–107

Chapter 6

Getting locked up to get free in colonial Cuba
Rachel Price
Atlantic Studies: Global Currents, volume 18, issue 1 (2021), pp. 108–128

Notes on Contributors

Camillia Cowling is Associate Professor of Latin American History at the Department of History, University of Warwick, UK. Her research has focused on the history of slavery, emancipation, and gender in Cuba and Brazil.

Daylet Domínguez is Associate Professor in the Department of Spanish and Portuguese at the University of California, Berkeley, USA.

Thomas Genova is Associate Professor of Spanish at the University of Minnesota Morris, USA.

Víctor Goldgel Carballo is Professor in the Department of Spanish and Portuguese at the University of Wisconsin, Madison, USA.

María de los Ángeles Meriño Fuentes is member of the Academia de la Historia de Cuba. She holds a PhD in history.

Aisnara Perera Díaz is member of the Academia de la Historia de Cuba. She holds a PhD in history.

Rachel Price is Associate Professor in the Department of Spanish and Portuguese at Princeton University, USA. Her research interest lies in communication technologies and slavery in the Iberian Atlantic.

Introduction

Daylet Domínguez and Víctor Goldgel Carballo

ABSTRACT
In the midst of a major economic restructuring known as Second Slavery, which included important debates between abolitionist and proslavery interests, Cuba experienced the emergence of new forms of mobility and networks. After being forcibly moved across the Atlantic, enslaved Africans were moved within Cuba, and sometimes sold to owners in other Caribbean islands or the U.S. South. A significant fraction of them managed to move on their own will – running away, defending their right to self-purchase, or making money that would help alleviate their situation or that of their friends and relatives. The essays included in this special issue, written by historians and literary critics, pay special attention to the ways in which human actors and ideas moved from the countryside to the city, from one Caribbean island to the next, and from the United States or the coasts of West Africa to the sugarcane fields.

Introduction

Focusing on nineteenth-century Cuba, this collection of essays brings together scholars working across different disciplines to examine understudied forms of mobility and networks. Our essays examine how enslaved persons moved and were moved; how they ran away or were captured and coerced to relocate; how they mobilized information and ideas to ameliorate their situation, and how they were used to advance other people's interests. Movement was regularly deployed to reinforce enslavement and the suppression of rights, while at times it helped others in their struggles for freedom.[1] All of this happened, to a great extent, thanks to new technological, epistemological, and political networks. In the midst of a major economic restructuring known as Second Slavery,[2] the Atlantic saw the emergence of new sellers and buyers, new navigation strategies implemented to evade British surveillance, and new discursive networks to defend proslavery ideologies against the advance of abolitionism.

As analytical frameworks, the notions of "networks" and "mobility" allow us to examine entanglements of local, transnational, and global histories. They foreground, for example, the material conditions of the massive surge of enslaved Africans that characterizes the period, as well as how physical displacements were differently experienced, represented, and contested. They also show that the big picture of Atlantic slavery is not just about large distances, as in the case of the Middle Passage, and not just about enforced bodily immobility in ships and plantations, but also about enslaved people moving autonomously within the island, owners relocating and selling them, and exiles writing in the United States to move the dial of public opinion. Always already uneven, space calls for modes of analysis that can account for heterogeneous experiences and help us perceive the extent to which mobilities were racialized, gendered, class-based, and intensified or restricted by emotions.[3] While this might be true in general, it was especially the case in Caribbean regions. Cuba, in particular, constitutes a rich example of what geographer Tim Cresswell has called a "constellation of mobility" – that is, "historically and geographically specific formations of movements, narratives about mobility and mobile practices."[4]

Beginning in the first decades of the nineteenth-century, Cuba was a fundamental node in the Atlantic world. In that sense, it constitutes an object of study with an exceptional capacity to highlight wider networks of transatlantic exchanges, as well as the many routes and events that connected the Spanish Caribbean with Saint-Domingue, the United States, Africa, and Europe. As slavery started to decline in other areas as a consequence of the Haitian Revolution and British abolitionism, the Cuban economy grew at a hectic pace, and by the 1830s it had transformed the island into the world's richest colony and its major producer of sugar. This dramatic change, as Ada Ferrer points out, was far from being a contradiction but, rather, the attack on slavery in some parts of the world and its immediate growth in places like Cuba were different manifestations of a global division of labor.[5] Moreover, while in the Francophone and Anglophone Caribbean the apogee of the plantation preceded and was a condition for the constitution of industrial capitalism in Europe, the institutionalization of plantation slavery in Cuba led to the colony's integration into an already existing global market.[6] This integration softened colonial ties with Spain. Even though Cuba would remain under Spanish control until 1898, the United States became its most important economic partner (tellingly, Cuba became a recurrent theme in U.S. foreign policy by the mid-nineteenth century). Within the island, and reflecting the complexities of "racial capitalism," enslaved workers were forced to develop the sophisticated infrastructures required by sugar and other commodities.[7] Until 1886, when it was finally abolished, Cuban slavery coexisted with the most modern technologies, other forms of labor, and liberal ideologies.

Mobility and networks were actually part of the foundational scene of Cuba's economic expansion. As the historian Manuel Moreno Fraginals elucidated in his groundbreaking study *El ingenio*, sugar growth on the island and the type of plantation slavery it entailed were to a certain extent the result of an eminently *criollo* project – unlike the French and English Caribbean colonies, where the process was orchestrated by their respective metropoles. Through a transatlantic journey led by Francisco Arango y Parreño in 1794, a handful of Cuban *criollos* collected information and prepared the logistics. Their trip included visits to sites that had been essential for the articulation of slavery in the past: Portugal (slave trade), England (the steam engine), Barbados and Jamaica (raw sugar). This foundational "intellectual adventure," as Moreno Fraginals called it, helped to establish the new technological and epistemological networks that would drastically escalate slavery in Cuba, devastate its ecology, and transform the ways in which its population experienced mobility.[8] The railroad, for example, began to operate in the colony before it did in the metropolis, while the capital accumulated by those involved in the illegal slave trade was used to establish some of the steamboat routes that served to transport mail, goods, and slaves along the coast.[9]

The consolidation of the Second Slavery main regions – Cuba, the U.S. South, and Brazil – took place amidst of a strong antislavery campaign led by the English, who in 1807 had abolished the slave trade and in 1834 repealed slavery in their Antillean colonies. Between 1815 and 1820, the British Empire also managed to outlaw Spanish, French, and Dutch trafficking. As a result, and until the 1860s, the extensive Cuban coastline became the point of entry of hundreds of thousands of contraband captives, who arrived alongside the news about abolition in other parts of the world. After being forcibly moved across the Atlantic, enslaved Africans were moved within Cuba, and sometimes sold to owners in other Caribbean islands or the U.S. South. A significant fraction of them managed to move on their own will – running away, defending their right to self-purchase, or making money that would help alleviate their situation or that of their friends and relatives.

With abolitionism on the rise, proslavery interests sought to reconfigure hemispheric and transatlantic networks to extend both the trade and slavery well into the second half of the nineteenth century. Ships made in Baltimore or New York, for example, were regularly used for the illegal slave trade, and the same was true of U.S. capital, goods, flags, and papers. Organized around the two most significant themes of Atlantic abolitionism – the natural rights of man and sentimental rhetoric – proslavery arguments circulated extensively through the Atlantic public spheres in the form of speeches, pamphlets, newspaper articles, and manifestos. Sectors of the three most important slave societies of the continent – Cuba (sugar), the U.S. South (cotton) and Brazil (coffee) – formed a common front that has been referred to as "the proslavery international" – a pan-American alliance to stop the advancement of abolitionism.[10] Cubans and Southern planter elites, in particular, were bound together as members of a hemispheric slaveholding class.[11] As they could not afford to isolate themselves from the rest of the world, they engaged in a global struggle through foreign policy, filibustering, and propaganda campaigns that attempted to justify, legitimize, and humanize slavery.[12] Cuban exiles tried to shape the debates on annexation before the Civil War in the hopes of incorporating the island as a new state of the Union. In order to achieve this, they developed a strong print culture in both English and Spanish, which operated as a rich network between Cubans and North Americans.

The essays

Like a contrast dye, movement makes visible not just infrastructures and social relations but also their disparate scales. While this is true of the Atlantic more broadly, the revolution in mobility that marked the Cuban nineteenth-century calls for methods that go beyond national frameworks. In particular, this volume pays attention to the ways in which human actors and ideas moved from the countryside to the city, from one Caribbean island to the next, and from the United States or the coasts of West Africa to the sugarcane fields. Bringing together analyses from historians and literary critics, we aim to highlight different forms of engaging with the archive and of examining the circulation of bodies and texts. In that sense, while focusing on cases specific to Cuba, we will reflect upon many of the broader processes that defined the century: the immediate and long term consequences of the Haitian revolution, the parallel rise of abolitionism and proslavery ideologies, legal and illegal forms of slave trade, U.S. imperialism and its concurrent dreams of a "Caribbean empire," and the Cuban wars of independence, among others. Paying attention to the uneven meanings of mobility, we examine the variety of scales of time and space complicating the very meanings of "region" and "period."

In her essay, which focuses on the life of a West African woman known as Teresa Mina, Camillia Cowling analyzes the journeys that enslaved people made or were forced to make within the island in the context of an expanding economy. As she demonstrates, moving people to new locations – "slave-moving" – was a fundamental slaveholding practice that served disciplinary purposes, severing people from their kin and social ties. The practice was intimately tied to "place-making," or the social construction of space. Unfree people like Teresa, however, sometimes found ways to contest this. Either by foot, steamship, or railway, they moved or were forcibly moved as their masters transferred or sold them, but also as their tried to ameliorate their lot.

Engaging with a previously unstudied testimony, Víctor Goldgel Carballo examines the process by which a black man who claimed to have been born free in the United States was enslaved in Cuba for forty-one years. This process, he shows, depended on the constant reproduction of a certain type of active ignorance – "agnosia" – around the myriad fabrications that bolstered illegal slavery. Going over a series of autonomous movements and strategies through which the man reached the U.S. consulate in his efforts to surmount enslavement, the author directs his attention to one: storytelling. With a focus on 1853 and 1854, Goldgel Carballo's and Cowling's respective essays examine how different forms of coerced and autonomous movement shaped the lives of two individuals who were able to reach Havana and petition for freedom or improvement of their conditions.

In the decades preceding the U.S. Civil War, Cuban and Southern planters, as well as politicians and journalists from the Northern states and the island, began to envision new geopolitical cartographies caused by the expansion of the abolitionist movement driven by England. As Daylet Domínguez demonstrates, Ambrosio Gonzales, Cristóbal Madan, and John Thrasher formed part of a transnational community that resided between Cuba and the southern U.S. states. They comfortably communicated in both languages and aspired to merge these two spaces into a new political domain. In the mid-nineteenth century, she argues, slavery had the capacity to forge hemispheric alliances. Going beyond cultural and political links, these alliances served to imagine alternative futures for the region.

In his essay, Thomas Genova examines the entangled histories of race, gender, and imperialism in U.S. discourse on Evangelina Cisneros, a Cuban creole imprisoned in a Havana jail during her country's War for Independence from Spain. He analyzes the multi-authored *Story of Evangelina Cisneros* (1897), as well as various articles on the affair published in *The New York Journal*, looking at how this text network engages with the events through racial and gender paradigms specific to the post-Reconstruction era. The discursive imbrication between the U.S. and Cuban post-slavery regimes implicit in the Evangelina texts demonstrates how the southward migration of Reconstruction-era racial and gender constructs influenced the rise of formal U.S. imperialism in the Hispanic Caribbean. Genova and Domínguez's essays reveal that, starting in the mid-nineteenth century, the debates around slavery and race in the Caribbean took place in direct conversation with the United States. At this point in history, the idea of a circum-Caribbean began to gain prominence.

In their essay, Aisnara Perera Díaz and María de los Ángeles Meriño Fuentes examine the case of an enslaved Lucumí man named Víctor Chappotín who owned slaves in the 1830s. The few known cases of "slave/owners" in Cuba raise a number of juridical questions (in particular, if such ownership was recognized by the law), but they also prompt the authors to go beyond the dead letter of laws and analyze how this worked in practice. The life of Víctor Chappotín, they show, can teach us a lot about the entangled histories of West Africa, Cuba, and Saint Domingue, the forms of autonomy and social mobility that certain slaves could acquire by remaining loyal to their owners, and the goals and motivations of the free subjects consenting this form of slavery within slavery.

Focusing on the histories of two enslaved Africans sent to prison in Cuba and North Africa in the mid-nineteenth century, Rachel Price considers the ways in which prison could, paradoxically, serve as a path to freedom. The first case deals with the story of Gregorio Lucumí, imprisoned in Cuba for ten years. After being sentenced, his civil status was debated, as colonial authorities sought to discourage others from using incarceration as a conduit to freedom. The second case focuses on Isidoro Gangá, sent to prison in Melilla and who, post-sentence, appealed for freedom via free soil principles. Price studies the implications of understanding prison as a path towards and even a space of freedom in the midst of slavery. Price's and Perera Díaz and Meriño Fuente's essays focus on seemingly paradoxical strategies: slaves who used prison as a path to freedom, and slaves who sought a better life by enslaving others rather than by self-purchase. Like Cowling's and Goldgel Carballo's essays, they also engage with the possibilities and limits of the laws regulating slavery and freedom.

Our contributions, we hope, will also help scholars interested in understanding several key processes affecting slavery and abolition in other parts of the Atlantic; among others, the ways in which enslaved subjects contested hegemonic geographies; how wars and revolutions impacted networks of mobility, prompting the relocation of bodies and the transformation of their juridical statuses; how the abolitionist movement reconfigured the circulation of enslaved people and their strategies in fighting for freedom; and how representations of slavery and abolition taking place in one region could enter in dialogue with similar ones occurring in others.

Notes

1. Cowling, *Conceiving Freedom*, 123–148.
2. Tomich, *Through the Prism of Slavery*; Tomich and Michael Zeuske, "The Second Slavery," 91–100; Zeuske, "Out of the Americas."
3. Ahmed, *The Cultural Politics of Emotion*, 69.
4. Cresswell, "Towards a Politics of Mobility," 17.
5. Ferrer, "Cuban Slavery and Atlantic Antislavery," 134–157.
6. Williams, *Capitalism and Slavery*; Tomich, *Through the Prism of Slavery*, 75–94.
7. Rood, *The Reinvention of Atlantic Slavery*, 10–11.
8. Moreno Fraginals, *El ingenio*, 59–66.
9. García Martínez and Zeuske, *La sublevación esclava en la goleta Amistad*, 131.
10. De Bivar Marquese and Peixoto Parron, "Internacional escravista," 104–110.
11. Pratt Guterl, *American Mediterranean*, 6.
12. Karp, *This Vast Southern Empire*, 2–5.

Disclosure statement

No potential conflict of interest was reported by the author(s).

Bibliography

Ahmed, Sara. *The Cultural Politics of Emotion*. Edinburgh: Edinburgh University Press, 2014.

Cowling, Camillia. *Conceiving Freedom: Women of Colour, Gender, and the Abolition of Slavery in Havana and Rio de Janeiro*. Chapel Hill: University of North Carolina Press, 2013.

Cresswell, Tim. "Towards a Politics of Mobility." *Environment and Planning D: Society and Space* 28 (2010): 17–31.

De Bivar Marquese, Rafael, and Tâmis Peixoto Parron. "Internacional escravista: a política da Segunda Escravidão." *Topoi* 12, no. 23 (July–December 2011): 97–117.

Ferrer, Ada. "Cuban Slavery and Atlantic Antislavery." In *Slavery and Antislavery in Spain's Atlantic Empire*, edited by Josep M. Fradera and Christopher Schmidt-Nowara, 134–157. New York: Berghahn, 2013.

García Martínez, Orlando, and Michael Zeuske. *La sublevación esclava en la goleta Amistad*. La Habana: Unión, 2013.

Karp, Matthew. *This Vast Southern Empire: Slaveholders at the Helm of American Foreign Policy*. Cambridge, MA: Harvard University Press, 2016.

Moreno Fraginals, Manuel. *El ingenio. Complejo económico social cubano del azúcar*. Barcelona: Crítica, 2001.

Pratt Guterl, Matthew. *American Mediterranean: Southern Slaveholders in the Age of Emancipation*. Cambridge, MA: Harvard University Press, 2008.

Rood, Daniel B. *The Reinvention of Atlantic Slavery: Technology, Labor, Race, and Capitalism in the Greater Caribbean*. New York: Oxford University Press, 2017.

Tomich, Dale W. *Through the Prism of Slavery. Labor, Capital, and World Economy*. Lanham, MD: Rowman & Littlefield, 2004.

Tomich, Dale, and Michael Zeuske. "The Second Slavery: Mass Slavery, World Economy and Comparative Microhistories." *Review: A Journal of the Fernand Braudel Center* XXXI, no. 3 (2008): 91–100.

Williams, Eric. *Capitalism and Slavery*. Chapel Hill: University of North Carolina Press, 1944.

Zeuske, Michael. "Out of the Americas: Slave Traders and the *Hidden Atlantic* in the Nineteenth Century." *Atlantic Studies: Global Currents* 15, no. 1 (January 2018): 103–135.

OPEN ACCESS

Teresa Mina's journeys: "Slave-moving," mobility, and gender in mid-nineteenth-century Cuba

Camillia Cowling

ABSTRACT

This study tells the story of a West African woman, Teresa Mina, as a window onto a relatively unexplored aspect of nineteenth-century slavery in Cuba: the journeys around the island of Africans and their descendants, long after surviving the Atlantic slave trade. Coerced displacement, herein termed "slave-moving," was fundamental to the experience of slavery and to the contested process of "place-making" occurring on the island. Slave-moving served the practical needs of the expanding plantation economy, occurring via the same transport systems that enabled faster transfer of commodities, and became a key function of the colonial bureaucracy. It also served disciplinary purposes, deepening slaveholders' power and unfree people's subjection. Its effects were strongly gendered, exposing women to heightened, specific forms of subjugation. Throughout, the essay also explores how unfree people managed to travel of their own will, in ways that were nonetheless closely connected to the processes of slave-moving and place-making.

In late March 1854, a West African woman appeared before a *síndico* (legal representative) in the city of Cienfuegos on Cuba's southern coast.[1] She had been known by other names since her arrival in Cuba, but at this point she was called Teresa. She alleged that, although she had been working as a slave, she was really an *emancipada*: one of the group of Africans recognised as having been brought to Cuba after the slave trade became illegal in 1820. Theoretically, *emancipados* could claim a different status from that of enslaved people, although in practice their conditions differed little.[2] After surviving the horrors of the transatlantic journey, Teresa's movements continued, across western and central Cuba. Initially she spent a period in Havana at the Real Consulado, one of the colonial institutions that routinely used unfree labourers for roadbuilding and other public infrastructure projects. Later, she was transferred by road, to the house of one Doña Tomasa Martínez Valle in Cienfuegos, about 170 miles away, where she worked for around eight years. Her 1854 claim to be an *emancipada* prompted authorities to transfer her, by steamship, back to Havana to assess her claim. Around a month later, they rejected it, concluding she was in fact a slave, and returned her, probably by road, to Martínez Valle in Cienfuegos.

Yet she did not remain there long. In early July, she was discovered by the captain of a local steamship, the *Isabel*, when it docked in the port of Batabanó, due south from Havana.[3] Teresa had fled by steamship, retracing the same journey she had recently made under guard. When questioned, she said that she fled because Martínez Valle had inflicted harsh physical punishments on her – probably in retribution for her legal claim – and, in addition, threatened to move her from urban work in Cienfuegos to a sugar plantation.

Viewed from one angle, Teresa's case is simply one of the many legal claims that cumulatively helped shape unfree workers' relationship to Cuba's fast-changing slave society in the nineteenth century.[4] From the available documents, it is difficult to ascertain her true legal status – whether *emancipada,* as she claimed, or enslaved, as was alleged by one Don Mariano Poey, who testified that he had purchased her legally.[5] Instead, this essay explores a fundamental aspect of Teresa's experiences, shared with countless other unfree workers, which is not generally the central focus of histories of slavery in Cuba: her many journeys across the island. Long after surviving the Atlantic crossing, Teresa spent significant portions of her life travelling hundreds of miles across western Cuba, mostly in conditions of bondage, although at least once in flight. She travelled on the new transport networks that undergirded slavery's intensification and symbolised, for planters, Cuba's "modernity," and took thousands of steps along the island's dilapidated roads, witnessing the fast-changing physical spaces onto which slavery was being re-mapped.

The island Teresa had arrived to after her transatlantic voyage was experiencing an ongoing spatial, as well as social and economic, revolution. Sugar and coffee plantations crept over landscapes where previously forests or small farms had existed, radically altering the natural environment as well as social structures.[6] As ownership of lands and of bound people changed hands, power struggles raged locally over the positions of roads, fences, and plantation boundaries, as planters tried to contain and isolate their slaves while facilitating more efficient movement of goods. The upswing in production was fuelled by a transport revolution, which, by connecting Cuban products to North Atlantic markets, helped produce a "second slavery."[7] Steamship connections sprang up from the 1820s, followed by the first railways in Latin America from 1837, with rail links spreading across much of the island by the time of Teresa's 1854 case.[8] Yet we know more about the movement of sugar or coffee on these transport links than we do about the people – free and unfree – that they also carried. Built by variegated unfree workers, this infrastructure facilitated the coerced – and, sometimes, autonomous – transport of enslaved persons around the island.[9]

With increased movement of goods came an increasingly brisk movement of the human commodities whose work helped produce the material ones. This occurred, in the first instance, through the expanding, though illegal, Atlantic slave trade, which only ended around 1870. There was also a buoyant, if less well-studied, internal slave trade.[10] Far beyond actual sales, bound humans were regularly moved as a result of transfers, loans, rentals, or to accompany moving slaveholders as they went back and forth between city and country residences. Beyond private relationships of power between owners and the enslaved, the work of coercing sick, bound, resistive people into movement, and of documenting, measuring or attempting to control their movements, was also an important feature of the developing colonial bureaucracy. From a distance, the notion of so many people on the move lends itself to aquatic metaphors, recalling the water that surrounded the island – "flows," "waves," or "streams." Closer examination, though, quickly dispels the idea of this movement as easy or "natural." Instead, it reveals the exhaustion and horror of the "work" it required: thousands of steps taken by shackled legs; human hands that built the roads and railways; and minds that remembered the pain of these experiences and the companions lost on the way, even if the documentation left by enslavers referred only to "*brazos*" (arms).[11]

Forced movement also, of course, performed another important function: it helped to turn people into commodities.[12] The purposeful act of making other humans move against their will, as well as the experience of such journeys for the enslaved, are herein referred to as "slave-moving." Contrasting with the more sedentarist "slave-holding," the term underscores how such journeys actively heightened the power of the "slave-movers." Slave-moving destroyed transportees' precariously-established local social identities, and they were often kept in deliberate geographical ignorance, without knowing their route or destination. The subjection involved in forced transport was also gendered. Women transportees, whose occupations were less likely than men's to offer them mobility and access to geographic knowledge, were thrown into male-dominated transport environments, surrounded by male guards and male transport workers, as well as by majority-male fellow transportees.[13] Transport and displacement heightened their vulnerability to violence and sexual assault. Both for men and, particularly, for women, this kind of movement surely cannot be equated with any easy notion of "cosmopolitanism."[14]

Yet Teresa's steamship flight from Cienfuegos, repurposing slavery's transport infrastructure to new ends, also reveals much about enslaved people's ability to move for purposes of their own, even while their journeys were often connected to, rather than completely separable from, slave-moving processes. The purpose of Teresa's journey – avoiding forced displacement to a plantation – was also, in itself, spatial. In a small but collectively significant way, her actions contributed to an ongoing process – highly unequal, but nonetheless contested – of "place-making" in Cuba. "Place-making" emphasises how, rather than being simply pre-existing "co-ordinates on a map," "places" and their significance are made socially, through human movements through them and through relations of power.[15] Existing histories of nineteenth-century Cuba necessarily explore the ever-intensifying movements of sugar, coffee, and humans that propelled the island's transformations; they are by no means guilty of "sedentarism."[16] Nonetheless – as several historians have begun to explore – explicitly shifting our gaze toward the politics of space and human movement can offer fresh perspectives on the particular slave society that they helped produce.[17] People like Teresa did not necessarily think of themselves as "runaways." They may not appear in places where historians have often sought mobile slaves – maroon communities, or runaway advertisements – both of which, incidentally, usually feature more men than women. Yet such people – women as well as men – nonetheless employed mobility in creative, contestatory ways.

After a closer examination of Teresa's case, this study explores and contextualises her journeys in two ways. First, it considers the human histories of the mechanisms of movement that facilitated slavery's expansion and on which Teresa travelled. Second, it examines the broader politics of struggles over human movement as slavery was re-made in mid-nineteenth-century Cuba.[18]

Contested geographies in Teresa's legal claim

A closer look at the competing testimonies of Teresa and Don Mariano Poey, who alleged he had purchased her legally, reveals the politics of movement that affected the lives of *emancipados* and slaves alike. It is not possible to identify conclusively which claim, if either, was correct. Much of the documentation regarding the origins of Africans in Cuba after 1820 is closer to fiction than fact: it was generated in order to establish ownership over people who, as everyone knew, had been brought to the island illegally. In any case, the only difference between an *emancipado* and any other illegally-imported African was that the *emancipados'* ships happened to have been among the small number captured, usually by the British navy, while policing the illegal trade. If, as is likely, Teresa was imported after 1820, her claim to be an *emancipada* certainly appealed to the spirit, at least, of the Anglo-Spanish treaties.

Teresa's declaration was given to Batabanó's *juez pedáneo* (local magistrate) after she was discovered as a stowaway. She stated she was a *emancipada*, of the *Mina* nation, but she was not given an opportunity to detail how she came to hold this status, for example by declaring which ship she arrived on.[19] On reaching Cuba, she said, she was held at the Real Consulado in Havana, "with other *emancipados*" – likely including companions from her Atlantic voyage – for an unspecified period.[20] Later, "the Government ordered that she be removed from that *depósito* [holding], and she was sent overland … until she reached Cienfuegos." There, she was taken to the house of Martínez Valle, for whom, she learned, she would now be working. She remained there until 1854, when her formal claim to be an *emancipada* brought her back to Havana. She was returned to Martínez Valle when the claim was rejected, but soon fled, and stowed away on the *Isabel*. Asked why, she said "around a month ago [Martínez Valle] had punished her severely and, in addition, she planned to send her to work on an Ingenio [sugar plantation]."

Spatial politics loomed large for the *emancipados*. In theory, they were supposed to undergo a period of "tutelage" and then be freed. In practice, few ever really were. There were "innumerable abuses" and "a genuine trade in *emancipados*."[21] *Emancipados* labored on public works projects from at least the early 1830s.[22] Others were assigned for five-year periods to private individuals, who could extend such assignations almost indefinitely, in practice obtaining slave labour at bargain prices. These de facto owners, known as *consignatarios*, often included widows like Martínez Valle, who employed them in urban domestic service.[23] Acting from Havana and other major cities, the British tried to enforce what they saw as the "spirit" of the slave trade treaties by requesting that the *emancipados* be kept in the capital.[24] Yet, increasingly, many met a fate like Teresa's, scattered across the island to locations that included *ingenios*, where they worked alongside slaves. Here, it was harder to trace them, and harder for them to seek redress. Devastating for those involved, this process of forced dispersion nonetheless allowed "fugitive speech" to pass among different categories of unfree workers across the island, as a by-product of slave-moving itself.[25] This oral information was likely responsible for the canny timing of Teresa's claim, which coincided closely with a brief change in Spanish policy relating to the *emancipados*.

The year before Teresa's claim, the decades-long British-Spanish contention over the *emancipados* had taken a new turn, thanks to Spanish need for British support following the election of expansionist U.S. president Franklin Pierce. In March 1853, all *emancipados* who had served at least five years were nominally freed. A new captain general, Juan de la Pezuela, arrived in December to showcase, for British eyes, Spanish determination to tackle the slave trade question. Over the coming months, Pezuela's initiatives sent Cuban slaveholders into a panic. Efforts were made to free those who had served five years, with their *consignatarios* ordered to come forward or face fines. Linked to this was an inflammatory announcement that officials could henceforth search private properties for recently-imported Africans. This would close the legal/spatial loophole that had long facilitated the illegal Atlantic trade: since it was illegal to enter plantations or other private properties to check for new African arrivals, they could be quickly hidden there after disembarking, emerging "re-packaged" as legal possessions. Allowing searches of private properties thus threatened the viability of the entire trade.[26] Unsurprisingly, this opening was quickly closed down, before the end of 1854. Planters raised the spectres of "Africanization" and U.S. annexation, helping prompt Pezuela's replacement by José de la Concha in September 1854.[27] In the end, *emancipados*' fortunes changed little. Nonetheless, the timing of Teresa's petition certainly suggests she got wind of the brief change in policy.

Teresa's account was contradicted by Don Mariano Poey, in a declaration made to the same *juez pedáneo* soon after hers, in early August 1854. Questioned in the comfort of his home, where he was in bed with a mild fever, he declared he had purchased her and others in 1827 from a Havana trading company. Her name was then, he said, Quintina Mina. In 1830, he travelled to the Isla de Pinos in the employ of the Real Hacienda, taking her with him. However, "since the *negra* had become prone to drinking," he sold her to a local man, Don José Pastrana. He swore that "he has not owned, and does not own, any *negra emancipada*; and if Quintina Mina had had such a status, certainly the company ... would never have sold her." A baptism certificate declared that "Teresa, *morena*, the slave of Don Mariano Poy [*sic*], born in Guinea, parents unknown" had been baptised in Nueva Gerona, Isla de Pinos, by a Carmelite priest in 1835. She was then "over 21." Unsurprisingly, no date was given for her entry to Cuba, but it seems likely that she was then a recent arrival, brought by Poey or his associates to the slave-trading hub of the Isla de Pinos. This document stated she was originally named Luiciana – not Quintina – and re-named Teresa upon baptism; this discrepancy was not discussed. Baptism documents were regularly forged, with local priests' collusion, in order to document ownership of illegally-imported people, so we have little reason to trust this one. Certainly, the onus was squarely on Teresa to prove her status, not on Poey or Martínez Valle to prove ownership rights.

Scattered throughout Teresa's and Poey's competing declarations are multiple, sparse references to the hundreds of miles Teresa travelled over several decades of her life in Cuba. Collectively, they demonstrate that – whether she was "really" an *emancipada* or a slave – neither her subjection nor her resistance to it occurred in stasis. Yet – as often happens with infrastructure that moves or contains humans – the processes by which such movements occurred are rendered relatively invisible in these documents.[28] The next section probes the experience of some of these forms of movement, which in turn affected relations of power, from individuals to the level of the colonial state.

Mechanisms of movement

"Learning that the ship was coming here, she boarded it, and fled": Steamships[29]

Teresa was no stranger to the "modern" form of transport that was steamship travel. As well as regular lines linking Cuba with multiple destinations in Europe and the Americas, steamships were of course integral to the expanded African trade that carried her across the Atlantic in the first place. Steamships had also become the fastest means of journeying around the island itself, taking her from Cienfuegos to Batabanó in only a day.[30] Local steamships – *vapores de cabotaje* – operated regularly from the 1830s, first along the more navigable north coast and later along the trickier shallow southern coastline.[31] New wharves and warehouses handled the increased volume of shipping. These grandiose socio-spatial projects deliberately boosted the power of the wealthiest planter-merchants.[32]

As well as free passengers and cargo, local steamships routinely transported bound people. These included recently-arrived cohorts of Africans. Mariano Poey and other traders, for example, received a shipment of newly-imported *congos* a few years after Teresa's claim, who were then transferred to the *cabotaje* ship *Cubano*, which served the slave-trading hubs of Batabanó and the Isla de Pinos.[33] British consuls in Havana confirmed, the year before, that this was a regular use for the *Cubano*.[34] Similarly, a few years before Teresa made her complaint, the British denounced an illegal landing of Africans at Juraguá, near Cienfuegos. Fifty of these people were allegedly transferred to Havana on the local steamship *Cárdenas*.[35]

Steamships also transported unfree people who were not necessarily new arrivals. On 21 August 1864, two *criollo* (Cuban-born) slaves, owned by the same person, embarked at Batabanó for the Isla de Pinos. One had set out from Havana; the other, like Teresa, had journeyed (presumably also by steamship) from Cienfuegos, bearing a pass signed there just the previous day. Perhaps they met a twenty-year-old enslaved African woman on board, who was being transported on the same ship. This young woman was the only person named as female among these groups of male bound transportees. We have no information about whether any attempt was made to segregate male and female bound passengers, but travelling in conditions of bondage, surrounded by unknown men among both captives and crew, undoubtedly posed a heightened threat of rape and sexual abuse, perhaps not dissimilar to some elements of the traumatic Atlantic crossings, where rape was a central part of the process that turned women into slaves.[36] Travelling on the same local ships were other groups of men who were deeply connected to the Atlantic slaving world. In November 1859, for example, a slaver arrived on Cuba's south coast, near the city of Trinidad, from its Atlantic voyage. It deposited its "human cargo," who were soon transported to a nearby sugar estate and sold "to the highest bidder."[37] Then the ship's crew went on to Trinidad and boarded the "Rápido" – one of the regular local steamships serving the southern coast – to continue their journey around the island.[38] Women in bondage who were being transported around the island would do so on vessels alongside such groups of men.

When this gendered context is borne in mind, Teresa's case hints at the heavy price she is likely to have paid for mobility – by sea and also in the other forms it took in her case. After she was discovered on board by the ship's captain at Batabanó, she was taken to the local *juez pedáneo* for questioning. It behoves us to try to reach beyond the formal written record of this procedure, and consider some of the things it does not say. An African woman is discovered by a group of male sailors at a notorious slaving port. She is alone, presumably illiterate, and not a native speaker of Spanish. She has no protection against violence, sexual or otherwise. She is interrogated by three white, powerful, local men. As far as we know, she is the only woman in the room at the time. After the questioning, the men search her physically for any undeclared possessions. The details of how they undertake this are not written down, but we can take some clues from their social world. These men very likely own, and probably trade in, slaves themselves. They are accustomed to handling and evaluating commodified black bodies. This quotidian commodification is hinted at by the trader Mariano Poey's use of the derogatory "*negra*" to describe Teresa, in contrast with the more neutral "*morena*" of the baptism document. Surely, this daily physical familiarity informs the way they carry out their task. By the time they finish, they are "left with no doubt" that she is not hiding anything on her body. The neutrally-worded document can be assumed to mask experiences of physical violation. This was only one of countless dislocations that Teresa had undergone since her arrival on Cuban shores. Each time, she lost any precarious social protection that partial insertion into a local community might have afforded her.

Nonetheless, by throwing groups of different people together, such journeys also allowed clandestine knowledge to travel around the coasts. This information might be about legal openings, like that created by Pezuela's arrival in 1853, or about the business of geography and travel itself. It was surely no coincidence that, soon after her initial steamship voyage to Havana under guard, Teresa escaped by that same route: "[…] learning that the Steamship, was coming [to Batabanó], she fled, and boarded the ship."[39] Her shipboard escape should be located within the broader contestatory world of black Atlantic seafaring mobility.[40] It was common for fugitive slaves in the Hispanic Caribbean to board not just local, but international, ships. In just one example, in 1844, Pedro Rosa, an enslaved black man, fled Puerto Rico by boarding a ship in the coastal city of Ponce, bound for Boston. News of his escape was circulated to Cuba, with an instruction to prevent such incidents, as part of the wider crackdown on black mobility that was then underway in the wake of the Escalera conspiracy.[41] Teresa's story, a decade later, reminds us that such clandestine journeys nonetheless continued to be undertaken. Yet a key difference emerges between the two stories. Pedro Rosa had colluded with, and paid, a black dockworker, who persuaded the ship's captain to allow his passage.[42] Unlike Teresa, he managed to disembark without capture on arrival. In Teresa's case, although she was carrying some money, she was not able to buy the crew and captain's silence. Among many possible reasons, we might speculate that, as a woman, she was less able to draw on the masculine networks that operated in the social worlds of Atlantic ports.

Teresa's story, then, tells us several important things about the steamship journeys taken by unfree people in Cuba. Given the close connections between the social worlds of the Atlantic trade and of local shipping routes, simply boarding a ship exposed non-white travellers to the world of the illegal trade. Women's exposure to specific, heightened forms of violence and displacement further complicates any easy notions of seafaring "cosmopolitanism." Nonetheless, Teresa apparently thought this was a price worth paying. Despite the additional limitations she faced, she had clearly attained some of the geographic knowledge and mobility that seafaring connections offered to those whose more efficient enslavement they were designed to uphold.

"As if a port had opened up at every station": Railways[43]

We do not know what Teresa intended to do after the *Isabel* docked at Batabanó, but it seems unlikely that this was her final destination. If she hoped to live anonymously as an urban runaway, the long shadow of the illegal slave trade in this small port town would make this difficult. If she planned to approach authorities again about her legal status, this was best done in the capital, with which she would have some familiarity and perhaps acquaintances from her time working at the Consulado there. It thus seems likely that, as she had probably done on her recent journey from Cienfuegos to Havana under guard, she planned to make use of the railway line that linked Batabanó to Havana – whether travelling openly as a passenger, or clandestinely as a stowaway as she had on the ship, or by walking along the lines as a means of orientation. Since the line opened in 1843, it had become standard for Havana-bound steam passengers from the south coast to disembark at Batabanó and complete their journey by rail, thus avoiding sea travel around the dangerous waters of the San Antonio Cape. Reflecting the railways' role in "place-making," Batabanó's new position as rail/ shipping interchange meant it mushroomed from a "sad hamlet" into a bustling town.[44]

The railway story most familiar to historians of nineteenth-century Cuba is about sugar. Circumventing the terrible roads and lack of navigable rivers, the railways facilitated the opening of new lands by allowing export commodities – especially sugar – to be transported more efficiently to local ports. The *social* history of these early railways is less well known. Yet the railways brought huge socio-spatial changes, for enslaved and free alike. As well as goods, they carried large numbers of passengers.[45] Getting around the island by rail was a complicated and undesirable, because – like colonial railways elsewhere – separate lines sprang up to facilitate exports from different ports, rather than being planned as a coherent network for internal travel. Nonetheless, by the 1850s, the Havana, Matanzas, and Cárdenas railroad companies agreed to allow passengers to travel on one ticket across all three sets of lines, which were by now interconnected, allowing an integrated, if slow and inconvenient, service across much of the west of the island.[46] Promoting the transformations brought by the railways in 1838, just a year after the first line opened, the Conde de Villanueva, who oversaw the project, discussed passengers first and cargo second. Comparing with the maritime transport on which Cuba had always relied, he enthused:

> As if a port had opened up at each station, the railroad is traversed by inhabitants of the most remote places on the southern coast, while the warehouses are filled with a variety of goods that previously never entered or left the capital.[47]

Everywhere they arrived in the nineteenth century, railways altered the social geographies of those who witnessed or travelled on them. In Cuba, these changes occurred within an expanding slave society. Serving slaveholders' spatial priorities, they were nonetheless built and run with *emancipado*, enslaved, and other unfree labour and knowledge.[48] They offered new routes for the mobility of unfree people, stretching far inland, as well as for the Caribbean and Atlantic seafaring mobility which is better known by historians.

New connections were formed even before the lines began running, through the process of construction itself. As the lines spread out across the countryside, construction workers mingled with the enslaved residents of the plantations alongside them, in ways that were difficult to police. In 1843, for example, the enslaved builders of the line that would later probably bring Teresa from Batabanó to Havana were accused of stealing pigs from the neighbouring *ingenio* Sonora. When questioned, they blamed an escaped slave from one of the neighbouring plantations, who, as they had evidently learned, was at large in the area. Through railway construction, these newcomers to the area had quickly acquired an intimate knowledge of the local slaveholding landscape.[49]

Local enslaved people lived in close proximity to the railway lines, both during and after their construction. Lines ran right into the plantations to facilitate the transport of sugar; freight trains were loaded by enslaved workers. The railways altered the social uses of physical space for ordinary people, whether enslaved or free, creating new navigation routes or meeting-points. One railroad official, in 1837, suggested that a night guard should protect the railway construction materials from "the people of all kinds who, mainly by night, walk along the lines out of curiosity or as a shortcut to where they are going."[50] The lines surely orientated fugitives, as they later would in other "second slavery" settings.[51] By 1844, instructions to railway guards stated that they should pick up escaped slaves found on the lines.[52] Yet this was complicated by the fact that those policing and maintaining the lines were often the enslaved themselves.[53]

Trains were also widely used for slave-moving. They were viewed as a more discreet alternative to shipping for transporting convoys of recently-imported Africans.[54] Twenty newly-imported African children, for example, were reportedly transported to the city of Trinidad by railroad in early July 1861.[55] Other enslaved people travelled individually, with owners or guards. They were exposed to the worst and most dangerous conditions on the railways. In an 1838 crash, caused by a collision with an ox just outside the town of Bejucal, one of the most seriously injured was an enslaved man. He was being transported on behalf of his owner by one Don Juan Antonio Fabré, who explained that the other passengers in his coach had refused to travel with a "*negro*," so they made him perch on the front, exposing him to injury when the train crashed.

At the time of the crash, incidentally, this slave-moving was itself being undertaken, not by steam power, but by slave-power. The engine had broken down earlier in the journey, and the interim solution found – logically enough, in a setting where technical innovation and slave labour were intimately intertwined – was to haul in a group of slaves who worked for the railway company, and make them push. It was the passengers' shouts to them to go faster that led to the accident, when the train ran away down a steep hill.[56] Slave-moving, then, was itself done by slaves. Villanueva's invocation of a natural, aquatic movement of goods and people masked the pain that railway building and operating brought for unfree workers, as well as the difficulties in making the early railways run.

As well as such coerced movements, however, enslaved people sometimes travelled independently by rail. In August 1843, an enslaved man called Juan Gangá journeyed to Havana from Puerta de la Güira, about forty miles southwest of the capital, to seek a new owner in the city for himself and his wife.[57] Carrying a travel licence signed by his owner, he headed first to the town of Bejucal, where he boarded a Havana-bound train. He travelled "without any obstacle impeding his journey, since although at some points before he arrived at Bejucal he was asked to show his licence and told that it was not valid, no-one prevented him from travelling."[58] While the licence was checked on the roads, apparently no-one checked it once he was on the train, suggesting that the "paradise of anarchy" that was Cuban train travel might subject enslaved travellers to less, not more, scrutiny than the roads.[59] Did he purchase a ticket and travel openly? Or did he stow away, hoping to blend in with free passengers of colour? It is very rare to find direct references to enslaved people travelling autonomously on the trains, and perhaps this is because they did not often do so. Yet the documentary silence may also be because it was common enough to be seen as unworthy of comment. Surely, if ever the news of an enslaved West African calmly travelling by train across western Cuba ought to have sparked some discussion among colonial officials, it was in the summer of 1843, as slave rebellions broke out in Matanzas that would shake white slaveholding Cuba to the core – with the important participation of railroad slaves.[60] Yet Juan Gangá's journey was recounted as an incidental detail, not as significant in itself. If enslaved people used the railways – even as a means of orientation, without actually boarding the trains – this might help explain the large numbers of enslaved people who travelled long distances quickly and accurately to arrive in Havana to make legal appeals there.[61] The small towns and villages from which they had travelled were often connected to the capital by rail. Indeed, by 1868, there was no point in Cuba's western region between Artemisa and Macagua that was further than about 12 miles from a railway line.[62]

Juan Gangá probably would not have looked out of place on the trains. Most passengers were not members of the elite; many were probably people of colour. Racial segregation barred passengers of colour from first-class coaches (in a stark reminder of the racialised nature of train travel, animals could accompany their owners in first class, but their slaves could not, except in the case of wet-nurses accompanying their charges).[63] However, people of colour could travel in second and third class. Many passengers were illiterate – unsurprising, perhaps, in a majority illiterate society, but, nonetheless, indicative of their relatively low social status.[64] Often journeying by train for the first time in their lives, passengers continually got lost, and they found the whole concept of train travel difficult. If placards were placed on the trains, indicating their final destination, they were unable to read them; if they did read them, they assumed the train *only* went to that destination, rather than stopping at points in between. Yet, if the stops were called out by a guard, his voice was drowned out by the deafening, disorientating noise of the engines.[65] Fights broke out among drunk passengers, leading to warnings that if policing did not improve, "those of ill intent will think that the trains are a neutral space, where disorder is permissible."[66] On these confusing, chaotic journeys, struggling just to get from place to place in one piece, people of different social groups were obliged to coexist and, surely, share information. In this sense, it was perhaps was not so ambitious of Teresa to think she could travel by train from Batabanó to Havana.

However, the "paradise of anarchy" was surely much less paradisiacal for unaccompanied women travellers than for men like Juan Gangá, whose wife did not accompany him on his railway journey. Regardless of their legal or class status, railway workers appear to have been universally male. It is also likely that the majority of the passengers were men. If guards were unable to prevent fights among drunk male passengers, they were unlikely to prevent bodily violations of travelling women of colour; indeed, there was little to stop them from using their power to commit such acts themselves. Elite women had access to at least some sex-segregated spaces on railway journeys, such as "ladies' waiting-rooms" at some stations where they could pass the long hours between connections; yet the racial segregation on the networks suggests that most women of colour were unable to access these.[67] Given these barriers to non-elite women's travel, it is particularly striking and impressive that – at least in later decades, when railway links proliferated across western Cuba – enslaved people arriving in the capital to make legal petitions were at least as likely to be women as men.[68]

As well as moving sugar, then, the railways were also a slave-moving project. They spilled the blood of unfree workers in their building and running, and served planter "place-making" by facilitating the movement of bound humans. Yet, simultaneously, they also helped to formulate contestatory geographical practices. These practices were necessarily conditioned by gender, with women of colour experiencing significant barriers and gendered threats while travelling. Nonetheless, at least in Teresa's case, it is likely that she still saw the railways as a means, however difficult, to contest her geographic and gendered subjection.

Slavery and roads

Although Teresa experienced the "modern" transport mechanisms that underpinned the sugar revolution, at least one of her long-distance journeys from Havana to Cienfuegos, and possibly as many as three, were made on the island's dilapidated roads. Together, such journeys would involve a distance of at least 504 miles. While injured and sick slaves might be transported by cart or on horseback, the standard method for slave-moving by road was walking, reinforcing associations between slavery and walking that existed in other Caribbean settings.[69] Assuming a brisk pace of three miles per hour, and seven hours per day, that totalled around twenty-four days spent on the road. Yet the tortuous, poorly maintained roads, which were impassable in the rainy season, made such journeys far slower.[70] The Caribbean sun added significant physical hardship. The pitiful sight of groups of shackled, emaciated people – particularly convoys of recently-landed Africans – was commonplace on Cuba's roads, shaping the island's visual landscapes.[71] For the writer, and for most of those readers who will be able to access this essay, the experience of travel has largely been separated from physical exertion. Thus, the exhaustion, hunger and pain of these journeys – the "work" behind the "flows" of commodities and commodified humans – bears emphasising.

Documentary records of slave-moving are stubbornly silent about the conditions in which it occurred, but we should assume it routinely involved violence, including sexual violence.[72] Occasional glimpses suggest a broader hidden picture. In one 1863 case, a white soldier complained that the guards who arrested him on a Havana street one night for being drunk and disorderly had subjected him to a beating. The Gobierno Superior Civil did not stipulate any punishment for the guards, merely admonishing them that "when they capture any military individual, they should treat him with appropriate consideration, without harming him more than is necessary to avoid him running away."[73] Such "consideration" was only proposed for military personnel. We can only guess at the violence perpetrated against unfree transportees. For women like Teresa, spatial and sexual subjection were surely melded together as she traversed the island's streets and roads.

While roads to transport goods and unfree workers were fundamental to the expansion of the slave economy, they often also hampered plantation owners' quest for socio-spatial control. Roads also brought individual slaveholders (and slave-movers) into conflict with the priorities of the colonial state. Disputing heatedly with local officials, travellers, and each other, planters aimed to police the positions and uses of the roads that ran along or across their lands, citing, for example, the danger of their slaves being exposed to external influences.[74] Controlling the roads was necessary to achieve the "closed" plantation ideal, in which owners might completely control workers' movements. This notion was generally closer to fantasy than reality.[75] Yet it was a powerful fantasy nonetheless, linked to planters' self-image, honour, and social status. "Place-making" had strong emotional connotations. One land-holder, for example, complained in 1836 that the position of a road that bordered his lands meant that travellers cut across his lands. Constant invasion by outsiders meant that "the crops are not safe, and nor are the slaves free from the seduction of some of the passers-by [...]" This damaged his "sacred" property rights, making "a mockery of all the hopes he entertained" when he bought the property. Travellers even passed right by the *casa de vivienda* where he and his family lived, risking their "personal modesty."[76] Undesired road usage threatened several elements of his patriarchal control over "place": physical space, bound humans, and subordinate family members.

Like other transport connections, roads were closely bound up with the politics of slave-moving even before they were built. The problem of how to maintain, and expand, Cuba's dilapidated roads led to clashes between individual slaveholders and the institutions of the colonial state. For example, slaveholders who needed the roads nonetheless resisted the exhortations of local officials to contribute some of their slaves, as was customary, for annual road maintenance. They resented the lost work hours, but especially "the damages they suffer when their slaves are removed [from their plantations], the abuses they may commit when not with their overseers, the contact they experience with other slaves, and the distance" of the works from their plantations.[77]

Meanwhile, many roads were more directly built or maintained by forced labour under the remit of colonial state institutions. Thus, as well as spending months of her life walking the roads, Teresa herself may well have contributed to such work during her stints at the Real Consulado in Havana, along with other unfree workers who were not under the direct control of private individuals, such as *emancipados*, runaway slaves or those undergoing litigation or sale, and prisoners.[78] Men were the prime targets for roads and other public works projects, but some women were used too. Doing work defined as primarily "men's" work, in a small female minority among large heterogeneous groups of men, must have exposed women to gendered, as well as racialised, threats and subjection.[79]

The gendered subjection that forced roadbuilding produced becomes clearer if we remember that, while roadbuilding was an urgent practical necessity, it was also a disciplinary tool. Enslaved sugar workers – already doing some of the harshest work on the island – were punished for supposed misdemeanours through roadbuilding. For example, after an alleged conspiracy was uncovered among enslaved plantation workers in Remedios in 1864, the ringleader was sent for hard labour on local public works, which most often meant building roads.[80] This disciplinary function led to significant movement of mixed, but majority male, gangs of workers being transferred serially from work on one form of infrastructure to another. In 1837, for example, the builders of the first railroad on the island included the *emancipado* Francisco Carabalí, who ran away. As a punishment for unsanctioned mobility, he was transferred to roadbuilding.[81] In this very harshest of existences, different groups were thrown together and forced to coexist in new ways, probably sharing geographic and other information as they did so, in ways that would have included someone like Teresa Mina. Nonetheless, she surely paid a heightened gendered price for this peripatetic existence among groups of male strangers.

For Teresa Mina and those like her, then, Cuba's roads held significances far beyond planters' frustrations about the flooding and potholes that prevented them from getting their produce to port. They held memories of gendered physical and psychological pain, generated in their building and maintenance, as well as in forced journeys along them. Nonetheless, they also offered the possibility of contestatory movement for unfree people. When Teresa fled Cienfuegos, it was likely her knowledge of the roads that took her to the port and the waiting ship.

On the way, however, she would also need other forms of knowledge than simply knowing which direction to take. She also needed some appreciation of the complex relationships between human movement and power, which connected individual slaveholders, the workings of the colonial state, and unfree people themselves.

The politics of human movement: slaveholders, the state, and enslaved people

Teresa's legal claim reflected her attempt to use the developing functions of the colonial state to negotiate her situation with her purported owner. This was a spatial interaction as well as a legal one. The state was responsible for several of her coerced journeys, moving her from Cienfuegos to Havana and back again after the claim was rejected. Such journeys occurred through a formal, routinised process. In the journey back to Matanzas, for example, her transfer was signed off by Havana's chief of police and she was then passed to the custody of a police official, then sent back overland (*"por tierra"*), in a movement described in her case as *"por cordillera."* The term's literal meaning, "over a mountain range," is geographic. However, it developed a specific meaning in nineteenth-century Cuba:

> the method of conducting a prisoner, by passing him, with an official document, to the Juez Pedáneo … [who] gives a receipt to the person conducting him, and has the prisoner taken to the next Pedáneo, and so on, until he arrives at his destination.[82]

The daily business of moving bound people, then, combined both infrastructures of transportation and infrastructures of paper.[83] Transport of unfree persons was, by the 1850s, supported by the *rondas* (night patrols) and *guardia civil*, performing what was called *servicio de cordillera*.[84] Slave-moving, then, was closely bound up with the expanding bureaucratic apparatus of the colonial state.[85]

Slave-moving appears to have become more efficient as both transport systems and the colonial bureaucracy expanded. In 1834, for example, twenty years before Teresa's case, the Real Hacienda in Havana assigned six *emancipados* to work as oarsmen on the boats that ferried people and goods back and forth across Matanzas Bay. Of twenty *emancipados* sent from Havana four years previously, six had died. The surviving fourteen were working "day and night" to compensate for their loss, their exhausted bodies serving the port's growing transport needs.[86] Despite the urgency, transporting the additional six people from Havana to Matanzas was very slow – for bureaucratic reasons as much as for transport-related ones. A suitable conductor for them needed to be found, and a passport emitted for him. A delay of almost a year ensued.

By the 1850s, slave-moving seemingly functioned more smoothly. In January 1850, for example, an enslaved *criollo*, Andrés, did like many other enslaved people and somehow travelled from the Pinar del Río tobacco plantation where he normally worked to Havana to allege ill-treatment.[87] Because he was not resident in Havana, the *síndico* there refused to hear his case, and he was returned *"por cordillera"* to Nueva Filipina (now Pinar del Río city), around 130 miles away. He arrived just ten days later. The efficiency of this process is striking, given that the poor, rural folk who often accompanied bound travellers did so for very poor pay and conditions.[88] Frequently illiterate, they carried written permits allowing them to transport their human cargo, which neither they nor their transportees could read.[89]

As the existence of such permits implies, as well as ultimately facilitating slave-moving by private individuals, the colonial state also sought to control it. Such controls reflected, in particular, the ongoing, if very half-hearted, policing of the illegal African trade. Those transporting slaves were required to carry a transit pass for each slave and, from December 1854, an identity document called a *cédula de seguridad*. Mostly, such documents did the opposite of what they were designed to do: instead of clamping down on the African trade, in practice they functioned to create property rights in illegally-imported people, magically transforming them, with a few drops of ink and the requisite bribes, from *bozales* (newly-imported Africans) into *ladinos* (those who had been on the island longer), who could be bought, sold, and – of course – moved.[90] If a modern-day passport acts both to facilitate movement and to document individual identity, these documents could be seen as the opposite of a passport: in facilitating coerced movement, they gave legally free people a new fictive identity as chattel.[91]

While there was general collusion on the trade between the state and owners, there were also frequent moments when owners fell afoul of an overzealous local official, or of the vagaries of Spanish policy. Checks on their slave-moving powers provoked angry outbursts from slaveholders, who saw them as an affront to their authority.[92] This anger reflected another of the crucial functions of slave-moving: it was explicitly understood by slaveholders and slaves alike as a disciplinary tool, at least as powerful as whips or shackles. Geography itself played a part in this. Cuba's archipelago comprises 68,885 square miles; it surpasses the size of all the other Caribbean islands put together.[93] It is dwarfed by the other "second slavery" settings – namely Brazil and the United States – where internal slave trades saw enslaved people transferred thousands of miles.[94] Yet Cuban distances were sufficient that, when traversed in conditions of bondage, they frequently severed people permanently from kin and social ties, creating a "family diaspora" across western Cuba, and forcing them to adapt multiple times to new environments.[95] Such dislocations inspired constant fear in the enslaved, whether or not they ever happened to them personally.[96]

The threat also responded to the divisions understood to exist in this Spanish colonial setting between rural and urban work. In punishment for her legal claim, Teresa's purported owner threatened her not just with displacement in general, but specifically with transfer to a sugar plantation. Such a transfer was dreaded by urban workers in general, but it carried specific weight for a woman who had long worked in a city. It would move her from a space where sex ratios were relatively balanced to one where women were greatly outnumbered by men, and into work that was thought of as being primarily for men.[97] It was this threat of transfer into the "psychic space" of the sugar plantation that helped prompt Teresa to flee, using movement to counter the weaponizing of location by Martínez Valle.[98] Although Teresa said she had no children and was not asked about other family links, we know that the task of trying to preserve family ties through such geographic manoeuvres was undertaken in particular by women.[99]

Thinking about the connections between the ostensibly separate categories of slave-moving and the travel that unfree people undertook independently helps highlight the many similarities between the experience of each kind of movement. Whether they travelled at their own, or at someone else's, initiative, travel for unfree people – especially for women – surely involved "emotional geographies" of trauma and loss.[100] It was dangerous and physically painful, carrying the risk of rape and other violence, displacement, and the severing of kinship ties. It was performed via infrastructure designed by slaveholders, often in the company of people being moved coercively. On the other hand, thinking about the close connections to slave-moving helps us understand why enslaved people's "rival geographies" were so significant.[101] Place, and the human movement that helped "make" it, were not simply the terrain on which these struggles played out, but a vital part of what was being fought over. Enslaved people like Andrés sought to use the geographic distribution of colonial power to their advantage, journeying from distant rural locales to the capital. Here, they could make legal claims to higher authorities, knowing that those of their local towns were often in league with their owners. Temporary relocation to a city was also a strategy for carving out an urban social identity, with the hope of being able to remain there after the case was resolved.[102] This geographic logic was shared with other categories of unfree workers, disseminating across the island through the slave-moving process itself. *Emancipados*, for example, often knew of the British attempts to keep them in Havana and away from the *ingenios*; this kind of knowledge likely influenced Teresa. Her contestatory movements, and those of countless others like her, derived their power precisely from the challenge they presented to slaveholders' ability to weaponize place and human movement.

Conclusion

After Teresa was questioned in Batabanó in July 1854, she still had some slave-moving to endure. First, she was sent about twenty miles by road, probably on foot, to Bejucal, where she was incarcerated. In September 1854, she made a last coerced journey before disappearing from our view, back to Cienfuegos to serve the woman who had brutally punished her and planned to send her to an *ingenio*. Her attempts to resist Martínez Valle's physical and geographic power over her had failed.

Teresa's many journeys around Cuba, long after surviving the Atlantic crossing, were typical experiences for unfree workers on the island in the mid-nineteenth century. In a rapidly-expanding plantation economy, the daily remaking of "place" was inseparable from coerced human movement. The transport systems that permitted the upswing in sugar and other production were also "slave-moving" systems – built and operated with unfree labour, and used in a quotidian way to transport unfree people. The infrastructure of transport was connected to an infrastructure of paper, in the form of the developing colonial bureaucracy: the promotion, control, or prevention of enslaved movement became an important part of colonial officials' jobs. The ability to make other people move was also central to individual slaveholders' power and status, producing collaboration, but also conflict and discord, with state officials. In this sense, "mobility and control over mobility both reflect and reinforce power."[103] It was precisely the challenge to these geographic forms of power that lent such significance to unfree people's creative, diverse efforts to move of their own accord, often using the same infrastructures of transport and paper that were built for their more efficient containment and subjection.

Both slave-moving and unfree people's mobility were gendered phenomena. Whether coerced or in flight, Teresa's journeys were made alongside groups of mostly male strangers, whether fellow transportees or guards. The physical and social vulnerability associated with travel was greater for her than for men, while accessing the geographic and social knowledge that travel might offer was harder. Given the gendered costs of movement, her ability and willingness to move are testament to her resilience and courage.

Teresa's story also suggests that we should be wary of drawing too sharp a line between unfree people's experiences of coerced and autonomous movement. Her aim was probably less to achieve movement in its own right than to use it to do the opposite: to avoid forced transfer to a plantation out of the city she had come to know. Fixity, then, was a resistive, strategic aim, countering the ravages of forced displacement. Thus, if we appreciate the context of slave-moving and place-making, we can form a better understanding of unfree people's diverse uses and experiences of mobility, as well as its contestatory power.

Notes

1. "Expediente sobre haberse embarcado sin licencia en el vapor 'Isabel' la negra Teresa Mina," Archivo Nacional de Cuba (henceforth ANC), Gobierno Superior Civil (GSC), legajo (leg.) 949, expediente (exp.) 33581, 1854. Unless otherwise referenced, all subsequent discussions of Teresa's case are based on this reference. On the *síndicos procuradores*, see Perera and Meriño, *Estrategias de libertad*, vol. 1, 137–180.
2. *Emancipados*, nominally under government "protection," were supposed to receive full freedom after a period of apprenticeship, but very few did. 26,000 people were declared *emancipados* between 1824 and 1866 – under 5% of 551,991 Africans estimated to have been disembarked between 1820 and 1866. Roldán de Montaud, "En los borrosos confines," 161; and Eltis et al., "Estimates."
3. The *Isabel* was one of five local steamship lines that ran along Cuba's southern coast. It ran twice a month between Batabanó and Santiago de Cuba. García de Arboleya, *Manual*, 221.
4. Perera and Meriño, *Estrategias de libertad*; de la Fuente, "Slave Law"; Scott, *Slave Emancipation*; Cowling, *Conceiving Freedom*.
5. The Poeys were a prominent slaveholding Creole family. However, Mariano Poey himself was a little-known Catalan slave trader. Perera and Meriño, *Contrabando de bozales*, 127, 236–237.
6. Balboa, *De los dominios del rey*, chapters 4–5; Funes, *From Rainforest to Cane Field*; On the soil exhaustion that helped create sugar's moving frontier, see *Cartilla práctica*, 14.
7. On the importance of transport networks to the "second slavery," see Tomich, "The Second Slavery"; Tomich and Zeuske, eds., "The Second Slavery," parts 1 and 2; Zeuske, "Out of the Americas."
8. Zanetti and García, *Sugar and Railroads*; Moyano, *La nueva frontera*; Curry-Machado, *Cuban Sugar Industry*.
9. As Daniel Nemser explores, physical infrastructure played a key role in Spanish colonial strategies of governance, organising urban populations along spatial/ racial lines. In Cuba's expanding slave society, infrastructure organised people according to free/ unfree status, as well as race – through its operations once built, but also in the construction process itself. See Nemser, *Infrastructures of Race*.
10. On the Atlantic trade, see Franco, *El comercio clandestino*; Murray, *Odious Commerce*. For the workings of the Atlantic trade within Cuba itself, see Perera and Meriño, *Contrabando de bozales*; Barcia et al., *Una sociedad distinta*. On the internal market see Bergad, Iglesias, and Barcia, *The Cuban Slave Market*; Joda, "Mujer y esclavitud doméstica."
11. For an argument against the language of "flows," which elides "work," see Sedgewick, "Against Flows."
12. Johnson, *Soul by Soul*, chapter 4.
13. For want of a better term, enslaved autonomous movements are referred to herein as "mobility," despite its rather presentist and Global North-ist connotations of choice and ease of travel, which are a world away from Teresa's experiences.
14. On the pitfalls of equating movement with "cosmopolitanism," see Lightfoot, "Plassy Lawrence." For feminist critiques of the tendency to reify mobility, see McDowell, *Gender, Identity*

and *Place*, 208; Wolff, "On the Road Again." On digital sources' privileging of mobile historical subjects, see Putnam, "The Transnational and Text-Searchable."

15. On "place-making," see Sheller and Urry, "New Mobilities Paradigm," 216.
16. Sheller and Urry critiqued "sedentarist" analytical tendencies in the social sciences and a failure "to examine how the spatialities of social life presuppose (and frequently involve conflict over) both the actual and the imagined movement of people from place to place, person to person, event to event ("New Mobilities Paradigm," 208).
17. For example: Cowling, *Conceiving Freedom*, chapter 5; Finch, *Rethinking Slave Rebellion*; García, *Beyond the Walled City*; Lucero, *A Cuban City, Segregated*; Sartorius, "Travel, Passports"; Scott, *Degrees of Freedom*; Tezanos, "Architecture"; Walker, *No More, No More*, chapter 2.
18. This study is part of a forthcoming book, *People Out of Place: Space, Slavery and Human Movement in Nineteenth-Century Cuba*.
19. *Mina*: traded from the Gold Coast, today's Ghana. See Barcia, *Seeds of Insurrection*, 19.
20. On *emancipados* who re-encountered their *carabelas* – companions from the Atlantic voyage – at such institutions, see Perera and Meriño, *Contrabando de bozales*, 213.
21. Roldán, "En los borrosos confines," 169.
22. Havana's Ayuntamiento, Consulado, and Sociedad Patriótica petitioned Madrid to be able to use *emancipados* on public works from at least 1829. Archivo Histórico Nacional, Madrid (AHN), Estado, leg. 8033, exp. 18, 4 November 1829. By 1831, *emancipados* worked on various public works projects: "Estado general que manifiesta el número de los negros emancipados existentes … ," AHN, Estado, leg 8033, exp. 26, doc 4, 12 March 1831.
23. Roldán, "En los borrosos confines," 168.
24. For example, George Villiers to D. Eusebio de Bardají y Azara, Madrid, 25 August 1837, AHN, Estado, leg. 8035, exp. 11, doc. 2.
25. On "fugitive speech," see Derby, "Beyond Fugitive Speech," 127.
26. Perera and Meriño, *Contrabando de bozales*, 15–19, 104–110; Roldán, "En los borrosos confines," 180–182.
27. Urban, "Africanization of Cuba Scare."
28. On infrastructure's tendency to become "invisible" – at least for some people at some moments – see Nemser, *Infrastructures of Race*, 16–17.
29. "Expediente sobre haberse embarcado sin licencia en el vapor 'Isabel' la negra Teresa Mina," ANC, GSC, leg. 949, exp. 33581, 1854.
30. By 1859, there were eleven steamship lines. Most operated on either the north or south coast; two linked the two coasts. García de Arboleya, *Manual*, 205; Zanetti and García, *Sugar and Railroads*, 412 (n. 20). For the social, financial and ecological transformation wrought by steamships in another "second slavery" setting, see Johnson, *River of Dark Dreams*, chapter 3.
31. García de Arboleya, *Manual*, 217.
32. Rood, *The Reinvention of Atlantic Slavery*, chapter 3.
33. Perera and Meriño, *Contrabando de bozales*, 236–237. *Congo*: a broad term for a person embarked from West-Central Africa. Like other "nation" names, this encompassed a vast multiplicity of ethnic and linguistic groups. See Finch, *Rethinking Slave Rebellion*, 24–25, 237, n. 22–24.
34. John V. Crawford to Captain General, Havana, 1 November 1860, National Archives, UK (NA), FO 313/54.
35. The authorities in Havana concluded, unsurprisingly, that this was not a shipment of newly-arrived Africans, but simply of 50 "legal" slaves, being transported around the island with the correct *pasaportes* having been emitted for them. AHN, Estado, leg. 8044, exp. 11, doc. 3, 27 November 1850.
36. Dorsey, "It Hurt Very Much."
37. Joseph T. Crawford to Captain General, Havana, 29 November 1859, NA, FO 313/54, p.1.
38. Ibid.
39. The *Isabel*, the ship Teresa boarded, was listed in 1859 as connecting Batabanó with Santiago de Cuba, operating along the south coast twice a month. García de Arboleya, *Manual*, 221.
40. Among numerous references, the classic text remains Scott, *Common Wind*.
41. On this crackdown, see Reid-Vázquez, *Year of the Lash*.

42. AHN, Estado, Leg. 8039, exp 8, 1844, doc. 1, p. 2.
43. Conde de Villanueva to Antonio María de Escovedo, Havana, 29 November 1838, in: "Expediente sobre la llegada del Camino de Hierro a Güines, comunicada por el Ingeniero Director a los Sres. De la Comisión," ANC, Real Consulado y Junta de Fomento (henceforth JF), leg. 131, exp. 6422, 1838.
44. Zanetti and García, *Sugar and Railroads*, 53, 102. An inn in Batabanó even offered "meals coinciding with the train's arrival" for steam travellers with connections to Havana; see García de Arboleya, *Manual*, 203.
45. While freight, and particularly sugar, generally generated higher revenues than passengers, there were exceptions. The Havana-Matanzas railroad company reported in 1865, for example, that passenger revenue in 1864 for its trunk line was just over 244,055 pesos, while freight brought in just over 228,768. *Informe con que la Junta Directiva*, 16.
46. García de Arboleya, *Manual*, 204. The inconveniences of rail travel meant that passengers often preferred to travel between these three cities by steamship or stagecoach (Zanetti and García, *Sugar and Railroads*, 55).
47. Conde de Villanueva to Antonio María de Escovedo, Havana, 29 November 1838, in: "Expediente sobre la llegada del Camino de Hierro a Güines, comunicada por el Ingeniero Director a los Sres. de la Comisión," ANC, JF, leg. 131, exp. 6422, 1838. For a sycophantic biography of Villanueva, then president of the Junta de Fomento, see *Biografía de … Claudio Martínez de Pinillos*.
48. For example, in 1836, the workforce employed on the Havana-Güines line comprised *emancipados* – previously employed in building the Fernando VII aqueduct – plus white indentured workers from the Canary Islands and prisoners. See *Cuadro del camino de hierro de La Habana a Güines*. Thanks to Jorge Macle for passing me this document. Three decades later, the Havana-Matanzas railroad company cited a similarly mixed workforce, including white labourers, slaves, Chinese indentured workers and *emancipados*: *Informe … de la administracion económica de la Empresa … 1864*, 5. These included contracted Irish workers, brought from the US, who made multiple complaints to the British consul about brutal physical punishments and other ill-treatment. See, e.g., Joseph T. Crawford to Captain General, 9 May 1859, NA, FO 313/54. On enslaved knowledge that fed into broader Atlantic networks of technical knowledge, see Rood, *Reinvention*, chapter 4.
49. "Causa criminal para averiguar quiénes fueron los autores del robo de cerdos del ingenio 'La Sonora' (Escribanía de Martín)," ANC, Miscelánea de Expedientes (ME), leg. 2488, exp. L, 1843.
50. "Expediente sobre solicitar del Gobierno la soltura de un negro que, hallándose de guardiero en la ciénaga, paradero del camino de hierro, fue aprehendido como cimarrón," ANC, JF, leg. 151, exp. 7497, 1837.
51. The railways that came to south-eastern Brazil a couple of decades later helped link urban abolitionists and rural plantation slaves, while slave fugitives followed the lines for orientation (Machado, *O plano e o pânico*, 92, 152).
52. "Sobre la formación de un reglamento para los celadores del camino de hierro de Güines," ANC, JF, leg. 133, exp. 6526, 1844.
53. "Expediente instruido en virtud del oficio del Esmo Sor Presidente de la Junta de Fomento, sobre el reglamento adoptado para evitar los perjuicios y excesos en el Camino de Hierro," ANC, JF, leg. 131, exp. 6248, 1838; "Causa criminal por la muerte del negro Miguel Carabalí ocasionada por los carros de vapor," ANC, ME, leg. 2488, exp. Ll, 1843. Enslaved people acted as repairmen, watchmen, signalmen, and switchmen well into the 1850s: see Rood, *Reinvention of Atlantic Slavery*, 103.
54. Perera and Meriño, *Contrabando de bozales*, 210.
55. John V. Crawford to Captain General, Havana, 6 July 1860, NA, FO 313/54.
56. "Expediente sobre averiguar las desgracias ocurridas en el camino de hierro y el orden en que se halla establecido," ANC, JF, leg. 131, exp. 6429, 1838.
57. "Gangá:" a person embarked in the region of Sierra Leone and Liberia. See Basso, *Los gangá*.
58. "Expediente promovido contra el negro Juan Gangá, esclavo de D. Antonio de la Peña, prendido por falta de licencia con los requisitos prevenidos," ANC, ME, leg. 4286, exp. F,

1843. Thanks to Aisnara Perera Díaz and María de los Angeles Meriño Fuentes for sharing this document with me. They discuss it briefly in Perera y Meriño, *Estrategias de libertad*, vol. 1, 336-337.

59. For this term see Zanetti and García, *Sugar and Railroads*, 84–85. Attempts at greater regulation of the railways were made after about the mid-1850s, but regulations were usually not respected in practice. On the enslaved knowledge that was used to carry out attempts at greater legislative control, see Rood, *Reinvention*, 105–108.
60. Guerra, *Manual de historia*, 436; Finch, *Rethinking Slave Rebellion*, 84–85.
61. Cowling, *Conceiving Freedom*, chapter 5.
62. Zanetti and García, *Sugar and Railroads*, 79.
63. *Compañía de caminos de hierro de la Habana*, 2–6; *Tarifa provisional del ferro-carril de la Bahía de la Habana a Matanzas*.
64. Illiteracy was around 80% by 1861. Fornet, *El libro en Cuba*, 111.
65. "Expediente a propuesta del Excmo. Ayuntamiento de esta Capital (Habana) sobre que se ponga a los trenes prontos a salir una muestra que indique el punto a donde se dirigen," ANC, JF, leg. 137, exp. 6684, 1852.
66. "Expediente relativo a la conducta de un cabo de guardias municipales de San Antonio al entregarse de un detenido en el camino de hierro," ANC, GSC, leg. 1378, exp. 53792, 1857.
67. For example, plans for a waiting-room for "*señoras*" (ladies) at Guanabacoa station are discussed in *Ferro-carril de la Bahía de la Habana a Matanzas*, 5.
68. Cowling, *Conceiving Freedom*, chapter 5.
69. On injured slaves, see, for example, "Expediente sobre la aprehencion de 7 cimarrones por el capitán del Partido de Guamutas de la propiedad de Dn N Lascano … ," ANC, JF, leg. 151, exp. 7471, 1832. On slavery and walking see Lambert, "Master-Horse-Slave."
70. On extra distances travelled due to Cuba's winding roads, see Saco, *Memoria sobre caminos*, 69–73.
71. Perera and Meriño, *Contrabando de bozales*, 170–172.
72. This formed part of a larger issue of judicial torture of enslaved deponents. For Andrés Pletch, this was linked to changing concepts of sovereignty during Cuba's "second slavery." See Pletch, "'Coercive Measures.'"
73. "Expediente promovido por el E. S. Capitán General para que se prevenga a los empleados de seguridad y serenos, que cuando conduzcan presos a individuos del ejército no le causen mayor vejación que la precisa para evitar la fuga," ANC, GSC, leg. 1388, exp. 54160, 1863.
74. For example: "Sobre los perjuicios que dice D. José Antonio Días Bustamante le origina la serventía que pasa por los linderos de su finca 'Dos Hermanos' en el partido de Alquízar," ANC, GSC, leg. 683, exp. 22310, 1841.
75. Gloria García, *La esclavitud*, 40–41.
76. "Sobre la queja de Dn. Miguel Fernández [sic; the petition the file contains refers instead to Dn. Manuel Melis], dueño del tejar situado entre el Cano y Arroyo Arenas que los vecinos de ambos pueblos dejan el camino real para pasar por sus terrenos ocasionándole grandes daños," ANC, GSC, leg. 683, exp. 22270, 1836.
77. "Expediente formado en virtud del oficio del Marqués de San Felipe en que se queja de los perjuicios que le ocasiona el mal estado del camino que conduce al paradero del vapor 'San Felipe' a su ingenio de este nombre," ANC, GSC, leg. 683, exp. 22283, 1839.
78. The British complained about the terrible conditions for *emancipados* engaged in road-building. Henry Bulwer to D. Francisco Martínez de la Rosa, Madrid, 18 March 1845, AHN, Estado 8040, leg. 4, doc. 25. On *emancipados* and public works, see Roldán, "En los borrosos confines," 164–165; Varella, "Esclavos a sueldo," 196–197.
79. A list of *emancipados* captured between 1824 and 1830 showed 218 men and 14 women working at the Consulado: "Estado general … de los negros emancipados … ," AHN, Estado, leg 8033, exp. 26, doc 4, 12 March 1831. Women slave runaways worked on the roads too: "Expediente sobre el parte dado por el administrador del Depósito, de haber una carreta de Don José Ramon Hernandez atropellado a una negra cimarrona nombrada Felipa," ANC, JF, leg. 151, exp. 7470, 1832. Nonetheless, one Junta de Fomento administrator stated that women and young children were not ideal for roadbuilding: "Expediente promovido por el

Sr Coronel Dn Evaristo Carrillo para que la Junta le venda el negro Feliciano, o se le compre una negra que este dice ser su consorte," ANC, JF, leg. 151, exp. 75328, 1841.

80. "Expediente instruido con motivo de un conato de rebelión en la dotación del ingenio 'La Luisa,' Remedios," ANC, GSC, leg. 961, exp. 34038, 1864.
81. "Expediente relativo a la fuga del emancipado Francisco Carabalí, destinado a la obra del camino de hierro," ANC, JF, leg. 151, exp. 7495B, 1836.
82. Pichardo, *Diccionario provincial*, 70. I'm grateful to María de los Ángeles Meriño and Aisnara Perera for this reference.
83. On the connections between spatial and bureaucratic techniques for governing colonial populations, see Nemser, *Infrastructures of Race*, 118–132.
84. "Memoria que al Exmo Sor Gobernador y Capitán General, le dirige el ayudante de la Guardia Civil, Comandante de una Partida en persecución, de las observaciones que en el desempeño de su cometido ha hecho," ANC, GSC, leg. 1364, exp. 53242, 1852.
85. On the development of colonial administrative and judicial functions and their relationship to slavery, see Perera and Meriño, *Estrategias de libertad*, vol. 1, chapter 2.
86. "Expediente formado sobre proporcionar seis emancipados para tripular la falúa de rentas reales de Matanzas," ANC, JF, leg. 151, exp. 7488, 1834.
87. Expediente sobre remitir por cordillera al Juzgado de Pinar de Rio al negro Andrés criollo que se queja del maltrato que le da su dueño," ANC, GSC, leg. 946, exp. 33373, 1850.
88. For example, rural guards who accompanied convict labourers being transported by train in the 1850s had to pay, out of their own pockets, half the regular ticket price charged by the Havana Railroad Company. "Sobre si los guardas rurales pagan el pasaje por entero," ANC, JF, leg. 137, exp. 6720, 1857.
89. "Memoria [del] ayudante de la Guardia Civil ... " 1852.
90. On the *cédulas* and the slippery distinction between *bozales* and *ladinos*, see Perera and Meriño, *Contrabando de bozales*, 18, 117–120, 210, 228.
91. On passport history, see Kolla, "History of the Passport"; Sartorius, "Finding Order"; Sartorius, "Susceptibility in Transit."
92. For one such case, see Cowling, "Esclavitud."
93. Martínez-Fernández, "Geography."
94. For a comparative angle on internal slave trades, see Johnson, ed., *Chattel Principle*.
95. On the "family diaspora," see Perera and Meriño, "The African Women," 898.
96. For this point on the U.S. South, see Johnson, *Soul by Soul*, 19.
97. On plantations' gendered imbalances see, for example, Saco, *Memoria sobre caminos*, 165.
98. On "psychic space," see Finch, *Rethinking Slave Rebellion*, 51.
99. See Cowling, "Gendered Geographies," and Perera and Meriño, "The African Women."
100. On "emotional geographies," see Schivelbush, *Railway Journey*.
101. Building on the work of Edward Said, Stephanie Camp developed this term in exploring resistive uses of space by enslaved people in the U.S. South. Camp, *Closer to Freedom*, 7.
102. Cowling, *Conceiving Freedom*, chapter 5.
103. Skeggs, *Class, Self, Culture*, 49.

Acknowledgements

Many thanks to Mark Cowling, Leida Fernández Prieto, Edward Kolla, María de los Ángeles Meriño Fuentes, Diana Paton, Aisnara Perera Díaz, Daniel Rood, and two *Atlantic Studies* reviewers for their very helpful suggestions on this essay. Especial thanks to David Sartorius for his generous and insightful comments. I am very grateful to Daylet Domínguez and Víctor Goldgel Carballo for their useful comments on the text, and for their infinite patience and support.

Disclosure statement

No potential conflict of interest was reported by the author(s).

Funding

This research was partly funded by the Leverhulme Trust and British Academy. Many thanks to Mark Cowling, Leida Fernández Prieto, Edward Kolla, María de los Ángeles Meriño Fuentes, Diana Paton, Aisnara Perera Díaz, Daniel Rood, and two *Atlantic Studies* reviewers for their very helpful suggestions on this essay. Especial thanks to David Sartorius for his generous and insightful comments. I am very grateful to Daylet Domínguez and Víctor Goldgel Carballo for their useful comments on the text, and for their infinite patience and support.

References

Balboa Navarro, Imilcy. *De los dominios del rey al imperio de la propiedad privada: estructura y tenencia de la tierra de Cuba (siglos XVI–XIX)*. Madrid: Consejo Superior de Investigaciones Científicas, 2013.

Barcia, Manuel. *Seeds of Insurrection: Domination and Resistance on Western Cuban Plantations, 1808–1848*. Baton Rouge: Louisiana State University Press, 2008.

Barcia Zequeira, María del Carmen, Miriam Herrera Jerez, Adrian Camacho, and Oilda Hevia Lanier. *Una sociedad distinta: espacios del comercio negrero en el occidente de Cuba (1836–1866)*. Havana: Editorial Universidad de la Habana, 2017.

Basso Ortiz, Alessandra. *Los gangá en Cuba*. Havana: Fundación Fernando Ortiz, 2005.

Bergad, Laird W., Fe Iglesias, and María del Carmen Barcia. *The Cuban Slave Market, 1790–1880*. Cambridge: Cambridge University Press, 1990.

Biografía del Excmo Señor Don Claudio Martinez de Pinillos, Conde de Villanueva, publicada en el periódico titulado El Trono y la Nobleza, que dirige Don Manuel Ovilo y Otero (n.a.). Havana: Imprenta del Tiempo, 1851.

Camp, Stephanie M. H. *Closer to Freedom: Enslaved Women and Everyday Resistance in the Plantation South*. Chapel Hill: University of North Carolina Press, 2004.

Cartilla práctica del manejo de ingenios ó fincas destinadas a producir azúcar (n.a.). Irún: Imprenta de La Elegancia, 1862.

Compañía de caminos de hierro de la Habana (n.a.). Havana: Imprenta de J. M. de Eleizegui, 1844.

Cowling, Camillia. *Conceiving Freedom: Women of Colour, Gender, and the Abolition of Slavery in Havana and Rio de Janeiro*. Chapel Hill: University of North Carolina Press, 2013.

Cowling, Camillia. "Esclavitud, espacio físico y movilidad en Cuba, s. XIX." In *Orden político y gobierno de esclavos: Cuba en la época de la segunda esclavitud y su legado*, edited by José Antonio Piqueras, 205–228. Valencia: Centro Francisco Tomás y Valiente UNED Alzira-Valencia, 2016.

Cowling, Camillia. "Gendered Geographies: Motherhood, Slavery, Law and Space in Nineteenth-Century Cuba." *Women's History Review* 27, no. 6 (June 2017): 939–953.

Cuadro del camino de hierro de La Habana a Güines en 30 de noviembre de 1836. Havana: Imprenta del Gobierno y Capitanía General, 1836.

Curry-Machado, Jonathan. *The Cuban Sugar Industry: Transnational Networks and Engineering Migrants in Mid-Nineteenth-Century Cuba*. New York: Palgrave Macmillan, 2011.

De la Fuente, Alejandro. "Slave Law and Claims-Making in Cuba: The Tannenbaum Debate Revisited." *Law and History Review* 22, no. 2 (Summer 2004): 339–367.

Derby, Lauren. "Beyond Fugitive Speech: Rumour and Affect in Caribbean History." *Small Axe* 18, no. 2 (July 2014): 123–140.

Dorsey, Joseph C. "'It Hurt Very Much at the Time': Rape Culture, Patriarchy, and the Slave Body Semiotic." In *The Culture of Gender and Sexuality in the Caribbean*, edited by Linden Lewis, 294–322. Gainesville: University Press of Florida, 2003.

Eltis, David, et al. "The Transatlantic Slave Trade Database." Accessed 9 May 2019. https://www.slavevoyages.org/assessment/estimates.

Ferro-carril de la Bahía de la Habana a Matanzas: Informe presentado por su Administrador General para demostrar el estado de los fondos y de los trabajos ejecutados hasta el fin del mes de diciembre del año de 1858. Havana: Establecimiento tipográfico La Cubana, 1859.

Finch, Aisha K. *Rethinking Slave Rebellion in Cuba: La Escalera and the Insurgencies of 1841–1844*. Chapel Hill: University of North Carolina Press, 2015.

Fornet, Ambrosio. *El libro en Cuba, siglos XVIII y XIX*. Havana: Editorial Letras Cubanas, [1994] 2014.

Franco, José Luciano. *El comercio clandestino de esclavos*. Havana: Editorial de Ciencias Sociales, 1980.

Funes Monzote, Reinaldo. *From Rainforest to Cane Field in Cuba: An Environmental History Since 1492*. Translated by Alex Martin. Chapel Hill: University of North Carolina Press, 2008.

García, Gloria. *La esclavitud desde la esclavitud*. Havana: Editorial de Ciencias Sociales, 2003.

García, Guadalupe. *Beyond the Walled City: Colonial Exclusion in Havana*. Oakland: University of California Press, 2016.

García de Arboleya, José. *Manual de la Isla de Cuba: Compendio de su historia, geografía, estadística y administración*. Havana: Imprenta del Tiempo, [1852] 1859.

Guerra y Sánchez, Ramiro. *Manual de historia de Cuba desde su descubrimiento hasta 1868*. Havana: Instituto Cubano del Libro, 1971.

Informe con que la Junta Directiva de la Compañía del Ferro-Carril da cuenta a la General de Accionistas, de la administración económica de la Empresa durante el año de 1864. Havana: Imprenta La Antilla, 1865.

Joda Esteve, Beatriz. "Mujer y esclavitud doméstica: La Habana (1790–1844)." PhD diss., Universitat Jaume I, 2014.

Johnson, Walter. *Soul by Soul: Life Inside the Antebellum Slave Market*. Cambridge, MA: Harvard University Press, 1999.

Johnson, Walter, ed. *The Chattel Principle: Internal Slave Trades in the Americas*. New Haven, CT: Yale University Press, 2005.

Johnson, Walter. *River of Dark Dreams: Slavery and Empire in the Cotton Kingdom*. Cambridge, MA: Harvard University Press, 2013.

Kolla, Edward. "A (Global?) History of the Passport." Paper presented to Global History and Culture Centre, University of Warwick, 22 May 2019.

Lambert, David. "Master-Horse-Slave: Mobility, Race and Power in the British West Indies, c.1780–1838." *Slavery & Abolition* 36, no. 4 (2015): 618–641.

Lightfoot, Natasha. "Plassy Lawrence's Caribbean Freedom Journey." Paper presented at the annual conference of the Association for the Study of the Worldwide African Diaspora, Seville, 7–11 November 2017.

Lucero, Bonnie A. *A Cuban City, Segregated: Race and Urbanization in the Nineteenth Century*. Tuscaloosa: University of Alabama Press, 2019.

Machado, Maria Helena. *O plano e o pânico: os movimentos sociais durante a década da abolição*. Rio de Janeiro: UFRJ/EDUSP, 1994.

Martínez-Fernández, Luis. "Geography, Will it Absolve Cuba?" *History Compass* 2, no. 1 (January 2004): 1–21.

McDowell, Linda. *Gender, Identity and Place: Understanding Feminist Geographies*. Cambridge: Polity Press, 1999.

Moyano Bazzani, Eduardo L. *La nueva frontera del azúcar: El ferrocarril y la economía cubana del siglo XIX*. Madrid: CSIC, 1991.

Murray, David R. *Odious Commerce: Britain, Spain and the Abolition of the Cuban Slave Trade*. Cambridge: Cambridge University Press, 1980.

Nemser, Daniel. *Infrastructures of Race: Concentration and Biopolitics in Colonial Mexico*. Austin: University of Texas Press, 2017.

Perera Díaz, Aisnara, and María de los Ángeles Meriño Fuentes. *Contrabando de bozales en Cuba: perseguir el tráfico y mantener la esclavitud (1845–1866)*. San José de las Lajas, Cuba: Ediciones Montecallado, 2015.

Perera Díaz, Aisnara, and María de los Ángeles Meriño Fuentes. *Estrategias de libertad: un acercamiento a las acciones legales de los esclavos en Cuba (1762–1872)*. 2 vols. Havana: Editorial de Ciencias Sociales, 2016.

Perera Díaz, Aisnara, and María de los Ángeles Meriño Fuentes. "The African Women of the Dos Hermanos Slave Ship in Cuba: Slaves First, Mothers Second." *Women's History Review* 27, no. 6 (November 2018): 892–909.

Pichardo, Esteban. *Diccionario provincial casi-razonado de voces cubanas*. Havana: Imprenta del Gobierno, [1836] 1862.

Pletch, Andrés. "'Coercive Measures: Slave Rebellion, Torture, and Sovereignty in Cuba 1812–1844." *Slavery & Abolition* 40, no. 2 (June 2019): 271–294.

Putnam, Lara. "The Transnational and the Text-Searchable: Digitised Sources and the Shadows they Cast." *The American Historical Review* 121, no. 2 (2016): 377–402.

Reid-Vázquez, Michele. *The Year of the Lash: Free People of Colour in Cuba and the Nineteenth-Century Atlantic World*. Athens: University of Georgia Press, 2011.

Roldán de Montaud, Inés. "En los borrosos confines de la libertad: el caso de los negros emancipados en Cuba, 1817–1870." *Revista de Indias* 71, no. 251 (2011): 159–192.

Rood, Daniel B. *The Reinvention of Atlantic Slavery: Technology, Labour, Race, and Capitalism in the Greater Caribbean*. New York: Oxford University Press, 2017.

Saco, José Antonio. "Memoria sobre caminos en la Isla de Cuba." In *Colección de papeles científicos, históricos, politicos y de otros ramos sobre la Isla de Cuba*. vol. 1, edited by José Antonio Saco, 58–167. Paris: Imprenta de D'Aubusson y Kugelmann, [1829] 1858.

Sartorius, David. "Travel, Passports, and the Borders of Race in Nineteenth-Century Cuba." Presented at the meeting of the Latin American Studies Association, Rio de Janeiro, 14 June 2009.

Sartorius, David. "Finding Order, Inspiration, and Jose Martí in the Libros de Pasaportes." *Hemisphere* 27 (Winter 2018): 11–13.

Sartorius, David. "Susceptibility in Transit: Passports, Circulars, and Other Speculations in Nineteenth-Century Cuba." Unpublished paper passed to the author, 2019.

Schivelbush, Wolfgang. *The Railway Journey: Trains and Travel in the Nineteenth Century*. Oxford: Blackwell, 1986.

Scott, Julius S. *The Common Wind: Afro-American Currents in the Age of Revolution*. New York: Verso, 2018.

Scott, Rebecca J. *Slave Emancipation in Cuba: The Transition to Free Labour, 1860–1899*. Princeton, NJ: Princeton University Press, 1989.

Scott, Rebecca J. *Degrees of Freedom: Louisiana and Cuba After Slavery*. Cambridge, MA: Harvard University Press, 2005.

Sedgewick, Augustine. "Against Flows." *History of the Present: A Journal of Critical History* 4, no. 2 (Fall 2014): 143–170.

Sheller, Mimi, and John Urry. "The New Mobilities Paradigm." *Environment and Planning A* 38 (2006): 207–226.

Skeggs, Beverley. *Class, Self, Culture*. London: Routledge, 2004.

Tarifa provisional del ferro-carril de la Bahía de la Habana a Matanzas, con aprobación del Gobierno (n.a.). Havana: Imprenta La Antilla, 1861.

Tezanos Toral, Lorena. "The Architecture of Nineteenth-Century Cuban Sugar Mills: Creole Power and African Resistance in Late Colonial Cuba." PhD diss., City University of New York, 2015.

Tomich, Dale. "The Second Slavery: Bonded Labour and the Transformation of the Nineteenth-Century Economy." In *Rethinking the Nineteenth Century*, edited by Francisco Ramírez, 103–117. Stanford, CA: Stanford University Press, 1988.

Tomich, Dale, and Michael Zeuske, eds. "The Second Slavery: Mass Slavery, World Economy, and Comparative Microhistories," parts 1 & 2. Special issues, *Review: Journal of the Fernand Braudel Centre* 31, nos. 2 and 3 (2008).

Urban, C. Stanley. "The Africanization of Cuba Scare, 1853–1855." *Hispanic American Historical Review* 37, no. 1 (February 1957): 29–45.

Varella, Claudia. "Esclavos a sueldo: la coartación cubana en el siglo XIX." PhD diss., Universitat Jaume I, 2010.

Walker, Daniel. *No More, No More: Slavery and Cultural Resistance in Havana and New Orleans.* Minneapolis: University of Minnesota Press, 2004.

Wolff, Janet. "On the Road Again: Metaphors of Travel in Cultural Criticism." *Cultural Studies* 7, no. 2 (1992): 224–239.

Zanetti, Oscar, and Alejandro García. *Sugar and Railroads: A Cuban History, 1837–1959.* Translated by Franklin W. Knight and Mary Todd. Chapel Hill: University of North Carolina Press, 1998.

Zeuske, Michael. "Out of the Americas: Slave Traders and the *Hidden Atlantic* in the Nineteenth Century." *Atlantic Studies: Global Currents* 15, no. 1 (2018): 103–135.

Forty-one years a slave: Agnosia and mobility in nineteenth-century Cuba

Victor Goldgel Carballo

ABSTRACT

On the basis of a previously unstudied testimony, this study approaches the life of a slave from a methodological standpoint at the crossroads between Literary Studies and History. On 4 October 1853, a black man stepped into the U.S. consulate in Havana. According to the testimony he gave that day, he had been born free in Charleston, South Carolina. In 1812, at the age of ten or twelve, he was hired to work on a sloop that took him to Cuba, where he was kidnapped and sold as a slave. It would take him about forty-one years to reach the consulate and petition for his freedom. Opposing agnosia ("not-knowing") to anagnorisis ("to recognize"), I explore different ways of (not) knowing linked to complicity, hypocrisy, and illegal slavery, while at the same time analyzing the slave's storytelling as a form of mobility.

On Tuesday, 4 October 1853, a black man in his early fifties left the cigar factory where he had been recently put to work, walked through the streets of Havana, and stepped into the U.S. consulate. According to the testimony he gave that day, he had been born free in Charleston, South Carolina. In 1812, at the age of ten or twelve, he had been hired to work on a sloop that took him to Cuba. After a few days in Regla (right across the bay from Havana), he was kidnapped and sold as a slave. As a child, his name had been Ben. As a slave, he was rechristened Juan Criollo. It would take him about forty-one years to reach the consulate and petition for his freedom.[1]

I stumbled upon Ben/Juan's 8-page testimony at Cuba's *Archivo Nacional* while doing research on illegal slavery for a book on race and open secrets. Transcribed in the first person at the consulate, a Spanish version was immediately sent to the Captain General of the island. It is now the first document in a 48-folio file that resulted from the investigation. As I found out later, the testimony is also preserved in English as part of the consular dispatch sent from Havana to Washington, D.C.[2] To my knowledge, neither the Spanish nor the English versions have been previously studied.

In the Anglophone world, with more than 6,000 texts of this sort, narratives by slaves or former slaves, quickly became the most prominent genre in Atlantic diasporic literature, whereas just a few miles southeast of Cuba, in the former colony of Saint Domingue, no first-person slave narratives have been preserved.[3] Due to the relative frequency with which slaves reached the courts, Cuba is somewhere in between, but it looks very different from the standpoint of historiography than from that of literary studies. While historians regularly engage with first-person accounts of slaves found in Cuban or Spanish archives, literary scholars have focused solely on the one extant slave autobiography written in Spanish, Juan Francisco Manzano's.[4] One of my main objectives in writing this essay is to show that approaching other Cuban slave testimonies from the field of literary studies is not only possible but necessary. Greater attention to language and storytelling, I argue, would translate into new insights into the lives of slaves, and, in particular, into the relationship between slavery and fiction.

There are many things we will probably never know about Ben/Juan (for reasons that will soon become clear, I will refer to him using both names). In particular, the evidence gathered during the investigation carried out by colonial authorities is insufficient to state with any degree of certainty that he had in fact been born in Charleston or that he had been born free. The task of finding baptismal records or witnesses in the U.S. was undertaken almost half a century after he and his family had supposedly left the city. Proving that a black man had been born free, furthermore, might have seemed futile to people living in Charleston – a place where black seamen from the North or Britain could be legally jailed and then sold as slaves.[5] Ben/Juan's story, nevertheless, was plausible enough to prevent his return to his owner. In the pages that follow, I frame his narrative as part of a wider effort to overcome the fabrications regularly imposed on slaves during this period. Such an effort was characterized by a series of autonomous movements – most importantly, as I will show, those of his tongue – through which he tried to surmount confinement and coerced displacements.

The period from 1812 to 1853 can be summarized in a few words: a very long time. How could the suspicious origins of a slave who at first only spoke English remain unattended for that long? As Ben/Juan made clear, people were aware of his situation: "Every body^{almost} in the neighborhood knew and know my history."[6] The word "almost" was added right above the line, with the symbol placed in between "body" and "in," as if to rectify: not *really* everybody. How can we conceptualize this type of knowledge that, although held by (almost) everybody, did not prompt any action? With respect to those who could have helped him, it seemed to consist precisely in not wanting to know, in turning a blind eye to what was most evident, whether because of self-interest, cynicism, indifference, fear, or other reasons. Indeed, this is a very peculiar way of (not) knowing linked to complicity, hypocrisy, repression, and the open secret of illegal slavery that I will describe as a vernacular form of agnosia (from the Greek "not-knowing") and oppose to anagnorisis (a fundamental term in Aristotle's *Poetics,* which literally means to recognize or make known again). The word "agnosia" is often used in medicine to describe the loss of the ability to recognize certain things, such as faces (prosopagnosia).[7] I am borrowing it here to characterize not individuals and their neuro-psychology but rather a social order that required the constant reproduction of ignorance around the myriad illegal and unjust acts that bolstered slavery. This ignorance was in great part a response to the emergence of legislation – in particular, the ban of the slave trade – that contradicted customary practices. Far from being monolithic, it was an everyday language (i.e. vernacular) used in a wide array of situations by a variety of subjects to pretend that they did not know certain things – from the highest officials, who were bribed to make the illegal trade possible, to the poorest of slave owners, who needed fake documentation to protect their property, and even to the slaves themselves, who had a lot to lose if they testified against their owners.[8] In fact, as we will see, Ben/Juan declared not only that (almost) everybody knew his story but also that he was punished every time he brought it to the attention of his masters and, at least once, the local authorities. The very existence of his testimony, however, demonstrates that agnosia gave way under certain conditions – for example, when illegally-held slaves were able to reach Havana and compel a recognition on the part of the state. Correspondingly, agnosia – no matter how extensive or how fundamental for social reproduction – can be only perceived and studied when it fails. It is only because Ben/Juan was able to effectively seek redress that we know about his otherwise silenced bondage.

This is how his testimony begins: "I was born free in the city of Charleston – my parents were freemen. My father was named Joseph and was generally called *Uncle Joe* – my mother's name was Lizzie (Elizabeth)."[9] He then goes on to explain that his father was a fisherman and names the different locations where they lived and worked after leaving Charleston in or around 1808. The last one of these was the isle of New Providence, where the captain of a small trading sloop hired him as a cabin boy and took him to Cuba. This is how Ben/Juan describes the moment of his kidnapping:

> Captain Jim and myself used to sleep in Regla in the house of a person called Cordero. Some fifteen days after, one afternoon, Señor Cordero called me and told me to follow him. I did so, and he took me up the Calle Real to a grocery store (bodega), where a man came behind me, caught hold of me and dragged me along. I took hold of Cordero who allowed himself to be dragged along by me and said *let go and I'll go and call Captain Jim*. I let go and was taken to a room and put in the cepo (stocks). This occurred, as I have said, in the afternoon. I have never seen Cordero again. At midnight I was on my way, in charge of the person I have presented today (called Don José Hernández who lives in Regla and a mason by trade) to the *sitio* where I have been kept in slavery and pretty much the whole time in irons, till some two months ago.[10]

The crime of kidnapping and enslaving a person – known as *plagio* (plagiarism) – was a common occurrence in nineteenth-century Cuba. Just three days before Ben/Juan's visited the consulate, the *Gaceta de La Habana* informed readers about Eusebio, a four-year-old black boy who had recently disappeared; it was presumed that he had been tricked into going with his kidnappers. A few days later, the same newspaper wrote about an ongoing investigation on the *plagio* of a black woman, Felipa Criolla.[11] Ben/Juan's story, however, was peculiar, as it involved a potential diplomatic conflict during a particularly tense moment in Cuban history. An "Africanization scare" had started in March 1853, when Spain had promised to free all *emancipados* (ostensibly liberated Africans who, in spite of their name, were for all practical purposes still slaves) and the annexation of the island to the U.S. was very much on the table.[12] These factors, combined with the evidence that Ben/Juan presented (mostly his own testimony and a witness account), was strong enough to give him a chance in the extremely tilted playing field in which slaves fought to obtain freedom.

As soon as he was informed about the case, Captain General Valentín Cañedo started an investigation. On 6 October, he ordered that the slave be taken to what was known as the *depósito* (warehouse) of the Junta de Fomento (Development Board), where he joined captured runaways from all over the island. We do not know why Cañedo chose this *depósito*, rather than the judicial one where slaves who sued for their freedom were normally held. Captured runaways were regularly employed in road construction and other public works, and maybe Ben/Juan was no exception. However, given the relative notoriety of his case, which would reach the New York press a few days later, it was likely that he was at risk of being illegally sold once again – as was often the case with slaves kept in that location.[13] In the days that followed, a number of witnesses were interviewed, including Ben/Juan himself and his current and previous owners. Antonio Pedroso, his master during most of his life, had died in 1846, and his estate had been distributed among his heirs. In 1853 Ben/Juan found himself under a new master, who took him to Havana on a steamboat and rented him to a cigar factory at no. 12 Oficios Street, near the intersection with Sol Street. On 4 October, he was able to exert his right as a slave to receive a document that granted him three days to move freely within and without the city walls (including Regla) to try to find a new owner willing to pay 750 pesos.[14] He reached the consulate the same day, and he finally found receptive ears. He had also found a key witness: José Hernándes, a construction worker from Regla, who was first interviewed by the acting consul and a few days later by the colonial authorities, who were trying to verify Ben/Juan's claims.[15] Hernándes was the "slave-mover" who had taken him to his first owner about forty-one years earlier.[16]

Why did Ben/Juan decide to seek help at the consulate, rather than through the usual legal channels (i.e. by resorting to the *síndico*, or the municipal official in charge of protecting slaves)? And why were the diplomats representing a U.S. administration with no sympathies for abolitionism willing to help him? Before meeting the consul, William H. Robertson, Ben/Juan was interviewed by his secretary, Thomas Savage. While not an abolitionist, Savage would eventually become known as an enemy of the slave trade, so Ben/Juan might have expected to find in him a sympathetic interlocutor.[17] Robertson, on the other hand, owes his prominence in the historical record to his efforts in promoting annexation. In contrast to the previous administration, Franklin Pierce favored acquiring the island, to the point that several of the people he chose for key diplomatic posts believed that U.S. foreign policy pivoted around Cuba. His Secretary of State, William L. Marcy, for example, was an outspoken expansionist who would soon authorize the U.S. ambassador in Spain to offer $130 million for the purchase of the island.[18] As for Robertson, he was convinced that Cuban slave interests favored a U.S. military intervention. Just a few months later, in April of 1854, he would draft an invasion proclamation reassuring Cubans that "the Am. Eagle will defend you from their [your oppressors'] rapacity & vengeance, because the Sons of Washington are your brothers. *The Eagle will protect your lives, your families, your properties and the social condition of your country.*"[19] By "social condition" he probably meant the subjugation of blacks and the continuation of slavery. The consul would also complain about "the growing insolence of the negroes." As he scornfully pointed out in May of 1854, blacks referred to the newly appointed Captain General, Juan de la Pezuela "as 'tití Juan,' or 'Papá Juan,' the Patron of Liberty and Equality."[20] So even though protecting the peculiar institution both in Cuba and in the U.S. was one of the main goals of annexation, Ben/Juan could be used as ammunition. The story of a freeborn American boy kidnapped and then held in bondage for decades under the auspices of a despotic metropolis could, for example, help convince some northern abolitionists of the moral virtues of a U.S. intervention.

In late October, the *Weekly Herald*, owned by James Gordon Bennett in New York, published an article entitled "Late and Interesting from Cuba." It was dated October 6 and told the story of how Ben/Juan "found his way to the office of the American Consulate, and there claimed protection as a free-born citizen of the United States." [21] As the Havana correspondent pointed out, this "case of most extraordinarily character, of the many that undoubtedly exist, is now being exposed to the light, after a concealment of forty years."[22] The tension between the extraordinary and the common ("the many that undoubtedly exist"), or between daily suffering and spectacular exposure, would have been familiar to readers of abolitionist literature. By then, such literature included not just classics like Olaudah Equiano's 1789 *Interesting Narrative* but also recent best-sellers like Frederick Douglass' memoir (which, published in 1845, had sold 30,000 copies by 1850) and Harriet B. Stowe's *Uncle Tom's Cabin* (which sold about 300,000 copies in just one year after being published in book form in 1852).[23] Furthermore, the fugitive slave law of 1850 had reignited the U.S. abolitionist movement and put the figure of the runaway in the minds of the public. Bypassing the norms of the free states, the law not only criminalized any help offered to fugitive slaves but also encouraged the kidnapping of free blacks, which made hundreds of them flee to Canada. In this context, Ben/Juan's story probably struck a chord among readers in the Northeast. [24] In Havana, meanwhile, colonial authorities confronted the unsightly prospect of a rapacious bird indignant at their own rapacity.

Ben/Juan was finally close to having a shot at freedom.

On the move, or a convincing tongue

In order to understand the forms of agnosia that enveloped Ben/Juan's story, we should first go over the dialectics of movement and confinement that made his bondage possible. In comparison to most other slaves in Cuba, who were brought from West Africa, he had traveled a short distance. His family was in New Providence, about 380 nautical miles away from Havana; with good winds and a speed of 8 knots, traveling that far would only take two days. Neither his testimony nor the rest of the file contain information about his journey within Cuba right after his kidnapping, other than that the man in charge of transporting him was the above-mentioned Hernándes and that they started it at midnight. The *Weekly Herald* correspondent, however, noted that they were on horses and arrived at dawn. Even though he would spend about forty one years in just two locations – Peñalver and Arcos de Canasí, about nine and forty miles east of Havana, respectively – Ben/Juan's testimony also tells us very little about that time. Did he have any friends? A new family? A sense of community? A new self-understanding as someone living in a Spanish colony? His testimony does not say. Proving that he had been free and describing the injustices he suffered as a slave was evidently more important to him than sharing details about the new senses of identity he surely developed as a "Cuban" subject.[25] At any rate, those few miles that separated him from Havana were enough to facilitate his ongoing captivity, as they meant fewer legal and practical opportunities. When his new owner took him to Havana and hired him out to the cigar factory, he was suddenly in a position to adopt the tactics and movements of other slaves who appealed to the law.[26]

Just a couple of weeks later, on 4 October, he managed to get the abovementioned three-day *papel* (permit) authorizing him to move around the city. His testimony does not describe his movements, but it seems likely that he first went to Regla to find Hernándes. The cigar factory was almost next to the Luz dock, where boats regularly crossed the bay. If either before or after his visit to the consulate he was anywhere near the Paseo de Isabel II in the afternoon, he must have seen or at least heard the big military parade with which the ever-faithful island celebrated the saint's day of the consort King. If the recurrence of these topics in the local news are a good indicator, the cholera epidemic and the unseasonably hot weather were part of the conversations he had or overheard during those days. And although he makes no reference to this, there were surely people at the cigar factory and in the streets or the harbor who helped him. Otherwise, how could he have found Hernándes, more than forty years after his kidnapping? While we are in the dark about these networks of solidarity and information exchange, other slaves who came into archival view help us imagine them.[27]

The story Ben/Juan told on 4 October also shows that his coerced displacement involved a dialectics of de-territorialization (his being severed from his English-speaking community) and re-territorialization (as exemplified by the forgery of documents required to sell him and keep him enslaved under a new legal identity). This occurred spatially as much as symbolically. As he told Robertson, once in captivity he was forbidden from talking about his origins. He declared, for example:

> When I grew up, I once told my master that I was a free man – he put me in irons and kept me with them some six months – when released, I again said that I was a free man and was again put me in irons. In this manner I was kept in irons pretty much the whole of my life.[28]

Whether his owner aimed to repress his story or the more general sense of rebelliousness involved in any invocation of freedom, Ben/Juan's loose tongue caused the increased restraint of his body – a sign of his (repressed) power to extract himself symbolically from the territory of slavery. Mobility and confinement, from this perspective, operated verbally and psychologically as much as in space.

His tongue, moreover, was to be later presented as evidence of his origins. At the end of his testimony, Ben/Juan points out that since the year of his kidnapping to his arrival in Havana two weeks before, "I have not seen or spoken to any person that spoke English." The next day, the *Weekly Herald* correspondent would write: "He says he kept himself from losing the knowledge of the English language he had at twelve years, by con[s]tantly repeating th[e] story of his life, to himself in English, enumerating every incident and all the names of his family and friends."[29] This intimate scene described by the journalist is not part of Ben/Juan's testimony. However, even if we were to understand it as just fictional, the scene is so plausible that leaving it unattended would probably hurt the truth more than it would protect it. In particular, it suggests that Ben/Juan's native tongue was perceived (if not by him, at least by others) as being one and the same with his subjectivity, so that by using it "he kept himself," period. The inalienability of the language with which he had learned to speak was strained by his alienation as a slave, but it was not destroyed. Lacking other Anglophone interlocutors on the site where he was held for decades, he doubled as storyteller and listener, as the one giving testimony and the one receiving it. English was a metonymy for his origins and his freedom, and speaking it kept him in touch with both. But even when he spoke in Spanish he was dangerously close to his freedom. Whenever he told his story to his masters, he was put in shackles, as if the sheer mention of his past were a form of flight. It was probably was. Unless we misconceive the potential as not real, Ben/Juan's physical flights should be understood as the heightened forms of that flight-as-potentiality which kept him telling his story. Storytelling, in this sense, was a form of mobility, as his masters seem to have feared.

Slavery had transformed him into Ben/Juan: someone who was simultaneously himself – the one who kept repeating his origins – and somebody else's property – the fungible not-subject who could be renamed at will. How could he interrupt this abstract logic of fungibility (of being replaceable, exchangeable, renamable)? And if he had a story that (almost) everybody knew but nobody wanted to hear, under what conditions could he tell it in a way that mattered to his pursuit for freedom? Arriving in Havana was of course a fundamental step. Had it not been for his tongue, however, he would have probably achieved very little. In the same way that the famous poet-slave Juan Francisco Manzano had earned his freedom thanks to his skill at writing, Ben/Juan also approached his because of a linguistic ability. British abolitionists often argued that "country marks" (the product of West African scarification practices) could be used to demonstrate that slaves of a certain age had been introduced into the island illegally – as they were proof of having been born in Africa and arrived after the ban of the slave trade.[30] Similarly, Ben's speech organs had been shaped before his bondage and, in that sense, transcending all of the legal farces that accompanied slave holding in Cuba, showed who he had been before. As the consul put it, Ben/Juan "still speaks sufficient English to be fairly understood," and with the same accent as blacks in the south of the United States. While other slaves also spoke English, most of them either were from the British West Indies or had learned the language from people born there, so his accent was a significant form of evidence.[31] His origin was indelibly inscribed in his body: in the strength and shape of the tissues of his lips, tongue, and palate, as well as in those parts of his nervous system with which he had learned to coordinate the movements of his speech organs as a child. As an objectified subject, he had little or no voice. As embodied evidence, however, his voice became an objective and weighty form of proof. It showed that before being Juan he had been Ben; that the last names "Criollo" and "Pedroso" did not characterize but an aspect of his life (being somebody else's possession), which was more fully explained by foreign names (Joseph, Lizzie, Charleston, etc.). Under the favorable conditions offered by the consulate, the plot of Ben/Juan's life was finally close to having its moment of anagnorisis.

Like a performative speech act and a shibboleth, the slave's testimony in his native tongue transformed him back into Ben. When he forwarded the slave's testimony to the Captain General, the consul stated that he believed him and pointed out that the least that could be done to redress his ordeal would be to offer him back wages for his forty-one years of unpaid labor. When he wrote to Washington, he highlighted the "straightforwardness and earnestness in his manner."[32] As the *Weekly Herald* put it, "his tongue was evidently touched with the fire of truth, for all that heard believed."[33] This verbal fire was implicitly presented as having a much higher truth-value than any documents that may be found showing that he was a Cuban-born slave. It allowed him to embody both selfhood and truth in a context in which falsification was the condition for the continuity of slavery.[34]

It would be difficult to overstate the importance of fakery during this period of Cuban history. All of those forms of actively not-knowing linked to complicity, hypocrisy, and self-preservation that I characterized earlier as a vernacular form of agnosia depended on forged documents, bribes, and spurious legal ceremonies. When he was asked if he had ever seen the document proving that Ben/Juan was a legally held slave, his current owner declared that he had not *"por la confianza que le inspiraba el conocimiento de la familia de Pedroso*" (because of his trust in the Pedroso family).[35] When the immediately previous owner, Guadalupe Pedroso, was asked a similar question, she declared that the bill of sale of the then 12-year old boy "*se extravió con otros papeles en un temporal*" (were lost along with other documents during a storm).[36] Ben/Juan's bondage, as countless others', did not even require forged documents; pretending that such documents had existed was often enough.

I just wrote that his speech act transformed Juan back into Ben; that, under the weight of undeniable, embodied evidence, agnosia and falsification finally gave way to anagnorisis. However, was this what really happened? Or am I presenting as fact what is just a possibility among many, as truth what is only partially true, and as an actual outcome what was for the most part a demand for justice? As someone who works on literature, I should not be asking these questions. They suggest that words matter little – or, worse, that I am a closeted positivist. Am I seriously asking if something "really happened"? As someone interpelated by Ben/Juan's testimony, however, I cannot but wonder. His speech act might very well have been felicitous in the presence of some, convincing Thomas Savage or the readers of the *Weekly Herald* that he was in fact Ben. But in the investigation ordered by the Captain General, he is still "Juan Criollo" and "Juan Pedroso," and this is the case even while his belonging to the "English nation" or to the United States is taken as fact. After being interrogated on 17 October, he is called "*el moreno Juan Pedroso natural de Charleston*" (the black Juan Pedroso, a native of Charleston).[37] The same had happened half a century earlier, in 1827, the day of his second baptism, when a priest referred to him as "Juan Antonio de la Asunción, *adulto de nación Inglés, esclavo*" (adult of the English nation, slave).[38] Being from Charleston and belonging to the "English nation" was clearly not enough to avoid being Juan. No matter how many times he tried, and no matter how fired up his tongue was, his speech would amount to very little. As we learn from his testimony, for example, a priest gave him his new name despite his protesting that he already had one. He declared to Robertson: "I was told that I was going to be baptized. I said that I had already been baptized in Charleston, but was answered *eso no sirve* [that's no good] – so I was baptized in the town of Peñalver and named *Juan*. My original name was *Ben* (Benjamin)."[39] This was a standard legal procedure to launder the slaves of the illegal trade – one that erased their clandestine origin, or the scene of abduction. As Michael Zeuske and Orlando García have observed, there existed two ways of entering slavery: the real and silenced one (the illegal trade), and the symbolic and written one (as moral persons baptized in the Catholic community of a given region).[40] The scene of the second baptism shows the deep interdependence of anagnorisis and agnosia: the ritual gesture of the priest demonstrates the existence of Ben/Juan's previous identity in the very act of erasing it. No matter how preposterous, Juan's juridical identity was being forged to bury the person he had been before. His words, in that sense, mattered very little. Given the right context, however, they could matter enough.

Literature/history: an interregnum

What is the value of words? And how do historians and literary scholars value them differently? The available sources force us to grapple with Ben/Juan's effectiveness as a narrator as much as with his impotence. By emphasizing the former, we risk obscuring the latter.

Conversely, by insisting that his story was systematically ignored we risk downplaying his power to move countless people – other slaves working alongside him, seamen at the harbor, or the slave-mover who was in charge of him in 1812 and whom, for example, he convinced to testify at the consulate more than forty years later. In the same way, my cautious characterization of him as a white-sponsored witness of his own tragedy rather than as a skillful storyteller able to shape his destiny might be an aftereffect of the systemic ways of silencing that allowed for his continuous enslavement – or of the racialized ways in which words were assigned value. For all we know, Ben/Juan could have made up parts of his story – as the slave Bárbara Falero had done in 1832 when she impersonated another African of her same name to gain freedom.[41] If this were the case, believing his story would account to missing who he really was and how much value he could extract from words.

As Aristotle put it his *Poetics,* a historian "relates what actually happened" and the poet "the kind of events that would happen."[42] What happens, however, when generalized agnosia pushes someone's freedom away from the *actual*, erasing it almost altogether not just from the person's life but from historical memory? Should we become poets to set the record straight? Or at least consider the extent to which slaves themselves might have been poets? Inasmuch as he lived in such a context, understanding Ben/Juan as both a historian and a poet of his own freedom – as someone relating things that happened and/or would happen – may bring us closer to the truth than either stopping where the empirical evidence ends or reading his testimony as a literary fiction.[43] I would therefore suggest, as a general hypothesis, that poetic and historical readings of a text like Ben/Juan's may productively converge when two conditions are met. The first one is that the focus on what "would happen" does not make us indifferent to available evidence to the contrary; for example, to the fact that Ben/Juan continued to be Juan in the eyes of Spanish authorities and was kept as a captured runaway. Given that what mattered to him was actual liberation, offering him an imaginary one would be little more than an anachronistic declaration of good will. The second condition is that we avoid relying excessively on what sources prove, as this could make us disregard those dimensions of the text that indicate potentiality. Wasn't his desire to become Ben, after all, the force that took him to the consulate? And wouldn't this be true even if he had never actually been Ben, or free? Imagining freedom is certainly not the same as achieving it, but there is some meaningful overlap. Taking a cue from Marx's *Grundrisse,* Barbara Foley has observed that documentary fiction not only recreates historical process and structures but also tries to convince readers "of the legitimacy of the author's specific conception of those processes and structures."[44] Similarly, in providing his testimony, Ben/Juan not only painted a picture of his life as a free child but also prompted his audience to view it from his own eyes and thus evaluate his own understanding of the social world – including both his rights and desires. The following is the question that, according to the consul, Ben/Juan asked Thomas Savage as soon as he greeted him: "Sir, is it just and proper that a man born free in a civilized country should be kept in slavery and bondage without having committed any crime?"[45] The question is obviously rhetorical, in both senses of the word: Ben/Juan was making a point and creating suspense, and he most likely used a less grandiloquent style – that is, if he asked the question at all. Regardless, the story he told that day led Savage and others to see the world from his perspective. Freeborn or not, Ben or Juan, his tongue was able to transport some people and move them to the point of helping him. No matter, the objective limitations, one's tongue can take one a long way – this much historians know as well as poets.

Competing stories

In several occasions throughout his testimony, Ben/Juan refers to his legal rights as a slave, which he intended to use to prove his status as a freeborn person. He declares, for example, that he unsuccessfully requested a permit to look for a new owner many times, so that he could use it – as he would eventually do in Havana – to reach the authorities and inform them about his plight. Around 1849, three years after the death of Antonio Pedroso, the man who had been his master during most of his life, Ben/Juan escaped, looked for the *teniente* (Deputy Mayor) of his jurisdiction, and told him his story. The scene, theoretically, could have been one of anagnorisis, with the representative of the law suddenly gaining knowledge of Ben/Juan's true identity – or at least recognizing him as a slave who had been denied his right to look for a new owner. The *teniente*, however, was reluctant. He contacted his current owners (the daughters of Pedroso), whose answer, as Ben/Juan puts it, was "that *they could not give me the paper I asked because it was not possible.*"[46] Ben/Juan kept running into the brick wall of a willfully reproduced ignorance of the law. No matter what his rights were or how convincing his claim might have been, the *teniente* remained impassive and the Pedroso family could respond with a simple refusal. So he was sent back with an overseer, punished, and put in shackles once again.

In this sense, his story resonates with that of many other slaves and free people of color for two main reasons. First, because the laws protecting him could only be activated if he first learned about them, became fluent in their logic, and had enough mobility, support, and luck to request redress to the proper authorities. Secondly, because planters had their customary rights, and they protected them by manipulating the law as much as they could. As the ban of the trade transformed every single newly arrived slave into a liability, this had to be done with increased frequency.[47] Ben/Juan's experience of the legal system as little more than (but not merely) a charade, therefore, was increasingly shared by others, as in the span of a few decades the expansion of plantation slavery brought more slaves to Cuba than in all previous history. From the early colonial period up until 1812, when he was kidnapped, about 130,000 Africans had disembarked on the island; in just ten years, that number would double; and by 1853, when he showed up at the consulate, the total had risen to 645,000. His condition as an illegally-held person, anticipated that of most slaves during this period. At the moment of his kidnapping, the slave trade had just been outlawed in the British colonies and the U.S. Just a few years later, in 1817, Spain signed a treaty agreeing to prohibit the introduction of new African slaves that would take effect in 1820. After that date, all Africans brought into Cuba – about 419,000 until 1853 – were introduced in a clandestine way, usually with the complicity of colonial authorities.[48]

So, calling him Juan appears to endorse the legal farces and the captivity from which he struggled to escape. And yet, calling him just Ben would be almost as problematic, as the story of his life – like those of most slaves – was to a great extent one of people in positions of power not wanting to know, or of willful disavowal. If in his *Poetics* Aristotle defined anagnorisis as a dramatic change "from ignorance to knowledge" (as when Oedipus realizes that he has married his mother and killed his father), Ben/Juan's case shows that, in the case of oppressed and exploited subjects, revelation does not necessarily dispel ignorance.[49] Most certainly, the ethical interpellation produced by his testimony demands that we undo the agnosia that served to perpetuate his bondage and that we acknowledge his struggle to stop being Juan. This, in turn, forces us to consider that the sources that call him "Juan Criollo" or "Juan Pedroso" might be obstacles rather than vehicles in our search for the truth, and to question the objectification reproduced in the archive by arguing that his actions and movements reveal the existence of subaltern circuits for the production and circulation of knowledge. My point, however, is that even if we believe his testimony down to the last detail and, attentive to the need to read the colonial archive against the grain, we treat all other documents with utter suspicion, the fact remains that the silencing of his story not only defined his life but also shaped his struggle for freedom. And this silence, I would like to emphasize, was not monolithic. Rather, there were many, intricate, amalgams of silence/story. Or, to put it differently, Ben/Juan's story was actually many different, competing, ones: the one his owners did not want to hear but (almost) everybody knew, the one imposed on him through the new baptism, the one the consulate forwarded to the Captain General and Washington, D.C., the one the colonial authorities in charge of the investigation believed would please their superiors, and the "interesting" one presented in the press, among others. In a few of them, he was Ben – in particular, in the eyes of witnesses who were or pretended to be sympathetic. In most, he was Juan. In all of them, however, his identity was defined by the possibility of being somebody else.

Acknowledging the presence of these competing stories is key because the people who saw him as Ben did so not just in spite of his putative legal identity but also because of it – as the burial of his origins under his Spanish name was the reason why his life was "interesting" in the first place. Ben/Juan's is likely the story of a freeborn boy named Ben who was kidnapped and enslaved. This, however, is more certain: it is a story about both the fascination and the reluctance that he elicited – about people moved by a mix of solidarity, politics, sense of duty, and masochistic voyeurism who wanted to hear or read about such an interesting life, as well as about people who were equally eager to know nothing about it.[50] It was because some of them worked hard to ignore the slave's origins that others were open to and even eager for anagnorisis – that decisive moment when Ben would be finally recognized as a person who should have never been a slave (whether this recognition implied that it was acceptable to enslave other people is, of course, an equally interesting question).

The disjunction between reality (Ben?) and appearance (Juan?) is also present in the archive as one between voice and convention. Ben/Juan's testimony should be treated as a palimpsest that includes a lot more words than the ones he used. Even though it is the only known remainder of a unique life, his testimony is not just his, as the white interlocutors who heard and transcribed it shaped it with their own questions, comments, doubts, facial expressions, and silences, and as the hand that put it in writing could not but borrow from available discursive genres and respond to ongoing debates. As for the latter, we should recall that Ben/Juan's story was inscribed in a decades-long ideological struggle between English-speaking abolitionists (most notably, British officers such as David Turnbull) and Spanish Caribbean pro-slavery interests. Havana was at the very epicenter of these struggles. As for the available discursive genres, we should point out at least in passing that a long-dated fear and fascination with captivity had bred many similar stories across time in the New World. It has been even argued that "the single narrative form indigenous to the New World is the victim's recounting of unwilling captivity."[51] In the U.S. context, as well as in others, this form was being repurposed into slave narratives, in which the roles of the "savage" and the "civilized" were inverted: the supposedly civilized now reduced to slavery and tortured the presumed savages. When viewed from this perspective, whole sections of Ben/Juan's 1853 testimony fit easily in a robust and growing corpus of slave narratives. "I was born in … ", the phrase with which it begins, was one of its most recurring tropes. The same can be said about his quick account of his parents, the references to the cruelty of his masters, and the mention of his previous, failed attempts at gaining freedom. Even its episodic and rambling nature can be understood as generic. From this perspective, most of the claims we could make about the experience of the slave based on his testimony are little more than tentative, as his voice – no matter how fundamental in his constitution as a subject and his pursuit of freedom – reaches us through this maze of conventions.[52]

This said, conventions were also the means for constructing a sense of veracity and authenticity. Ben/Juan's testimony has many of those "areas of hesitation" and those compressed, general accounts of the past that scholars have defined as constitutive of documentary prose, and, in that sense, as rhetorical indicators of truth.[53] He declares, for example: "I was so small when I left Charleston that I have no distinct recollection of any thing there, except that the gentleman who governed the place was tall and had the use of one eye only."[54] The very feebleness of his memory serves at this point as evidence, because not remembering in great detail can be more convincing than the opposite. A similar rhetorical strategy is at play in the news coverage. According to the *Weekly Herald,* Ben said that his plan had been to reach "the America" (quotation marks in the original) – by which he meant the consulate, as the amused journalist clarifies. Did he really speak that way or was this just one more instance of that blackspeech with which writers ventriloquized racialized others? Be it as it may, the phrase was presented as an indication of truthfulness, as the candidness that the quotation marks attributed to the slave was to be surely understood as a clue to his ineffectualness at lying. Even more crucially, however, all of these conventions were put in motion by Ben/Juan' own movements. Coerced displacements and confinement were the conditions that allowed a fabricated narrative to be imposed on his life. It makes sense, therefore, to think of his autonomous movements as a means of constructing a counter-narrative. Moving in space, in both cases, produced meaning.

Quietus

The investigation carried out by the authorities did not produce conclusive results. In December the Spanish consulate in Charleston notified Havana that they had still not been able to find any corresponding baptismal records. On 11 May, the new Captain General, Juan de la Pezuela, sent a report to Spain informing of the case and complaining about Robertson. In spite of the diligence with which the investigation had been conducted, he observed, the consul *"se ha mostrado de un modo tan destemplado en sus últimas comunicaciones dicho agente, sin precedente que pudiera conducirlo a tal estremo, que sobre ello llamo la superior atención"* (has been so ill-tempered in his most recent communications, without any reason for such extremes, that I call your superior attention to the matter).[55] Even though Pezuela was the nightmare of Cuban planters, as he seemed determined to stop the illegal trade and took a number of measures that were perceived as leading to abolition, his report does not show any particular interest in Ben/Juan but rather alarm at the consul's tone. Diplomatic tensions were at their worse. The *Black Warrior,* a U.S. passenger and mail ship, had been seized by Cuban authorities in late February 1854 for custom violations, and the Pierce administration seemed willing to make a *casus belli* out of it.[56] Just a few weeks before Pezuela wrote his report, the *New York Herald* had suggested to get "three or four war steamers, and despatch them to Cuba, with peremptory orders to obtain satisfaction for the injury done to the Black Warrior."[57] Cuban planters were of course major players in this design. On 14 May, Robertson informed the Secretary of State that the "cry is *Revolution* – arms are being procured as fast as possible."[58]

In passing, the report also mentions that Ben/Juan had died. It includes no details about when, how, or where. The name Ben is not used. Rather, he is referred to as "*un negro llamado Juan Criollo*" (a black man named Juan Criollo). The main purpose of the report was indeed to inform about the pressure being put on Cuba by the American consulate. Ben/Juan's story, at this point, once again, stops being his and becomes that of his white sponsors. He probably would have not been surprised. If his more than forty years in Cuba had taught him anything, it was that everybody could know his story as well as how to ignore it. Yet he managed to tell it in such a way that it still haunts us today.

Notes

1. "Expediente sobre haberse presentado el negro Juan Criollo esclavo de Martitegui y Ca. al agente comercial encargado del Consulado de los Estados Unidos, exponiendo ser natural de Charleston, de condición libre habérsele reducido a esclavitud desde muy pequeño." Archivo Nacional de Cuba (hereafter ANC), Gobierno Superior Civil (hereafter GSC), 948/33475, 1853.
2. William H. Robertson to Secretary of State William L. Marcy, Havana, 8 October 1853. In *Despatches from United States Consuls in Havana, Cuba, 1783–1906* (hereafter DUSCH), roll 26 (16 February 1853–29 December 1853).
3. Miller, *The French Atlantic Triangle*, 34–35. As Jenson has argued, however, limiting one's attention to the slave narrative obscures other genres produced in the French colonial and postcolonial worlds (Jenson, *Beyond the Slave Narrative*, 2). On slave narratives in the British West Indies, see Aljoe, *Creole Testimonies.*
4. Manzano, *Autobiografía de un esclavo.* A few examples that I cite in this article are Meriño and Perera, *Estrategias de libertad*; Cowling, *Conceiving Freedom*; Barcia, "Fighting"; De la Fuente, "Slaves and the Creation" and "Slave Law." On Manzano's autobiography, see Aching, *Freedom from Liberation.* In the realm of literary studies, Julio Ramos' "La ley es otra" constitutes a notable exception, as it engages with the testimony of a slave named María Antonia. See also Price, "African Interpreters." Other Cuban slaves' testimonies can be found in García, *Voices of the Enslaved* and Pérez de la Riva, "Antiguos esclavos." Also, on 2 October 1854 the *The British and Foreign Anti-Slavery Reporter* published "Cuban Slaves in England," including depositions from several *emancipados* sailing from Plymouth to the west coast of Africa.
5. Wilson, *Freedom at Risk,* 59–61 and Bolster, *Black Jacks*, 196.
6. Robertson, letter to Secretary of State, 8 October 1853, DUSCH, 282.
7. In 2008, with an eye on the history of science, the term "agnotology" was coined to frame the general study of socially-constructed ignorance (see Proctor and Schiebinger, *Agnotology*).

8. Meriño and Perera, *Contrabando*, 103. Regardless of the law, as Sidney Chalhoub has argued in reference to Brazil, the continuous enslavement of Africans "was legitimated by custom" (422).
9. Robertson, letter to Secretary of State, 8 October 1853, DUSCH, 279. Underlined in the original.
10. Ibid, 281. The parentheses and the underlining are part of the original, in which some Spanish words, like "cepo," are nevertheless not underlined.
11. *Gaceta de La Habana*, 1 Oct., 4 and 7 Oct, "De oficio," 2. See also Scott, "Paper Thin" and Scott and Venegas, "María Coleta." The two major nineteenth-century literary works that engage with plagiarism in the Cuban context are Cirilo Villaverde's *Cecilia Valdés* (1882), which does so incidentally, and Francisco Calcagno's *Uno de tantos* (1881; republished in 1891 as *Romualdo, uno de tantos*), which focuses on the issue. See Goldgel, "Plagio y anacronismo deliberado." For studies of free blacks kidnapped in the U.S., see Wilson, *Freedom at Risk*, Bell, *Stolen*, and Rothman, *Beyond Freedom's Reach*.
12. Urban, "The Africanization Scare." Alexander M. Clayton, the U.S. consul between 1853 and 1854 (absent from the island, however, when Ben/Juan visited the consulate), pointed out the following in a letter to a friend written a few years later: "When I reached the Consulate in December 1853, I soon became surrounded by persons, who were anxious to use every possible means to prevail on me, [sic] to induce our Government to take the Island" (Sydnor, "Letter," 366). In peninsular Spain, two versions of Stowe's *Uncle Tom's Cabin* were performed in 1853. As Surwillo observes, they were "part of a larger 'Black Tom' phenomenon in Spanish social literature of the midcentury" (32–33).
13. Díaz Martínez, "Trabajo y negocio," 236–239.
14. While first just customary, the right of slaves to "pedir papel" and use it to seek a new owner was codified in the 1842 ordinance regulating slave-holding known as the "Reglamento de Esclavos." See Barcia, "Fighting," 168; De la Fuente, "Slaves and the Creation," 662; De la Fuente, "Slave Law," 367.
15. "Expediente sobre haberse presentado," ANC, GSC, 948/33475, 1853.
16. I borrow the term "slave-mover" from Cowling, "Teresa Mina's Many Journeys."
17. Howard, *American Slavers*, 113. Savage had grown up in Havana and assisted numerous consul generals. When his superiors were away, he was in charge of the Consulate. A few years after Ben's visit, he refused to provide suspicious vessels with the paperwork they regularly used to avoid British inspections in their travels to Africa (Howard, *American Slavers*, 114).
18. Guerra, *Manual de historia*, 532 and Pérez, *Sugar, Cigars, and Revolution*, 107
19. Foner, *A history*, II, 80 (italics in the original). Robertson sent it under the heading "Ideas that must be taken into consideration in composing the proclamation that will be addressed by the President to the Inhabitant of Cuba when the American Army shall come to the same." As Foner observes, several big slave-owners met with Robertson and urged him "that he persuade President Pierce to send American troops to Cuba" (80). Many Cubans were equally active in the U.S. (Domínguez, "Slaveholders in the South"). For an analysis of how annexationist conspiracies bloomed in the early 1850s, see Pérez, *Cuba*, 45–46.
20. Manning, *Diplomatic Correspondence*, XI, 787. On Pezuela, see also Urban, "The Africanization Scare."
21. "Late and Interesting from Cuba," n.p. The article also reappeared as "An American Free Negro in Cuba" in the *North American and United States gazette* (Philadelphia, Pennsylvania), Thursday, 27 October 1853; Issue 18,927 and, with the same title, in *The Friend. A Religious and Literary Journal.* Vol. XXVII, No. 18. 14 January 1854. Philadelphia: Kite and Walton, 143.
22. "Late and Interesting from Cuba," n.p.
23. Lee, *The Cambridge Companion*, 19; Stowe, *The Annotated*, xxxix.
24. Sinha, *The Slave's Cause*, 500–501. In Northern states there was a continuous interest in stories like Ben/Juan's. In 1844, for example, Elizabeth Hoar, who had been engaged to Charles Emerson (Ralph Waldo Emerson's brother), accompanied her father all the way down from Massachusetts to South Carolina to try to convince state officials to do something about the free blacks who were being regularly kidnapped from Northern boats (Wood, *Black Milk*, 100).

25. In his *Ever Faithful: Race, Loyalty, and the Ends of Empire in Spanish Cuba,* Sartorius has alerted us to the tendency in Cuban studies to overlook the variegated political subjectivities of people of African descent (see, for example, 60–61). Arguably, an American-born boy like Ben/Juan was as likely to become "Cuban" as African-born subjects. Focusing on the latter (including one, Olaudah Equiano, who at some point of his life also claimed to have been born in South Carolina). Sweet has shown that an either/or model of identity severely limits our understanding of the Black Atlantic ("Mistaken Identity," 283). While Ben/Juan invokes precisely that kind of model in his quest for freedom, his testimony also demonstrates that he was different things to different people.
26. Cowling, "Esclavitud," 219–227. In *Conceiving Freedom*, Cowling shows the prominence of women in legal struggles and the importance of being in Havana (128–132). For the U.S. South, see Camp, *Closer to Freedom*.
27. As the recurrence of the tropes of the black hole and black matter in black feminist scholarship shows, the fact that some lives and experiences are invisible to those exterior to them does not mean that they do not affect their environments in perceivable ways. See, for example, Browne, *Dark Matters*, and Hammonds, "Black (W)holes." As for the forms of solidarity that slaves found in Havana, a good example can be found in the 1843 testimony of James Thomson. Born in Nassau in 1812, he was kidnapped and kept enslaved in Cuba for 21 years until he successful ran away: "On going down to the wharf, I met a native of Jamaica, a former acquaintance, who advised me to go to the English Consul, Mr. Turnbull, and he accompanied me thither. Not finding him at the office, I had to go away and wait until the next day. While passing through the streets in search of a lodging, I saw Mr. --------, a native of Nassau, who kindly gave me shelter, and on the following day identified me to the Consul, as did also a coloured woman, another native of Nassau" (*The British and Foreign Anti-Slavery Reporter*, 3 May 1843, 72). On the spread of information in the Caribbean more broadly, see Scott, *A Common Wind.* On the specific topic of Haiti in this context, see Ferrer, "Speaking of Haiti." On the study of gossip and rumors as sources, see Derby, "Beyond Fugitive Speech."
28. Robertson, letter to Secretary of State, 8 October 1853, DUSCH, 282.
29. "Late and Interesting from Cuba," n.p.
30. Meriño and Perera, *Contrabando*, 244. On country marks, see Gomez, *Exchanging Our Country Marks.*
31. Robertson, letter to Secretary of State, 8 October 1853, DUSCH, 277 and 285. As one of the enslaved Bahamian brothers studied by Barcia observed in 1845, "The English language is common there [the district of Candelaria] where it is even spoken by Spaniards and African slaves" ("*The Kelsall Affaire*," 284–285). Barcia also quotes the British consul in Havana, Joseph T. Crawford, who in 1843 claimed that there were "several thousands" of slaves introduced illegally in Cuba from the Bahamas (Ibid., 280). The same year, citing an unnamed "highest authority," *The British and Foreign Anti-Slavery Reporter* repeated this information (3 May 1843, 71).
32. Robertson, letter to Secretary of State, 8 October 1853, DUSCH, 276.
33. "Late and Interesting from Cuba," n.p.
34. Zeuske, "The Names of Slavery," 63–65. Barcia, "*The Kelsall Affaire*," 282.
35. "Expediente sobre haberse presentado," ANC, GSC, 948/33475, 1853.
36. Ibid.
37. Ibid.
38. Ibid.
39. Robertson, letter to Secretary of State, 8 October 1853, DUSCH, 284.
40. Zeuske and García, "Estado, notarios y esclavos," para. 36. See also Meriño and Perera, *Estrategias de libertad*, Vol. 1, 270, Zeuske, "The Names of Slavery"; "Out of America." We don't know why his owners waited fifteen years to baptize Ben/Juan, but the fact that they did proves that they could, thus suggesting that not being "officially" Juan had little or no impact on his prospects for freedom during this early stage of his bondage.
41. Meriño and Perera, *Del tráfico*, 244–298.

42. Aristotle, *Poetics,* 28.
43. By "literary fiction" I mean an imaginative text that is not necessarily verifiable (Cohn, *The Distinction of Fiction*, 15). The bibliography on the relationship between fiction and history is too broad to reference here. Saidiya Hartman's *Wayward Lives* constitutes an interesting and recent example, as it re-presents or fictionalizes the lives of the black women she studies. For responses to Hartman's earlier calls and for "critical fabulation" on the part of scholars working on slavery, see the special issue of *History of the Present* edited by Connolly and Fuentes.
44. Foley, *Telling the Truth,* 85.
45. Robertson, letter to Secretary of State, 8 October 1853, DUSCH, 279.
46. Ibid., 282–283.
47. Referring to Brazil (but the same could be clearly argued about Cuba), Chalhoub has observed that the illegal trade also made freedom more precarious for people of African descent, "The Precariousness of Freedom," 424–427.
48. Eltis, "A Brief Overview."
49. Aristotle, *Poetics*, 30.
50. On the masochistic pleasure on the part of the person empathizing with slaves and the "economy of enjoyment" developed around them, see Hartman, *Scenes of Subjection*, 18–26.
51. Kolodny, *The Land Before Her*, 6.
52. On captivity narratives, see Pierce, "Redeeming Bondage," 85. On slave narratives, see Olney, "'I was born'," 50–51. On the rambling and episodic as generic, see Foley, *Telling the Truth*, 394. Among the vast literature that examines the tension between black subjectivity and white sponsorship and media in slave narratives in the U.S. context, Olney's "'I was born'" and Sekora's "Black Message/White Envelope" stand as two well-known examples. For Baker, similarly, slave narratives prevent access to "the authentic voice of black American slavery," as the individual is "transformed into a sharer in the general public discourse about slavery," *The Journey Back*, 43. Taking distance from this focus on the erasure of the black voice, scholars such as Andrews and Santamarina emphasize the collaborative nature of the practice. For the Cuban context, see Ramos, "La ley es otra" and "Cuerpo, lengua, subjetividad," as well as Aching, *Freedom from Liberation*.
53. Toker, "Toward a Poetics," 193 and 197–198.
54. Robertson, letter to Secretary of State, 8 October 1853, DUSCH, 284.
55. "Testimonio del espediente gubernativo formado sobre reclamo hecho por el negro Juan, Criollo, de nación Inglés, sobre su libertad" (ca. 80 folios), La Habana, Francisco de Castro, 29 de Abril de 1854." Archivo Histórico Nacional de Madrid, Estado, Trata de negros, 8047–2/19, no. 6.
56. Guerra, *Manual de historia,* 538–539.
57. *New York Herald*, 11 March 1854, n.p.
58. Manning, *Diplomatic Correspondence*, XI, 786.

Acknowledgements

I would like to thank Camillia Cowling, Daylet Domínguez, María de los Ángeles Meriño, Aisnara Perera, Julio Ramos, Daniel Rood, Francisco Scarano, James Sweet, and Sarah Wells for their generous comments on different drafts of this paper. Also, many thanks to Carlos Venegas for his guidance in the Havana archives and to the *Atlantic Studies* anonymous reviewers for their thoughtful suggestions.

Disclosure statement

No potential conflict of interest was reported by the author(s).

Funding

This work was supported by the American Council of Learned Societies, the Vilas Associate award (University of Wisconsin, Madison), and the National Humanities Center.

Bibliography

Aching, Gerard Laurence. *Freedom from Liberation: Slavery, Sentiment, and Literature in Cuba.* Bloomington: Indiana University Press, 2015.

Aljoe, Nicole N. *Creole Testimonies: Slave Narratives from the British West Indies, 1709–1838.* New York: Palgrave Macmillan, 2012.

Andrews, William L. *To Tell a Free Story: The First Century of Afro-American Autobiography, 1760–1865.* Urbana: University of Illinois Press, 1988.

Aristotle. *Poetics.* Oxford: Oxford University Press, 2013.

Baker, Houston. *The Journey Back.* Chicago: University of Chicago Press, 1980.

Barcia Paz, Manuel. "Fighting with the Enemy's Weapons: The Usage of the Colonial Legal Framework by Nineteenth Cuban Slaves." *Atlantic Studies* 3, no. 2 (March 2006): 159–181.

Barcia Paz, Manuel. "The Kelsall Affaire. A Black Bahamian Family's Odyssey in Turbulent 1840s Cuba." In *The Chattel Principle: Internal Slave Trades in the Americas*, edited by Walter Johnson, 275–290. New Haven, CT: Yale University Press, 2004.

Bell, Richard. *Stolen: Five Free Boys Kidnapped into Slavery and Their Astonishing Odyssey Home.* New York: Simon & Schuster, 2019.

Bolster, W. Jeffrey. *Black Jacks: African American Seamen in the Age of Sail.* Cambridge, MA: Harvard University Press, 1997.

Browne, Simone. *Dark Matters: On the Surveillance of Blackness.* Durham, NC: Duke University Press, 2015.

Calcagno, Juan Francisco. *Uno de tantos. Novela cubana.* La Habana: Imprenta del Avisador Comercial, 1881.

Camp, Stephanie M. H. *Closer to Freedom: Enslaved Women and Everyday Resistance in the Plantation South.* Chapel Hill: University of North Carolina Press, 2004.

Chalhoub, Sidney. "The Precariousness of Freedom in a Slave Society (Brazil in the Nineteenth Century)." *International Review of Social History* 56, no. 3 (2011): 405–239.

Cohn, Dorrit. *The Distinction of Fiction.* Baltimore, MD: Johns Hopkins University Press, 2000.

Connolly, Brian, and Marisa Fuentes. eds."[Special Issue]." *History of the Present* 6, no. 2 (2016).

Cowling, Camillia. *Conceiving Freedom: Women of Color, Gender, and the Abolition of Slavery in Havana and Rio de Janeiro.* Chapel Hill: University of North Carolina Press, 2013.

Cowling, Camillia. "Teresa Mina's Many Journeys: Between "Slave-Moving" and "Mobility" in Mid-Nineteenth-Century Cuba" (in this volume).

Díaz Martínez, Yolanda. "Trabajo y negocio: los cimarrones dentro y fuera del depósito." In *Orden político y gobierno de esclavos: Cuba en la época de la segunda esclavitud y de su legado*, edited by José Antonio Piqueras Arenas, 229–252. Valencia: Centro Francisco Tomás y Valiente Uned Alzira-Valencia, Fundación Instituto de Historia Social, 2016.

De la Fuente, Alejandro. "Slave Law and Claims-Making in Cuba: The Tannenbaum Debate Revisited." *Law and History Review* 22, no. 2 (2004): 339–369.

De la Fuente, Alejandro. "Slaves and the Creation of Legal Rights in Cuba: *Coartación* and *Papel.*" *Hispanic American Historical Review* 87, no. 4 (2007): 659–692.

Derby, Lauren. "Beyond Fugitive Speech: Rumor and Affect in Caribbean History." *Small Axe: A Caribbean Journal of Criticism* 18, no. 2 (44) (2014): 123–140.

Domínguez, Daylet. "Slaveholders in the South: The Networks of Cubans and Southerners in the Age of the Second Slavery" (in this volume).

Eltis, David. "A Brief Overview of the Trans-Atlantic Slave Trade." Voyages: The Trans-Atlantic Slave Trade Database. Accessed 15 July 2019. https://www.slavevoyages.org/voyage/about.

Ferrer, Ada. "Speaking of Haiti: Slavery, Revolution, and Freedom in Cuban Slave Testimony." In *The World of the Haitian Revolution*, edited by David Patrick Geggus and Norman Fiering, 223–247. Bloomington: Indiana University Press, 2009.

Foley, Barbara C. *Telling the Truth: The Theory and Practice of Documentary Fiction*. Ithaca, NY: Cornell University Press, 2018.

Foner, Philip Sheldon. *A History of Cuba and Its Relations with the United States. 2 Vols*. New York: International Publishers, 1962.

García, Gloria. *Voices of the Enslaved in Nineteenth-Century Cuba: A Documentary History*. Translated by Nancy L. Westrate. Chapel Hill: University of North Carolina Press, 2011.

Goldgel, Victor. "Plagio y anacronismo deliberado en la novela antiesclavista cubana." *Revista de Estudios Hispánicos* 53, no. 2 (June 2019): 563–584.

Gomez, Michael A. *Exchanging Our Country Marks: The Transformation of African Identities in the Colonial and Antebellum South*. Chapel Hill: University of North Carolina Press, 2000.

Guerra, Ramiro. *Manual de historia de Cuba: desde su descubrimiento hasta 1868*. Madrid: Ediciones Erre, 1975.

Hammonds, Evelynn. "Black (W)holes and the Geometry of Black Female Sexuality." *differences: A Journal of Feminist Cultural Studies* 6, no. 2–3 (Summer-Fall 1994): 126–145.

Hartman, Saidiya. *Scenes of Subjection: Terror, Slavery, and Self-Making in Nineteenth-Century America*. New York: Oxford University Press, 1997.

Hartman, Saidiya. *Wayward Lives, Beautiful Experiments: Intimate Histories of Social Upheaval*. New York: W. W. Norton, 2019.

Howard, Warren S. *American Slavers and the Federal Law, 1837–1862*. Berkeley: University of California Press, 1963.

Jenson, Deborah. *Beyond the Slave Narrative: Politics, Sex, and Manuscripts in the Haitian Revolution*. Liverpool: Liverpool University Press, 2012.

Kolodny, Annette. *The Land Before Her: Fantasy and Experience of the American Frontiers, 1630–1860*. Chapel Hill: University of North Carolina Press, 1984.

"Late and Interesting from Cuba". *Weekly Herald* [New York, New York], 22 October1853: n.p.

Lee, Maurice S. *The Cambridge Companion to Frederick Douglass*. Cambridge: Cambridge University Press, 2009.

Manning, William R. *Diplomatic Correspondence of the United States: Inter-American Affairs, 1831–1860. 12 Vols*. Washington: Carnegie Endowment for International Peace, 1932.

Manzano, Juan Francisco. *Autobiography of a slave. / Autobiografía de un esclavo*. Translated by Evelyn Picon Garfield. Detroit, MI: Wayne State University Press, 1996.

Meriño, Fuentes, María de los Ángeles, and Aisnara Perera Díaz. *Contrabando de bozales en Cuba. Perseguir el tráfico y mantener la esclavitud (1845–1866)*. San José de las Lajas, Mayabeque, Cuba: Ediciones Montecallado, 2015.

Meriño, Fuentes, María de los Ángeles, and Aisnara Perera Díaz. *Del tráfico a la libertad. El caso de los africanos de la fragata Dos hermanos en Cuba. 1795–1837*. Santiago de Cuba: Editorial Oriente, 2014.

Meriño, Fuentes, María de los Ángeles, and Aisnara Perera Díaz. *Estrategias de libertad: un acercamiento a las acciones legales de los esclavos en Cuba (1762–1872) 2 vols*. Havana: Editorial de Ciencias Sociales, 2015.

Miller, Christopher L. *The French Atlantic Triangle: Literature and Culture of the Slave Trade*. Durham, NC: Duke University Press, 2008.

Olney, James. "'I Was Born': Slave Narratives, Their Status as Autobiography and as Literature." *Callaloo* 20 (Winter 1984): 46–73.

Pérez, Lisandro. *Sugar, Cigars, and Revolution: The Making of Cuban New York*. New York: New York University Press, 2018.

Pérez, Louis A. *Cuba and the United States: Ties of Singular Intimacy*. Athens: University of Georgia Press, 2003.
Pérez de la Riva, Juan. "Antiguos esclavos cubanos que regresan a Lagos." In *Contribución a la historia de la gente sin historia*, edited by Pedro Deschamps Chapeaux and J. Pérez de la Riva, 163–190. La Habana: Editorial de Ciencias Sociales, 1974.
Pierce, Yolanda. "Redeeming Bondage: The Captivity Narrative and the Spiritual Autobiography in the African American Slave Narrative Tradition." In *The Cambridge Companion to the African American Slave Narrative*, edited by Audrey Fisch, 83–98. Cambridge: Cambridge University Press, 2007.
Price, Rachel L. "African Interpreters in the Cuban Courts: The Case of an Uprising on the Cafetal Salvador in Banes, Cuba, 1833." Manuscript.
Proctor, Robert N., and Londa Schiebinger. *Agnotology: The Making and Unmaking of Ignorance*. Stanford, CA: Stanford University Press, 2008.
Ramos, Julio. "Cuerpo, lengua, subjetividad." *Revista de Crítica Literaria Latinoamericana* 19, no. 38 (1993): 225–237.
Ramos, Julio. "'La ley es otra': Literatura y constitución de la persona jurídica." *Revista de Crítica Literaria Latinoamericana* 20, no. 40 (1994): 305–335.
Rothman, Adam. *Beyond Freedom's Reach: A Kidnapping in the Twilight of Slavery*. Cambridge, MA: Harvard University Press, 2015.
Santamarina, Xiomara. *Belabored Professions: Narratives of African American Working Womanhood*. Chapel Hill: University of North Carolina Press, 2005.
Sartorius, David. *Ever Faithful: Race, Loyalty, and the Ends of Empire in Spanish Cuba*. Durham, NC: Duke University Press, 2014.
Scott, Julius. *A Common Wind: Afro-American Organization in the Revolution Against Slavery*. New York: Verso Books, 2018.
Scott, Rebecca J. *Slave Emancipation in Cuba: The Transition to Free Labor, 1860–1899*. Pittsburgh, PA: University of Pittsburgh Press, 2000.
Scott, Rebecca J. "Paper Thin: Freedom and Re-Enslavement in the Diaspora of the Haitian Revolution." *Law and History Review* 29 (November 2011): 1061–1087.
Scott, Rebecca J., and Carlos Venegas Fornias. "María Coleta and the Capuchin Friar: Slavery, Salvation, and the Adjudication of Status." *The William and Mary Quarterly* 76, no. 4 (October 2019): 727–762.
Sekora, John. "Black Message/White Envelope. Genre, Authenticity, and Authority in the Antebellum Slave Narratives." *Callaloo* 10 (1987): 482–515.
Sinha, Manisha. *The Slave's Cause: A History of Abolition*. New Haven, CT: Yale University Press, 2016.
Surwillo, Lisa. *Monsters by Trade: Slave Traffickers in Modern Spanish Literature and Culture*. Stanford, CA: Stanford University Press, 2014.
Stowe, Harriet Beecher. *The Annotated Uncle Tom's Cabin*. New York: W. W. Norton, 2007.
Sweet, James. "Mistaken Identities? Olaudah Equiano, Domingos Álvares, and the Methodological Challenges of Studying the African Diaspora." *The American Historical Review* 114, no. 2 (April 2009): 279–306.
Sydnor, Charles S. "Letter from Alexander M. Clayton to J. F. H. Claiborne Relative to Cuban Affairs." *The Hispanic American Historical Review* 9, no. 3 (1929): 364–368.
Toker, Leona. "Toward a Poetics of Documentary Prose – From the Perspective of Gulag Testimonies." *Poetics Today* 18, no. 2 (Summer 1997): 187–222.
Urban, C. Stanley. "The Africanization of Cuba Scare, 1853–1855." *The Hispanic American Historical Review* 37, no. 1 (1957): 29–45.
Villaverde, Cirilo. In *Cecilia Valdes or El Angel Hill*. Translated by Helen Lane, edited by Sibylle Fischer. Oxford: Oxford University Press, 2005.
Wilson, Carol. *Freedom at Risk: The Kidnapping of Free Blacks in America, 1780–1865*. Lexington: The University Press of Kentucky, 1994.
Wood, Marcus. *Black Milk: Imagining Slavery in the Visual Cultures of Brazil and America*. Oxford: Oxford University Press, 2013.

Zeuske, Michael. "Out of the Americas: Slave Traders and the *Hidden Atlantic* in the Nineteenth Century." *Atlantic Studies* 15, no. 1 (January 2018): 103–135.

Zeuske, Michael. "The Names of Slavery and Beyond: the Atlantic, the Americas and Cuba." In *The End of Slavery in Africa and the Americas. A Comparative Approach, Münster-Hamburg-Berlin-Wien-London*, edited by Ulrike Schmieder, Katja Füllberg-Stolberg and Michael Zeuske, 51–80. Berlin: LIT-Verlag, 2011.

Zeuske, Michael, and Orlando García Martínez. "Estado, notarios y esclavos en Cuba." *Nuevo Mundo Mundos Nuevos* (Online), Debates. Accessed 21 July 2019. http://journals.openedition.org/nuevomundo/15842.

Appendix

After publishing this article as part of the special issue "Slavery, mobility, and networks in nineteenth-century Cuba" (2021), I conducted research at Madrid's Archivo Histórico Nacional and read a number of documents that substantially changed my understanding of Ben's case (in particular, "El Cónsul de los Estados Unidos en la Habana reclama la libertad del negro Juan Criollo," Estado, 8047–2/19). U.S. diplomats, I learned, had been able to locate and interview Ben's mother, Elizabeth Newton, in the isle of New Providence. Lizzie, as Ben called her, declared that she had never set foot in Charleston. Before moving to the Bahamas, she and her family had lived in Florida "among the Indians" (see also *Bahama Herald*, 21 December 1853). Moreover, she said, Ben had been born in 1810 and kidnapped in 1819 or 1820. Having reflected on this new evidence, I still consider "Forty-one years a slave" an accurate title. It stems from the story that mattered the most: the one Ben told. Born in Charleston or among Black Seminoles in Florida, enslaved for forty-one years or for thirty-three, Ben was able to move key actors with his words and force authorities to put his story in writing.

Furthermore, like the Paris police in Edgar Allan Poe's "The Purloined Letter," when I was writing the article I overlooked something very important that was hiding in plain sight: Ben did not refer to himself in racialized terms but rather as "a man born free in a civilized country" and as the son of "freemen." In other words, as I point out in my forthcoming book on race in nineteenth-century Cuba, Ben showed no signs of wanting to be known as black – not, at least, when dealing with white people in positions of power. Paradoxically, the racist agnosia against which he struggled resurfaced even in my anti-racist efforts to avoid it: I mused about whether I should capitalize "black," without realizing that to belabor this point meant ignoring Ben's most explicit claim—that he was, quite simply, "a man born free."

The capitalized "B," as well as the longer and broader historical struggles through which people of African descent began reclaiming blackness with pride, transforming it into Blackness, are signs of empowerment. There was a time, however, when a counterhegemonic praxis could consist of the opposite – when enslaved people, as historians of Latin America have shown, tried to escape from the grip of race and embrace the language of natural rights as part of their struggles for emancipation. Ben died (or, as I am now more inclined to believe, was disappeared) without reuniting with his family or recovering the freedom that would have allowed him to embrace all aspects of his past, had he wanted to do so. Yet he managed to tell a powerful story, positioning himself as, and convincing others that he was, the person he claimed to be.

Slaveholders in the South: The networks of Cubans and Southerners in the age of the second slavery

Daylet Domínguez

ABSTRACT
This study examines the alliances between Cuban and Southern planters before 1861 as a means of counteracting the rise of abolitionism across the Atlantic. The massive expansion of slavery in Cuba and in the US South in the first half of the nineteenth century led Cuban and Southern planters to perceive new geopolitical cartographies that challenged existing cultural, linguistic, and political borders. These alliances were not solely fashioned to preserve slavery in the southern United States or in Cuba, but rather as a piece of the larger battle between the pro-slavery and abolitionist forces of the Atlantic world in which the future of slavery was at stake. By analyzing essays written by Ambrosio Gonzales, Cristóbal Madan, and John S. Thrasher, I argue that in the mid-nineteenth century, slavery had the capacity to forge hemispheric alliances that transcended cultural and political links, thus helping to imagine alternative futures for the region.

In the decades preceding the US Civil War, Cuban and Southern planters, as well as politicians and journalists from the Northern states and the island, began to envision new geopolitical cartographies of the region caused by the expansion of the abolitionist movement driven by England. As tensions between the North and the South as well as between Cuba and Spain increased, Cuban and Southern slaveholders turned to each other and imagined themselves as part of the same geographical cartography united by chattel bondage. Their commitment to the future of slavery allowed them to transcend imperial and national circuits. Both were bound together as slaveholders in the Americas, and they used a common vocabulary to respond to the rise of abolitionism in the Atlantic sphere. They likewise developed a pro-slavery argument that relied on scientific racism.[1]

While the idea that the Southern states of the United States and Cuba shared a common political destiny was quite novel in the early decades of the nineteenth century, this notion was not as far-fetched when considered from the standpoint of nature and geography. Given their shared climate and agricultural products, as well as the presence of slavery, the South had been understood as belonging to an extended Caribbean region for quite some time.[2] By the middle of the nineteenth century, many of these Cuban and Southern planters would come to fantasize about the idea of Havana becoming the capital of the Confederate States of America. With the defeat of the

Confederacy in 1865, the relationship between Southerners and Cubans did not cease to exist. For a brief period, Havana became a place of refuge for many prominent supporters of the Confederacy: politicians, soldiers, planters, merchants, and other businessmen from the South settled in the city, bringing their families and those they had enslaved with them. Although many ended up returning to their places of origin, others decided to establish themselves in one of the last redoubts of slavery in the Western Hemisphere.[3]

In what follows I will focus on the alliances that planters, members of the military, journalists, and politicians – both Cuban and Southern – devised and created before 1861 as a means of counteracting the rise of abolitionism across the Atlantic. The massive expansion of slavery in Cuba and in the southern United States in the first half of the nineteenth century, based in large part on the technological modernization of the plantation system and its integration into the global market, led those Cuban and Southern planters to perceive new geopolitical cartographies that challenged the existing cultural, linguistic, and political borders. These alliances were not solely fashioned as a way to preserve slavery in the southern United States or in Cuba, but rather as a piece of the larger battle between the pro-slavery and abolitionist forces of the Atlantic world in which the future of slavery was at stake.[4] In the mid-nineteenth century, slavery was not an institution in decline, as many historians have suggested. Rather, slavery had the capacity to forge hemispheric alliances that went beyond cultural and political links, thus helping to imagine alternative futures for the region.

But not all the narratives used to uphold this hemispheric alliance relied on an open defense of slavery. Cubans, for example, appealed to Spanish despotism to promote the incorporation of the island within the United States. Southerners raised the issue in terms of national security. In the decade prior to the Civil War, those supporting slavery, both in Cuba and the United States, approached the problem of annexation through a perspective that was not limited to just the US South. They deftly combined the interests of the South with the logic of North American expansionism, which granted the issue of Cuba a national dimension that had the mobilization of public opinion in favor of annexation as its objective.

Within the vast corpus produced by Cubans and North Americans during the 1850s, I specifically consider the manifestoes, essays, and pamphlets written by Ambrosio Gonzales, Cristóbal Madan, and John S. Thrasher for a variety of reasons. These three had known one another in Havana and began their annexation-related activities on the island at the end of the 1840s; the three were educated and lived in both the United States and Cuba, which allowed them to move within North American and Cuban circles with considerable ease, using English and Spanish. In their attempts to annex Cuba, the three experimented with filibustering, as well as with propaganda campaigns. By examining their interventions in the public sphere, it is possible to reconstruct the interweaving economic, political, and military networks between the US South and Cuba and discern the cartographies of a world to come.

This was not the first time that the Cuban elites had imagined other forms of sovereignty for the political future of the island. Since the beginning of the 1820s they had attempted to integrate Cuba into Gran Colombia or Mexico in an effort to free themselves from the Spanish yoke. By the end of the 1840s, annexation plans were pointing towards the United States and were aimed at favoring the predominance of the slave regime.[5] With this purpose, *El Club de La Habana* was formed in 1847, comprising planters and writers such as Madan, Gonzales, José Luis Alfonso, Miguel Aldama, Cirilo Villaverde, and Ramón de Palma. Of particular prominence among the members was Thrasher, of North American provenance. On behalf of the organization, Gonzales arrived in the United States in 1848 with the express purpose of contacting the US general William J. Worth, one of the most important generals in the Mexican-American War, in order to lead a foreign army against Spain in Cuba. That same year, in New York, the *Consejo Cubano* was established under the direction of Gaspar Betancourt Cisneros. *El Club de La Habana* and the *Consejo Cubano* worked together, even if they sometimes disagreed on what actions to take. Madan was not only an important agent of the *Club de La Habana* in New York, but also served as the president of the *Consejo Cubano* for three years.[6] Villaverde, after his escape from Cuba, also took part in the *Consejo Cubano*.[7]

After the arrival of Narciso López to New York in 1848, the links with Southern politicians and military intensified. Together with Gonzales, López secured meetings with Jefferson Davis, Robert E. Lee, and John Quitman in search of leadership and support for the military expeditions that he carried out between 1849 and 1851. Even after López's execution in Havana, the filibuster movement did not die down; he rapidly became a martyr, not only for the Cuban exile community, but also for the Southerners. He came to be a rather attractive figure for the culture of the Southern United States, even appearing as an important character in the novel *The Free Flag of Cuba* by Lucy Petaway Holcombe Pickens, known as "The Queen of the Confederacy." Most North American travelers who visited Cuba after 1851 wrote similarly about López's expedition and tragic end. They paid tribute to him by visiting the place where he was executed in Havana.[8] The Cuban writers, who were close to López in the United States, including Miguel Teurbe Tolón and Juan Clemente Zenea, dedicated multiple pages of their anthology, *Laúd del desterrado*, to glorify his life and death. From Spanish General, Mariscal de Campo, and Governor of Trinidad in Cuba, López ended up being the spearhead for filibusterism in the US South. His trajectory allowed the North American and Cuban supporters of annexation to have a common hero for their cause.

It was right after his death, in fact, when General Quitman, Governor of Mississippi and planter, replaced López as the leader of the filibuster movement. Through his negotiations with the *Junta Patriótica Cubana,* Quitman took up the role as the plenipotentiary leader of the Cuban invasion, endorsing annexation as a way to defend the rights of the Southern states: the fate of slavery in Cuba was thus understood as fundamental for conserving the institution of slavery in the US South.[9] As Jossianna Arroyo reminds us, the main conflict that joined US and Cuba's exile community was the possible end of slavery.[10] The moment in which the alliance between Southern and Cuban planters was at its greatest intensity was, precisely, from 1853 to 1854. Although the Cuban annexation movement lasted until the early stages of the Ten Years' War (1868–1878), when the Assembly of Guáimaro proclaimed annexation as the central objective of the Cuban rebellion, it is difficult to find another moment in which the interests of the Cubans and Southerners came together with such vigor.[11]

The trigger that led to this situation was the arrival of Juan de la Pezuela to the island as the Captain General in 1853. Known for his abolitionist tendencies, his appointment was understood on the part of the slave-holding class in Cuba and the United States as a concession to the pressure of the English government.[12] Pezuela was resolute in his efforts to eliminate the illegal trade of slaves, and with that objective, he issued various ordinances that caused great controversy among the Cuban planters. First, he decreed the liberation of all the *emancipados*, a group comprised of all the Africans who had entered illegally after the treaties signed with England in 1817 and 1820. This measure led to panic among the planter elites since most slaves on the island during the mid-1850s were there as a result of illegal trafficking. Second, Pezuela permitted investigations of plantations with the purpose of finding slave populations that had been introduced to the island illegally, and he ordered the creation of a registry of slaves on all the sugar plantations, or *ingenios*, of Cuba. Third, Pezuela favored the introduction on the island of Spanish, Yucatec, and Chinese farmers. Alongside these, he also stipulated the entry of African apprentices who would be freed after a short period of training. Fourth, Pezuela again organized the black and *pardo* militias and finally allowed interracial marriage. Many of these laws were printed in the *Diario de la marina*. Since this was the first time that abolitionist ideas were debated in the colonial public sphere on the island, these measures generated the perception that Spain had as its ultimate aim the abolition of slavery.[13]

Pezuela's administration marked the first conscious attempt to eliminate the illegal slave trade, to liberate the *emancipados*, and to give a new direction to diplomatic relations with England.[14] What ended up becoming an abolitionist experiment on the part of the Pezuela administration was perceived by the Cuban and the Southern planters as an attempt to Africanize the island. If, in fact, politicians and planters of the South deployed the term "Africanization" to describe the policies enacted by Spain over the course of the 1840s and 1850s, as Robert E. May confirms, they were to a large degree inspired by the Cuban elites who had used the same term in their efforts to justify annexation.[15] Facing pressure from both England and Spain, Cuban and Southern planters imagined being part of a common geopolitical space on which the future of slavery in the hemisphere depended.

Ambrosio Gonzales

Ambrosio Gonzales, who would come to be a colonel in the Confederacy, identified as North American both sentimentally and in terms of his education, but also as the first Cuban wounded in combat for the cause of Cuban freedom.[16] For Gonzales, there was no contradiction in his averring of both beliefs. He was born in Cuba but had received a good part of his education in New York. On the island, Gonzales had rubbed elbows with the prominent planters and writers that comprised the *Club de Habana*; very soon he would maintain relations with John C. Calhoun, Jefferson Davis, Robert E. Lee, John Sullivan, and Mirabeau B. Lamar, among others. Because of his fluency in English, he became the right-hand-man to Narciso López and was tasked with developing relations with the political and military spheres of the United States. Many of the proclamations written with the intention of galvanizing the North American soldiers who joined his expeditions, although signed by López, were written in English by Gonzales himself. Likewise, the second expedition commanded by López would be organized in large part by Gonzales from New Orleans. In less than two years, he went from being a mere collaborator to one of the central figures of the Cuban annexation movement.[17] By the time the Civil War began, he was a key member of the Southern elite. Coming from a slave-holding family in Matanzas, he had become a planter in South Carolina by virtue of his marriage with Harriet Elliot, the daughter of a wealthy landowner. Following the abolition of slavery in 1865, Gonzales would become, as his biographer Antonio Rafael de la Cova notes, "the first person to promote Chinese and European indentured farmers in South Carolina, a policy that was later embraced by state politicians."[18]

Throughout the 1850s, Gonzales made various forays into the North American public sphere with the objective of mobilizing support among the populace for the cause of Cuban annexation. In 1852, to commemorate the first anniversary of López's death, he wrote the *Manifesto on Cuban Affairs Addressed to the People of the United States*. The pamphlet was published the following year in the *Daily Delta* of New Orleans, which was considered the most enthusiastic of all the local presses for Cuban annexation.[19] Between November 1858 and January 1859, he was commissioned by the Speaker of the House, James L. Orr, to write a series of ten articles about Cuban annexation in the *Detroit Daily Free Press*.[20] If his *Manifesto* was intended for the North American people at large, the journalistic articles focused mostly on the reading public of the US North.[21] In both cases, Gonzales promoted the idea of Cuban annexation not from a regional, Southern, standpoint, but instead by appealing to a notion of US nationalism; one that was imbued with the ideology of republicanism, but also tolerated expansionism and slavery.[22]

In his public writings, Gonzales attempted to overcome the traditional distinction between northern abolitionism and southern slave ownership by employing a homogenizing rhetoric that appealed to all North Americans. In the decade prior to the Civil War, those supporting annexation, filibusterism, and Cuban separatism had to formulate their arguments while considering various blocs and interests. First, there were prominent northern abolitionists that favored the annexation of Cuba. Second, a large number of North Americans who owned plantations in Cuba were originally from the northern states.[23] Rather than settling in the slave-holding South, they preferred to establish their business in Cuba, revealing, on the one hand, the fluidity of relations between the northern states and the island while, on the other hand, complicating the idea of a wholly abolitionist North. Third, many planters from the South did not endorse annexation because they saw the Cuban market as a strong competitor for their products. As Tom Chaffin points out, Cuban annexation was not supported by every plantation owner in the South, and it was not renounced by every Northerner.[24] By identifying himself with North American nationalism, Gonzales sought to bring together all of these positions in favor of annexing Cuba.

The objective of the *Manifesto* was to allow North Americans to familiarize themselves with the causes and the trajectory of the revolutionary movement in Cuba. From the outset, Gonzales recounted the activities of López in Cuba and the United States through the lens of independentism. Throughout the *Manifesto*, he would employ the terms "independence" and "revolutionaries" to refer to the expeditions commanded by López and the men who participated in them, all the while eschewing the use of terms such as "annexation" or "filibustering." He legitimized the help received from important southern political and military figures like John Quitman through the emancipatory prism. Written for the North American public, the *Manifesto* walked a fine line between the independentist and the republican rhetoric. The most effective way to awaken the sympathies of the North Americans was to elicit an independentist reading of the Cuban filibuster movement that was at the same time infused with republican ideals. In his writing, Gonzales spoke from the place of enunciation of the patriot.

With this in mind, Gonzales included in the *Manifesto* the *Conspiración de la Mina de la Rosa Cubana* organized by López, as well as the account of his four subsequent expeditions, along with the independence conspiracies previously initiated on the island. In particular, he referred to *Soles y Rayos de Bolívar*, a secret society for Cuban independence, of which José María Heredia had been one the most significant participants. In this manner, Gonzales established an independentist genealogy, tracing the origins of the Cuban struggle back to the 1820s. He additionally recounted in detail the political, economic, and social conditions to which the colony of Cuba had been reduced. In this description, he attempted to awaken North American sympathies by alluding to topics that were likely to capture their interest. The issue of high taxes figured prominently, for example, appearing on the first page of the *Manifesto*: if the average English citizen was paying taxes of $12, the average Spanish citizen $9, the average French citizen $7, and the average US citizen $2, the average Cuban citizen was paying a total of $40. Gonzales also made a point of mentioning the quarrels between Spain and the United States. For instance, he mentioned how, in 1849, the Spanish Crown had prohibited young Cubans from receiving their education in the United States. Moreover, he highlighted comparisons between the American Revolutionary War and the Cuban fight for independence. If the North Americans in their fight against England had received help from various European monarchies, the Cubans – who were subjected to an even more despotic regime– would similarly benefit from the goodwill of the North American citizens contributing to the Cuban cause. In this way he justified the presence of these Cubans in the United States: even if the revolutionary schemes were being thought up in Cuba's northern neighbor, the goal was to bring the revolution back to the island.

While López emphasized the idea of independence by detailing the way in which these revolutionary campaigns had been organized and financed in the United States, it would become increasingly apparent how he had been drawn ever closer to the political and military supporters of slavery in the South. Although the first campaign was financed, in the words of Gonzales, with Cuban funds that came from the island as well as from the United States, by the second, third, and fourth campaigns, the money primarily came from North Americans.[25] After the failure of his first campaign, López broke away from the Cuban planters brought together by the *Club de la Habana* and the *Consejo Cubano* and, before long, the ex-general of the Spanish army had to further restructure his connections within the United States. For this reason, he decided to create his own organization, the *Junta Patriótica Cubana*, together with Cirilo Villaverde and Gonzales, and relocate to the US South. The change in center of operations – from New York and Washington DC to New Orleans – was dictated by the growing support of Quitman to the cause.[26] At that moment, the political alliances that López maintained were no longer with the Cuban slave-holding class, but instead came almost entirely from Southern planters and politicians. John Henderson came to contribute 40,000 dollars of his personal fortune; Laurent J. Sigur donated a substantial part of his wealth to López's campaigns.[27]

When referring to these allies, Gonzales nonetheless declined to use the term "Southerners," instead saying they were "United States citizens" without specifying whether they came from the North or the South, demonstrating yet another way in which he opted for the homogenizing rhetoric. However, when he spoke of his adversaries, he did not hesitate to identify them in the most precise fashion:

> We have against us not only Spain, but that very [*sic*] France and England, and the menace of the blacks [...] We have had, it is true [...] the encouragement, the aid, and the gallant devotion of very many of the generous citizens of this republic.[28]

The distinction between allies and enemies reproduced the logic of the pro-slavery and abolitionist blocs. While England, France, and Spain coalesced as partners into a unified front, Cubans and North Americans, who except for John Sullivan, were all Southerners, emerged as the other axis. For both, the population of African descent came to be seen as a threat not only to Cuba, but also to the South.

The rhetoric of the *Manifesto* contrasted sharply with the tone used in the proclamations written in English to the US soldiers that accompanied López and in the letters sent to Southern political and military figures. In conversation with the North American people, Gonzales relied on a rhetoric of independence, yet when he addressed the prominent public figures of the South he would appeal to annexation. But the difference did not lie so much in the distance between the rhetoric of annexation and that of independence, which would often become intermingled as they were similarly fueled by patriotic ideals, but rather in the fact that Gonzales would make Cuban annexation a strictly Southern cause when writing for Southern elites. In a letter to Lamar in 1851, Gonzales attempted to convince the Texan politician to join forces as a leader of the López campaign. He assured him that they had enough men and resources, and that there were countless planters who had sold their properties in Savannah and Florida to enlist in the expedition, waiting to serve under his direction.[29]

The fluctuations between the rhetoric of independence and that of annexation in Gonzales' discourse must be understood, first, in terms of his maneuvering within the political culture of the United States and, second, in terms of his need to consolidate networks that would traverse both regional and national circuits. His public and private writings incorporated both ideas in ways that consistently kept his target audience in mind. But most importantly, independence and annexation were both options being exploited by the Cubans living in the United States. As Rodrigo Lazo explains, they were often used interchangeably: "Those seemingly contradictory positions could coexist because of an antebellum US political culture that promoted the independence of US states. Supporters of annexation among exiles were particularly interested in states' rights positions within US revolutionary writings."[30] Thus, while Gonzales would distinguish between the two terms depending on his audience, others such as Gaspar Betancourt Cisneros defended a notion of annexation centered around the ideals of independence and autonomy as offered by US statehood.[31]

Herminio Portell Vilá, who made a colossal effort to read the life of López through an independentist framework, did not hesitate to locate Gonzales among the annexation wing because of his proclamations and his letters to those in Southern political and military circles.[32] According to the Cuban historian, the accusations against López as a supporter of annexation come directly from propaganda spread by Spain and the United States, for whom it was advantageous to promote this idea of the Venezuelan. Manuel Sanguily and Manuel de la Cruz repeated these ideas when they wrote about López, and the same perspectives were further maintained by historians such as José Ignacio Rodríguez and Elías Entralgo.[33] What Portell Vilá overlooked was how López and Gonzales both courted the North American expansionist wing as a means of gaining support. For that reason, Vidal Morales y Morales preferred to label López neither as an independentist nor an annexationist, but rather as a separatist.[34]

Although the tension between slave labor and wage labor would be brought up in the *Manifesto*, Gonzales did not make the topic of slavery his focus. This argument worked rather well to gain the support of the slave states, but in order to appeal to the entire nation, he needed to overcome this polemical issue that inflamed the tensions that were dividing the United States. Even if Gonzales approached the question of Cuba's "Africanization" as one of the reasons that had fostered alliances between Cubans and Southerners, it would not be him, but rather Cristóbal Madan who would emphasize this question in the face of the threat of Cuba becoming either African or Spanish. In contrast with Gonzales, Madan chose the planter, rather than the patriot, as the galvanizing figure; he even came to construct a defense of filibusterism in the face of Spanish governance and would grant the movement a political tradition within the anticolonial struggles.[35] In spite of the difference in their postures, Gonzales and Madan became, together with John Thrasher, a relatively homogeneous block that imagined an alternative political geography in which political – between Cuba and the United States – and linguistic – between Spanish and English – differences were tempered through the common cause of slavery.

Cristóbal Madan

No political figure devised a better defense for annexation based on the fears of Africanization and abolition of slavery than Cristóbal Madan. He was one of the most eloquent and brilliant annexationists in New York, together with Gaspar Betancourt Cisneros, with whom he also edited the annexationist newspaper, *La verdad*. Madan had moved to New York from Cuba in 1822 at the age of 15. Over the next three decades he would situate himself in the center of the interactions between the Cuban and North American communities there.[36] He would become a naturalized citizen of the United States and marry Mary O'Sullivan, sister of John O'Sullivan, the man who coined the term "Manifest Destiny." His case offers a paradigmatic example of how US expansionism, based on the narrative of Manifest Destiny, emerged simultaneously with the Cuban annexation movement and in conversation with its principal advocates.[37] O'Sullivan's definition of Manifest Destiny resonates with the central arguments articulated by Madan and the Cuban community in defense of Cuban annexation. As Caroline Levander explains in "Confederate Cuba," the expression "Manifest Destiny" was used to refer not only to the westward expansion of the United States, but also to the desire of Southern leaders to liberate Cuba from its despotic oppressor, Spain.[38] The Cuban annexationists themselves had characterized their movement as a way to liberate Cuba from Spain, and the expansionists in the United States were in many ways motivated by them. From his bicultural position, Madan would carry out a vigorous campaign in favor of annexation and slavery in the United States. He would come to live, in the words of Lisandro Pérez, "a true transnational life, dividing his time between Cuba and his home near Madison Square."[39]

Even though very little is known about his life, it is likely that he wrote *Llamamiento de la isla de Cuba a la nación española, dirigido al Excmo. é Illmo. Señor Don Baldomero Espartero, duque de la Victoria, presidente del Consejo de ministros, por un hacendado, en diciembre 1854* while living in Cuba. By this date, Madan had returned to the island where he remained until the end of the 1850s, before going back to New York.[40] The title of the pamphlet lays out two fundamental questions for the reformist and annexationist camps that dominated the Cuban political spectrum in the first decades of the nineteenth century. The first concerns the stark contrast between Cuba and Spain: whereas Cuba is defined with regards to its physical geography, as an island, Spain is defined as a nation. If the colonizer was known by its political designation, the colony remained reduced to its geography. The second issue lies in the names of the sender and the receiver of the pamphlet, which was addressed to Baldomero Espartero and signed by an anonymous "*hacendado.*"[41] Madan utilized a pseudonym when addressing the President of Spain's Council of Ministers, and placed himself in the role of the planter.[42] In this manner, he became a spokesperson for the *hacendados*, speaking on behalf of the sugar cane production establishment, whose capital resulted in their economic power, having made Cuba the most prosperous enclave of the Spanish peninsula. The difference between geography and politics was paralleled by the dissimilarities that separated the figure of the planter from that of the politician. Speaking from the position of the planter led to a necessary reference to the most fundamental problem of the pamphlet: slavery.

Writing from the perspective of the planter also allowed Madan to construct a hemispheric alliance insofar as it united the owners of the Cuban sugar plantations with the Southern planter elite. Addressing the abolitionist front on both sides of the Atlantic, the *criollo* imagined the Cuban and Southern planters united through slavery and geography:

> The empty declarations of those who have usurped the title of philanthropist will not cow us as they did those who came before us: thus emboldened, we, *the planters of the south*, will point with our own fingers towards those new roads marked with a destructive trace that is both shameful and humiliating, unworthy of our intelligence and of our civilization. Go forth and contemplate the fruits of your act, we say to Jamaica [...] look at the moral superiority with which you would like to guide us, and recognize that it is you who retrograde, while by sustaining the civil and legal institution of slavery, we are the ones who foresee a benevolent, patriarchal system, uniquely capable of consolidating peaceful and mutually-beneficial relations between two peoples who, by God's hand, were made so distinct, the one from the other.[43]

The use of the expression "planters of the south" and the personal pronoun "we" to allude to both Cuban and Southern planters reveals how the slave-holding societies of the nineteenth century organized a common front – an international pro-slavery front, as seen by historians Rafael de Bivar Marquese and Tâmis Peixoto Parron – whose objective was the creation of a continental axis that would stand in opposition to the advance of abolitionism.[44] This axis between the US South and Cuba took shape precisely through the creation of a new geopolitical space that defied national, linguistic, and colonial borders. Slavery came to define this new space comprising the US South and Cuba, while the fact that they occupied the same geographic enclave, supporting the formation of new economic, political, social networks. Through the phrase, "planters of the south," Madan advanced an identity that was neither Cuban nor Southern but was instead transregional and would come to define a future political community. Slavery came to shape identities of both Cubans and Southerners.

Among the plantation owners of the US South, Madan made special reference to those from Louisiana, from whom he included a document they had written supporting the incorporation of Cuba in the United States. Louisiana, which was annexed to the United States after having been both a Spanish and French colony, appeared as a political model that the Cuban planters could follow insofar as it would offer them the autonomy they so desired – but that Spain continuously denied them – and the possibility to maintain the institution of slavery. On the other hand, there was Jamaica – Louisiana's antipode. By the middle of the nineteenth century, the point of reference for the pro-slavery camp was not just Haiti, but rather included Jamaica, where slavery had been abolished in 1833. The English colony became an example of what would happen to Cuba if the abolition of slavery came to pass.

If the Southern planters, who were headed in the pamphlet by General Quitman, favored a new geopolitical order together with the Cubans, England and Spain thus appeared as allies in opposition.[45] Madan portrayed a Spain that, by favoring the apprentice system and the elimination of slave-holding, cast itself as philanthropist and abolitionist across the Atlantic, adopting the rhetoric similar to that of England and France.[46] Against Spain and Captain General Pezuela, the Cuban planters championed the preservation of legal slavery. While the Cubans made a pact with the Southerners, the Spanish crown reaffirmed its alliance with the free black and mulatto populations. The resumption of free *pardo* and *moreno* battalions, authorized by Pezuela and endorsed by the Queen due to the loyalty shown at various moments by the *pardos* and *morenos* in their defense of the Spanish flag, was received by the Cuban planters as an attempt to Africanize the island and subjugate the annexationists.[47] If, as Matt Childs affirms, in the concluding decades of the eighteenth century and the opening decades of the nineteenth, "the rise of slavery caused a decline in esteem for black and mulatto soldiers in Cuban society," the threat of armed invasion from the US South obliged Pezuela to resume the black and mulatto militias, an institution that had been brought to a close ten years prior as a result of the *Conspiración de La Escalera*.[48] As occurred before against England during their occupation of Havana and was now occurring in the face of the allied Southern and Cuban annexationists, Spain would make a pact with the populations of African descent on the island.[49]

At the heart of the pamphlet was the tension between slave and indebted labor.[50] Madan declared himself in opposition to the replacement of the work of the enslaved with that of the indebted laborer. He also rejected the idea of substituting the work of Africans (enslaved or free) with that of Asians, arguing that indebted labor would lead to the abolition of slavery. For that reason, the pamphlet focused on attacking the system of African apprenticeship and the peonage.[51] The former would allow the entrance of Africans without limit, who would then become apprentices, earning a salary and, in a few years, becoming emancipated. The latter favored the entry of Galicians, Asians, and Mexicans from the Yucatan Peninsula as indebted laborers. Madan understood that indebted labor would be an experiment in emancipation, a plan to Africanize the island and, also, considered it the cause that had unleashed the persecution of legal slavery.[52]

Using abolitionist rhetoric, the pro-slavery elites did not hesitate to label the importation of indebted laborers and African apprentices as a moral crime. In this way they described both systems as the trafficking and forced-servitude of free men.[53] On the one hand, indebted labor would reduce Spanish farmers to a regime of barbarous servitude; on the other hand, it would condemn the peasants of the island because indebted laborers would end up taking their jobs. Among the other arguments they brandished against the system of African apprenticeship and the peonage, they stressed the high cost of paying a daily wage and the new heterogeneity that would be introduced with Asians workers. The pro-slavery elites were convinced of the need for forced or slave labor for tropical agriculture. In the words of Madan, it was much more productive than any system based on apprenticeship or day labor.[54]

In spite of the way in which Madan presented this tension between slave and indebted labor as a direct result of the agreements meant to stifle the slave trade that were signed between Spain and England in 1817 and 1820, which were then both ratified in 1835, in fact the work of enslaved persons had coexisted with that of indebted laborers and other wage earners since the final decades of the eighteenth century. Indebted labor and wage earning did not replace slavery. Rather, all these forms coexisted on the island since the end of the eighteenth century.[55] Having said that, indebted labor was never understood as a form of emancipated labor and was much more like slavery than wage earning. For this reason, the distinction between the enslaved and indebted laborers was one of the most ambiguous issues in the history of what has been called "The Second Slavery."[56]

The tension between slave and indebted labor was understood by the pro-slavery front as a confrontation between two opposing camps: between the Americas and Europe. The first camp was comprised of the Southern and Cuban planters who together defended slave labor; the second was composed of the abolitionist bloc: England, France, and Spain itself. By endorsing emancipation and apprenticeship, the second camp was undermining the rights of workers, as well as the development of science and industry.[57] Madan, for his part, legitimized his defense of slavery by coming out as a defender of workers' rights.

In his words, Southern and Cuban planters epitomized "progress" and "modernity" while Jamaica represented "chaos" and "disorder," forging his defense of slavery by extolling its "patriarchal" dimension. By portraying the abolitionists as regressive and lauding the slaveholders as benevolent, Madan revealed how the pro-slavery propaganda would appropriate many of the abolitionist arguments that were based around the very prevalent nineteenth-century ideals of philanthropy, morality, and humanity. Those defending slavery did not try to ignore the popularity that abolitionism had gained in the public sphere on both sides of the Atlantic, but it instead endeavored to see itself as part of a dialogue.[58]

Thus, by the end of the pamphlet, Madan contended that trying to impose the European way of thinking upon the Americas made the practice of filibustering seem conservative.[59] And he did not hesitate to declare to Espartero that it was Spain who had authorized rebellion, annexation, and even independence:

> By repudiating the white race's rights as a people, by stimulating the preponderance of the black race, by destroying the equilibrium established by slavery through a heedless integration of the institution with emancipated labor, and by endorsing and bolstering the troops of color in 1854 with the cry "Spanish or African" first proclaimed in 1851, the Spanish government has authorized rebellion, independence, annexation, and whatever other measure that may be needed to save the property and lives of the white race, because before our nationality stands one God, one religion, and one nature that ordains the preservation of our existence and of that of our children.[60]

Facing the rising tide of abolitionism on the island, Spain became the scapegoat in this longing for annexation. Under this line of reasoning, Madan entreated the President of the Council of Ministers to sell Cuba to the United States and to let island become incorporated to the Confederacy. He argued that if the incorporation were carried out with the approval of Spain and in a peaceful manner, Spain would spare Cubans of the uncertainties and dangers of the transitions and would thus favor the preponderance of the Hispanic lineage on the island and would attain the economic advantages could not achieve if a revolution were to occur. Conversely, Spain would not only lose its final trace of hegemony in the Americas but would additionally end up inciting a revolution. For Spain, the alternative to not selling Cuba was revolution, one that would be led and organized by the US South. Madan recognized that the military and political alliances between Cuban and Southern planters were no longer being planned merely to preserve slavery in Cuba, but also to save their lives. By writing from the perspective of the planter, he came to approach in a rather marked fashion the patriotic and independentist rhetoric of Ambrosio Gonzales in his political writings.

John S. Thrasher

In 1854, the same year that Cristóbal Madan published his pamphlet, John S. Thrasher met with Gaspar Betancourt Cisneros in New Orleans to commemorate the third anniversary of Narciso López's execution. In his remarks, addressed to the community of Cuban exiles in New Orleans as well as to the North Americans in attendance, Thrasher portrayed López and his army as martyrs for Cuban freedom. He insisted on the idea that the death of Cubans and North Americans together in battle foreshadowed the union of the two, "The Union of the Martyrs was the Union of the Races."[61] In the shared fate of Cubans and Southerners, Thrasher saw the foundations of Cuba's incorporation into the United States.

A journalist and a filibuster, Thrasher had settled in Havana in 1833 and, by 1850, he was the editor of the newspaper the *Faro Industrial de La Habana,* from which he would defend the annexation of Cuba to the United States by covering the confrontation between López and Spanish forces in 1851 as well as releasing the list of prisoners captured by the Spanish army.[62] He was charged by Captain General Concha of treason and sentenced to multiple years in prison in Ceuta. After being freed through some diplomatic maneuvering, in 1853 he took up residence in New Orleans, home to a sizeable community of annexation-supporting Cubans and Southerners, and where he would come to publish a newspaper, *The Beacon of Cuba*. Years later he became the superintendent of The Press Association of the Confederate States of America, continuing to defend the idea of including Cuba as a state in the Confederacy.[63]

In 1856, he published his English translation of Humboldt's *Ensayo político sobre la isla de Cuba* in New York, changing the title to *The Island of Cuba*, in order to foster public debate on the topic of Cuba's annexation. To do so, Thrasher updated Humboldt's essay by annotating it and adding a "Preliminary Essay." Given the importance of this revision, Fernando Ortiz included Thrasher's notes and introduction in his 1930 edition of *Ensayo político de la isla de Cuba* in the *Colección de Libros Cubanos*. In the opening pages, Thrasher assured his readers that, during his many years in Cuba, he had found no other book that contained such a comprehensive account of the social, economic, agricultural, commercial, and political conditions on the island. Without a doubt, he understood that by publishing the *Ensayo* first in French and then in Spanish, Humboldt had given the island unprecedented international recognition.

As an ardent supporter of slavery, Thrasher omitted Humboldt's antislavery chapter in his translation. This chapter was not only one of the most significant pleas for abolition published on either side of the Atlantic in the nineteenth century, but also a text that was, in some ways, "secretly" about Haiti.[64] In those pages, Humboldt offered a favorable reading of the Haitian Revolution, comparing it to other revolutions for independence across the Americas, but recognizing that it was unique in that it was the only revolution that had linked the anticolonial project with the abolition of slavery. Fundamentally, Haiti and its revolution gave meaning to Humboldt's anti-slavery project.[65] Despite Humboldt's public denouncement of Thrasher's annexationist motivations, the revised translation was repeatedly reedited in the United States, until 2011, when Vera M. Kutzinski and Ottmar Ette published a new, complete, critical edition.[66]

As Humboldt himself had done decades earlier, Thrasher read the island cartographically. Its position, connected with Central America, the Gulf of Mexico, other Caribbean islands, and the southern states, would guarantee the Union hemispheric control of the Americas.[67] But Thrasher added a detail that would be of vital importance for US expansionists: at a time when the United States was incorporating new states in the Pacific, the control of the island would ensure easy communication between the East Coast and the West Coast. Thrasher held that Cuba was a central piece of the expanding empire, given how its geographic position would secure and control the maritime routes between the Atlantic and the Pacific running through the isthmus of Panama. Cuba would ensure communication between New York and San Francisco.[68] Crucially, at this time, the United States shifted from focusing on policies of domestic republicanism to imperial power.[69]

Thrasher advocated for the annexation of Cuba in the same way that Ambrosio Gonzales had: through a nationalist perspective. The island's integration would not simply support the interests of the South, but rather the interests of the entire country: "The accession of Cuba to the Union is not, therefore, merely a Southern question, but it is a question of national government and of national power."[70] Attempting to give the impression of international unity, Thrasher swore that the interests of the South were the interests of the North. Thus, according to his logic, annexing Cuba was a matter that was incumbent on the South, the North, the East, and the West. Incorporating Cuba became an issue of national defense as well as in the interest of domestic business in the United States.

Just like the Cuban planters, Thrasher and other Southerners perceived the measures announced by Pezuela between December 1853 and May 1854 as an attempt to "Africanize" the island. On both sides of the Gulf, "Africanization" was understood as the adoption of a work system that had as its final objective the abolition of slavery and would lead to the decline in agricultural production, a bloody race war, and the extermination of the white population.[71] The alarm generated among the Southern planters resulted in the Louisiana legislature condemning the Africanization of Cuba and appealing to the federal government to prevent it at any cost.[72] Facing such a distressing predicament, Thrasher assured the Cubans that they could count on the United States as allies. Just like Gonzales, he would not use the word "Southerners," who were in fact organizing an armed intervention on the island under the command of John Quitman with the

Cubans living in New Orleans. He would instead use "Americans," with the express purpose of endowing the confrontation with an air of nationalism. In the same way, when referring to slavery at various moments, he would not speak of "Cuban slavery," but rather "slavery in the Americas," giving the topic a hemispheric quality. For Thrasher, the pressure placed upon Spain by England to implement abolitionist measures was in fact a means to block the advance of the United States in the island. He thus saw the conflict in the same way as Cristóbal Madan had: as a confrontation between the Americas and Europe, which was, above all, between Republicanism and Monarchism.

In 1859, Thrasher published his "Preliminary Essay," this time independently, under the title *Preliminary Essay on the Purchase of Cuba*. The differences between the two are minimal. For the new one, Thrasher added roughly fourteen pages in which he constructed a different context for this publication, which occurred in the middle of a campaign enacted by the administration of James Buchanan to reinvigorate North American efforts to purchase Cuba. He assured readers that, even if the desire for annexation had already been in existence for fifty years, the ultimate responsibility for doing so belonged to the US government, whose support had never materialized in such a way. In his last attempt before the outbreak of the US Civil War, Thrasher tried to mobilize the will of the North American people in favor of the annexation of Cuba.

Conclusion

In the mid-nineteenth century, the idea of "the South" did not only include the slaveholding states of the United States, but also comprised, to some degree, the Caribbean.[73] Ambrosio Gonzales, Cristóbal Madan, and John Thrasher formed part of a transnational community that resided between these two geographies; they comfortably communicated in both languages and aspired to merge these two spaces into one, forming a new political domain. Their mobility between these spaces and the networks that they developed across the southern United States and Cuba in some way brought into view an imaginary that became prevalent during the dawning moments and the first years of the American Civil War. But if the South saw itself, in the words of Matthew Karp, as a vast empire that would extend towards the south and that had already begun to expand westward with the recently-acquired Mexican territories in 1848, then Cubans would thus propose that the island, when incorporated into the United States, would come to be considered an empire within an empire.[74] In this case, US statehood did not represent a change from one colonial power to another, but rather a way to separate Cuba from Spain, obtain political autonomy, and preserve statehood.[75]

Facing the end of the illegal trafficking of slaves in 1820, the repeal of slavery in the English and French Antilles in 1833 and 1848, respectively, and the abolitionist experiment of Captain General Pezuela in Cuba between 1853 and1854, the pro-slavery classes in Cuba and the US South were forced to restructure their alliances and constitute themselves as a united front in opposition to England, France, and Spain. If at the end of the eighteenth century the growth of slavery in Cuba depended on negotiations between Francisco Arango Parreño and the Spanish Crown, then in the mid-nineteenth the preservation of this regime would occur not by virtue of a Spain that was giving in to pressure from England, but instead would be a result of their alliances with the Southern planters.

Through diverse means, Gonzales, Madan, and Thrasher defended the alliances between Cubans and Southerners. Gonzales recurred to the rhetoric of independence and he presented himself to the North American people as a patriot, even as he offered encouragement to the annexationist desires of his Southern allies. Madan, as an *hacendado*, appealed to the Spanish government to sell the island to the United States, and he did not hesitate to pressure them with the threat of filibusterism, independence, and revolution. In the midst of the tensions between pro-slavery and abolitionist forces, Madan put forth an important argument for the Southern planters: the most significant benefit offered by incorporating Cuba into the United States centered around the favorable influence that Spanish slave-holding legislation would have on the South.[76] Thrasher, for his part, directly addressed the government of the United States to urge for the incorporation of the island through purchase from Spain, defending Cuba's annexation from the nationalist perspective that had been employed by Gonzales before him.

Despite the underlying differences between the three, their interventions in the public sphere of the Atlantic were all directed towards the same end: preserving slavery. With this objective, they imagined new political cartographies for the region, unconcerned by the cultural and linguistic differences between the United States and Cuba; slavery, not language and not culture, became the catalyst for a new political order. The fact that Cubans and Southerners embraced this hemispheric identity reveals that "race," as Jossianna Arroyo points out, was not a crucial term by the 1850s in the US expansion politics, "it was still a period in which formative initial contacts with populations of color in émigré cities such as Louisiana, Key West, Tampa, and New York, and in the newly acquired territories from Texas to California began to open up a social space for linking the imperial mandate to race."[77] In this sense, slavery was fundamental in bridging identity politics in planters both the US North and South as well in Cuba. Even if our contemporary conceptions of political and linguistic differences may lead us to lose sight of the strength of slavery in bringing together groups or imagine alternative futures, it was the preservation of this institution that led Cubans and Southerners in the mid-nineteenth century to aspire to share a political future together.

Notes

Translated by Pedro Rolón.

1. Guterl, *American Mediterranean*, 5–9.
2. Iannini, *Fatal Revolutions*, 282–283.
3. Perez, Jr., *Cuba and the United States*, 19–22.
4. Karp, *This Vast Southern Empire*, 58–99.
5. As Portell Vilá reminds us, annexationism was not a homogenous movement: there was an annexation movement motivated by patriotic interests and one with a more economic bent. The latter defended the conservation of slavery; see, *Narciso López y su época*, Vol. 1, 167–192. One would have to add that even those annexationists with an abolitionist tendency – such as Gaspar Betancourt Cisneros, who allied himself with the pro-slavery wing in the South with the objective of separating Cuba from Spain – defended the incorporation of the island within the United States as a means of promoting white supremacy on the island.
6. Portell Vilá, *Narciso López y su época*, Vol. 2, 66.
7. For a detailed account of both organizations and the annexationist movements on the island and in the United States, see *Narciso López y su época* by Herminio Portell Vilá, and *Cuba and the United States* by Louis Pérez Jr., particularly chapter 2.
8. See, for example, Williams, *Sketches of the Old and New World*, 46.

9. May, *John A. Quitman*, 237.
10. Arroyo, *Writing Secrecy in Caribbean Freemasonry*, 57.
11. The First Cuban War of Independence, which broke out in 1868 on the island, began at the same time as the annexation debate. For this topic, see Pérez, Jr., *Cuba and the United States*, 51. In addition, the desire for annexation to the United States did not die with the Ten Years War but continued to be a matter with which José Martí had to address as late as 1890s.
12. Guerra, *Manual de Historia de Cuba*, 504.
13. For a detailed account, see Guerra, *Manual de Historia de Cuba*, 504–505.
14. Corwin, *Spain and the abolition of Slavery*, 121.
15. May, *The Southern Dream*, 35.
16. Gonzales, *Manifesto*, 11–12.
17. Cova, *Cuban Confederate Colonel*, 33.
18. Ibid., xxiii.
19. Urban, "The Ideology of Southern Imperialism," 56. The owner of this newspaper was the state senator Laurent J. Sigur, a friend of Gonzales', as well as a fervent ally and collaborator in the annexationist cause.
20. Cova, *Cuban Confederate Colonel*, 134.
21. Ibid.
22. Chaffin, "'Sons of Washington'," 91.
23. Dana, *To Cuba and Back*, 25.
24. Chaffin, "'Sons of Washington'," 93–94.
25. Ibid., 9.
26. May, *John A. Quitman*, 237.
27. Gonzales, *Manifesto*, 10.
28. Ibid., 6.
29. Portell Vilá, *Narciso López y su época*, Vol. 3. 149.
30. Lazo, *Writing to Cuba*, 65.
31. Lazo, "Filibustering Cuba," 11
32. Portell Vilá, *Narciso López y su época*, Vol. 3. 149.
33. Ibid., 243–246.
34. Morales y Morales, *Contribución*, 229–277.
35. Madan, *Llamamiento*, 173.
36. As Lisandro Pérez notes, Madan arrived in New York in order to learn English, but also learning firsthand the world of business in the big city. He came from a very wealthy family based in Matanzas. *Sugar, Cigars, and Revolution*, 40.
37. Portell Villá, *Narciso López y su época*, Vol. 2, 190.
38. Levander, "Confederate Cuba," 824.
39. Pérez, *Sugar, Cigars, and Revolution*, 76.
40. For the most information about the life and political activities of Madan, see Pérez, *Sugar, Cigars and Revolution*.
41. Madan appealed to Espartero as someone who represented "the principle of liberty" and was "the true mirror of the Spanish Progressive Party" (2). Espartero was Regent of Spain from 1840 to 1843 and on three separate occasions served as the President of the Council of Ministers.
42. As Pérez explains, one of the reasons why Madan, one of the chief defenders of annexationism, was capable of freely traveling between New York, Havana, and Matanzas was because of his use of pseudonyms when writing in the press and the fact that he placed himself in the role of a generic *hacendado* instead of being identified publicly for his writings. Pérez, *Sugar, Cigars, and Revolution*, 76.
43. Madan, *Llamamiento*, 125 (my emphasis).
44. Marquese and Peixoto, "Internacional escravista," 104–110.
45. Madan, *Llamamiento*, 40.
46. Ibid., 56.
47. Ibid., 84–85.

48. Childs, *The 1812 Aponte Rebellion in Cuba*, 91–94.
49. For a history of the black and mulatto militias in Cuba, see Sartorius, *Ever Faithful* and Schneider, *The Occupation of Havana*.
50. Madan, *Llamamiento*, 49.
51. Ibid., 40–41.
52. Ibid., 51.
53. Ibid., 106
54. Ibid., 124.
55. Moreno Fraginals, *El ingenio*, V I, 259.
56. Pezuela, who had been the Captain General of Puerto Rico before becoming that of Cuba, had established a system of semi-slavery that placed Puerto Rican farmers in a state of feudal relations with their hacienda owners. In 1849, Pezuela institutionalized wage labor in Puerto Rico through the *Reglamento especial de jornaleros*, which obliged farmers who did not own land or property to work under the authority of hacendados. For more information on the idea of "The Second Slavery," see Tomich, *Through the Prism of Slavery* Tomich and Zeuske, "Out of the Americas."
57. Madan, *Llamamiento*, 177.
58. Cowling, *Conceiving Freedom*, 101–103; Domínguez, "En los límites del discurso esclavista."
59. Madan, *Llamamiento*, 88.
60. Ibid., 222.
61. Thrasher, *Addresses*, 4.
62. Ortiz, "El traductor de Humboldt," 291–295.
63. Wilson, "Confederate Press Association," 161.
64. Zeuske, "Alexander von Humboldt," 77.
65. Domínguez, "Imaginarios antillanos," 50–52.
66. Regarding Humboldt's reaction and Thrasher's response, see Ortiz, "El traductor de Humboldt." For a study comparing the differences between the Spanish version and Thrasher's translation, see Kutzinski, "Translations of Cuba" [2006], 303–326, and Kutzinski, "Translations of Cuba" [2009], 111–134. See also Kutzinski, "Humboldt's Translator in the Context of Cuban history" and "Alexander von Humboldt's Transatlantic Personae."
67. Thrasher, "Preliminary Essay," 14–22.
68. Ibid., 20–21.
69. Arroyo, *Writing Secrecy*, 34.
70. Thrasher, "Preliminary Essay," 86.
71. Urban, "The Africanization of Cuba Scare," 29–30.
72. Ibid., 30.
73. Guterl, *American Mediterranean*, 32.
74. Lazo, "Filibustering Cuba," 11.
75. Ibid.,12.
76. Madan, *Llamamiento*, 225.
77. Arroyo, *Writing Secrecy in Caribbean Freemasonry*, 36.

Disclosure statement

No potential conflict of interest was reported by the author(s).

Bibliography

Arroyo, Jossianna. *Writing Secrecy in Caribbean Freemasonry*. New York: Palgrave, 2013.

Bivar Marquese, Rafael de, and Tâmis Peixoto Parron. "Internacional escravista: a política da Segunda Escravidão." *Topoi* 12, no. 23 (July–December 2011): 97–117.

Chaffin, Tom. "'Sons of Washington': Narciso López, Filibustering, and U.S. Nationalism." *Journal of the Early Republic* 15, no. 1 (Spring 1995): 79–108.

Childs, Matt. *The 1812 Aponte Rebellion in Cuba and the Struggle against Atlantic Slavery*. Chapel Hill: North Carolina University Press, 2006.

Corwin, Arthur. *Spain and the Abolition of Slavery*. Austin: Texas, 1967.

Cova, Antonio Rafael de la. *Cuban Confederate Colonel: The Life of Ambrosio José Gonzáles*. Columbia: South Carolina University Press, 2003.

Cowling, Camillia. *Conceiving Freedom: Women of Color, Gender, and Abolition of Slavery in Havana and Rio de Janeiro*. Chapel Hill: University of North Carolina Press, 2013.

Dana, Richard Henry. *To Cuba and Back*. London: Smith, Elder & Co, 1859.

Domínguez, Daylet. "En los límites del discurso esclavista: Retórica abolicionista, afectos y sensibilidad en *Los esclavos en las colonias españolas* de la condesa de Merlin." *Cuban Studies* 45 (2017): 252–272.

Domínguez, Daylet. "Imaginarios antillanos: Humboldt, Haití y la Confederación Africana en las Antillas." *Revista Iberoamericana* 84, no. 262 (2018): 45–64.

Gonzáles, Ambrosio. *Manifesto on Cuban Affair Addressed to the People of the United States*. New Orleans: Daily Delta, 1853.

Guerra, Ramiro. *Manual de historia de Cuba*. Habana: Cultural, 1938.

Guterl, Matthew. *American Mediterranean: Southern Slaveholders in the Age of Emancipation*. Cambridge, MA: Harvard University Press, 2009.

Iannini, Christopher J. *Fatal Revolutions: Natural History, West Indian Slavery, and the Routes of American Literature*. Chapel Hill: University of North Carolina Press, 2012.

Karp, Matthew. *This Vast Southern Empire: Slaveholders at the Helm of American Foreign Policy*. Cambridge, MA: Harvard University Press, 2016.

Kutzinski, Vera M. "Alexander von Humboldt's transatlantic personae." *Atlantic Studies* 7, no. 2 (2010): 99–112. doi:10.1080/14788811003700209.

Kutzinski, Vera M. "Humboldt's translator in the context of Cuban history." *Atlantic Studies* 6, no. 3 (2009): 223–243. doi:10.1080/14788810903264787.

Kutzinski, Vera M. "Translations of Cuba: Fernando Ortiz, Alexander von Humboldt, and the curious case of John Sidney Thrasher." *Atlantic Studies* 6, no. 3 (2009): 303–326. doi:10.1080/14788810903264779.

Kutzinski, Vera M. "Translations of Cuba: Fernando Ortiz, Alexander von Humboldt, and the curious case of John Sidney Thrasher." In *Alexander von Humboldt's Transatlantic Personae*, edited by Vera Kutzinski, 111–134. New York: Routledge, 2012.

Lazo, Rodrigo. "Filibustering Cuba: Cecilia Valdés and a Memory of Nation in the Americas." *American Literature* 74, no. 1 (March 2002): 1–30.

Lazo, Rodrigo. *Writing to Cuba. Filibustering and Cuban Exiles in the United States*. Chapel Hill: University of North Carolina Press, 2005.

Levander, Carolina. "Confederate Cuba." *American Literature* 78, no. 4 (December 2006): 821–845.

Madan, Cristobal. *Llamamiento de la isla de Cuba a la nación española, dirigido al Excmo. é Illmo. Señor Don Baldomero Espartero, duque de la Victoria, presidente del Consejo de ministros, por un hacendado, en diciembre 1854*. New York: Hallet, 1855.

May, Robert E. *John A. Quitman: Old South Crusader*. Baton Rouge: Louisiana State University Press, 1985.

May, Robert E. *The Southern Dream of a Caribbean Empire 1854–1861*. Baton Rouge: Louisiana State University Press, 1973.

Montes-Huidobro, Matías, ed. *El laúd del desterrado*. Houston, TX: Arte Público Press, University of Houston, 1995.

Morales y Morales, Vidal. *Contribución a la historia de la independencia de Cuba*. Habana: Avisador comercial, 1901.

Moreno Fraginals, Manuel. *El ingenio. Complejo económico social cubano del azúcar*. Barcelona: Crítica, 2001.

Ortiz, Fernando. "El traductor de Humboldt en la historia de Cuba." In *Ensayo político sobre la isla de Cuba*, edited by Alexander von Humboldt, 281–307. Habana: Fundación Fernando Ortiz, 1998.

Perez, Louis, Jr. *Cuba and the United States: Ties of Singular Intimacy*. Athens: University of Georgia Press, 2003.

Perez, Louis, Jr. *On Becoming Cuban*. New York: Harper Collins, 1999.

Pérez, Lisandro. *Sugar, Cigars and Revolution: The Making of Cuban New York*. New York: New York University Press, 2018.

Pickens, Lucy Petaway Holcombe. *The Free Flag of Cuba*. Baton Rouge: Louisiana State University Press, 2002.

Portell Vilá, Herminio. *Narciso López y su época*. Vol. 1. Habana: Cultural, 1930.

Portell Vilá, Herminio. *Narciso López y su época*. Vol. 2. Habana: Compañía editora, 1952.

Portell Vilá, Herminio. *Narciso López y su época*. Vol. 3. Habana: Compañía editora, 1958.

Sartorious, David. *Ever Faithful: Race, Loyalty, and the Ends of Empire in Spanish Cuba*. Durham, NC: Duke University Press, 2013.

Schneider, Elena. *The Occupation of Havana: War, Trade and Slavery in the Atlantic World*. Chapel Hill: University of North Carolina Press, 2018.

Thrasher, John Sidney. *Addresses Delivered at the Celebration of the Third Anniversary in Honor of the Martyrs for Cuban Freedom*. New Orleans, LA: Sherman, Wharton & co., 1854.

Thrasher, John Sidney, trans. "Preliminary Essay." In *The Island of Cuba*, edited by Alexander von Humboldt, 19–65. New York: Derby & Jackson, 1856.

Thrasher, John Sidney. *Preliminary Essay on the Purchase of Cuba*. New York: Derby & Jackson, 1959.

Tomich, Dale W. *Through the Prism of Slavery. Labor, Capital, and World Economy*. Lanham, MD: Rowman & Littlefield, 2004.

Urban, C. Stanley. "The Africanization of Cuba Scare, 1853–1855." *The Hispanic American Historical Review* 37, no. 1 (February 1957): 29–45.

Urban, C. Stanley. "The Ideology of Southern Imperialism: New Orleans and the Caribbean, 1845–1860." *The Louisiana Historical Quarterly* 39, no. 1 (January 1956): 48–73.

Williams, George W. *Sketches of the Old and New World*. Charleston, SC: Walker, Evans & Cosgwell, 1871.

Zeuske, Michael. "Alexander von Humboldt y la Comparación de las Esclavitudes en las Américas." *HiN* 6, no. 11 (2005): 65–89.

Zeuske, Michael. "Out of the Americas: Slave Traders and the *Hidden Atlantic* in the nineteenth century." *Atlantic Studies: Global Currents* 15, no. 1 (January 2018): 103–135.

Traveling tropes: Race, reconstruction, and "Southern" redemption in *The Story of Evangelina Cisneros*

Thomas Genova

ABSTRACT

This essay considers the entanglement of race, gender, and imperialism in U.S. discourse on Evangelina Cisneros, a white Cuban woman imprisoned in a Havana jail during her country's final War for Independence from Spain (1895–1898). I argue that, an event historically tied to the colony's abolition of slavery, Cuban Independence in writings about Cisneros becomes discursively imbricated with the reconsolidation of white supremacy in the U.S. South following the Civil War. The study establishes a dialogue between U.S. discourse on the events published in the late 1890s – the articles on the affair that appeared in *The New York Journal* and the multi-authored book *The Story of Evangelina Cisneros* (1897) – and Southern white supremacist author Thomas Dixon, Jr.'s *Trilogy of Reconstruction* (1902–1907) in order to explore the ways in which the Evangelina Cisneros text network mobilizes racial and gender paradigms typically associated with post-Reconstruction Southern "Redeemer" thinking.

This essay considers how the figure of Evangelina Cisneros, a white Cuban woman imprisoned in a Havana jail during her country's final War for Independence from Spain (1895–1898), becomes discursively assimilated to racial, gender, and imperial paradigms current in the United States in the period of Southern "Redemption" between Reconstruction and the Spanish-Cuban-American War. Born in Puerto Príncipe, Cuba, Evangelina Betancourt Cosio y Cisneros was the daughter of separatist Antonio Cosio Serrano, who had been deported to the Cuban Isla de los Pinos (present-day Isla de la Juventud), "*con la autorización de llevar en su compañía a sus dos hijas debido a su precaria salud*" (with authorization to bring his two daughters with him due to his poor health) as punishment for his activities against the metropole.[1] It was there that Evangelina, age 17, became involved in a planned uprising against the Spanish army, tasked with luring Lieutenant Coronel José Bérriz into an ambush with the promise of sexual favors.[2] The plan failed and Evangelina was imprisoned in a Havana jail while she awaited trial and probable deportation to Spain's North African penal colony in Ceuta. Though largely forgotten today, the events figured prominently in U.S. news reports on the Cuban conflict during 1897 and 1898. Renaming the protagonist "Evangelina Cisneros," William Randolph Hearst's *New York Journal* would dedicate no less than 375 articles to the affair.[3]

The Evangelina Cisneros story, then, was an integral part of a propaganda campaign in the popular press urging the United States to intervene in Cuba's anticolonial struggle against Spain. Washington eventually declared war against Madrid on 21 April 1898.[4] Race played a crucial role in the conflict, as "the Cuban-Hispanic-American War and consequent birth of the Cuban Republic [...] called for a reconfiguration of [the racial] discourse and race-defined inclusions and exclusions" prevalent during the colonial period.[5] The Independence struggle would open the door to definitive abolition in 1886, an Afro-Cuban rights movement under leaders such as Juan Gualberto Gómez and Rafael Serra during the late colonial period, and significant Afro-Cuban participation in the war against Spain.[6] These facts would force the country's elites to seriously (if begrudgingly) consider the question of racial equality in a post-war republic that, unlike the United States at the time, would extend voting rights to Afro-descendants. Cuban patriot and ideologue José Martí, for his part, would give voice to this interracial ideal in his notion of "*nuestra América mestiza*" (our mixed-race América), deliberately articulated as a counterdiscourse to the aggressive Anglo-Saxonism of "*el pueblo rubio de nuestro continente*" (the blond nation of our continent), where white supremacist ideologues feared the birth of a "mulatto citizenship" during the generation following Civil War and Emancipation.[7]

Given the fear of "mulatto citizenship" in the turn-of-the-century United States, it is not surprising that the Evangelina texts should represent Cuba's quest for independence in terms of racialized sexual violence. In an editorial published in the *Journal*, New England reformer Julia Ward Howe asks: "How can we think of this pure flower of maidenhood condemned to live with felons and outcasts, without succor, without protection, to labor under a torrid sky, suffering privation, indignity, and torment worse than death?"[8] Like much anti-Spanish propaganda, the question gestures at the possibility of interracial rape – a favorite trope of white-supremacist thinkers such of the period – through the euphemism "worse than death." Capitalizing on public disgust at Spain's behavior and seeking to draw attention to his newspaper, Hearst sent reporter Karl Decker to Cuba in order to smuggle Evangelina out of prison and into the United States. The following year, a team of writers including Julian Hawthorne, Decker, and Cisneros published *The Story of Evangelina Cisneros* to build support for the U.S. war against Spain and eventual annexation of Cuba.

By framing Cisneros' liberation from Spanish domination as a rescue from racialized rape, the Evangelina texts reflect a common fear in the post-Reconstruction United States that, in the words of Thomas Dixon, Jr., "Desdemonas may be fascinated again by an Othello!"[9] Begun during the U.S. occupation of Cuba (1898–1902) that followed North American involvement in the island's war with Spain, Dixon's *The Leopard's Spots: A Romance of the White Man's Burden, 1865–1900* (1902), *The Clansman: An Historical Romance of the Ku Klux Klan* (1904), and *The Traitor: A Story of the Fall of the Invisible Empire* (1907) – the first two of which inspired D.W. Griffith's now-infamous 1915 silent film *The Birth of a Nation* – are foundational works of the turn-of-the-nineteenth-century black rapist myth. As numerous commentators have shown, Dixon and other white-supremacist Southern-Redeemer writers would deploy the black rapist trope to preserve white hegemony against the perceived threat of black ascendency following Emancipation.

In the following, I will examine the Evangelina texts in relation to Dixon's *Trilogy of Reconstruction* (as the three novels collectively are known) and similar works of

Southern Redemptionist writing in order to explore the circulation of the white supremacist trope of the black rapist through the U.S. South and Cuba. My argument builds on Karen Roggenkamp's study of the Cisneros affair in the context of a "new journalism [that] operated explicitly within models of dramatic storytelling."[10] Expanding on the idea of a "broadly drawn literary culture" through which, as Roggenkamp explains, the nineteenth-century yellow press narrativized current events, I will show how the racial mythology of post-Reconstruction Southern Redemption shaped the telling of Evangelina's story in the United States during the late 1890s.[11] The assimilation of Evangelina to U.S. racial mythology that I describe functions as a facet of what Cuban historian Marial Iglesias Utset has identified as *"la confrontación de los valores y las costumbres coloniales con las representaciones políticas y culturales patrocinadas por las autoridades interventoras"* (the confrontation of colonial values and customs with the cultural and political representations sponsored by the Occupation authorities). This semiotic realigning of Cuban society under U.S. invasion and occupation *"afectó toda la simbología de la existencia cotidiana e hizo resurgir la dimensión política de las prácticas simbólicas"* (affected the entire symbology of daily life and brought the political dimensions of symbolic practices back to the surface).[12] By folding Cuba into the U.S. South through the black rapist trope, the yellow press of the time imperialistically articulated the island's independence struggle through the symbolics of white supremacy, which were uniting the Northern country after the divisive experiences of Civil War and Reconstruction. Through the black rapist trope, the propagandistic texts unify the U.S. national family following the Civil War by discursively adopting the Cuban *criolla* Evangelina. In this way, they present eventual North American military intervention in the Cuban conflict as an aspect of the white supremacist project of Southern Redemption.

Cuba in the South

Transnational studies of the U.S. South and the Caribbean have enjoyed a boom in recent years. The historian Matthew Guterl coined the term "American Mediterranean" to refer to the economic and cultural space defined by the circulation of masters, enslaved persons, and slaveocratic ideologies through the Caribbean and its littoral, a region that Southern planter society hoped to transform into its own slaveholding empire.[13] Similarly, literary scholar Martyn Bone, playing on Marxist theorist Immanuel Wallerstein's notion of an "extended Caribbean," has proposed the "extended South" as a frame through which to view the circulation of people and ideas among the Continental United States and the islands of the Antillean archipelago.[14] Inter-American scholar Kirsten Silva Gruesz has noted that, situated near the mouth of the Mississippi River in the Gulf of Mexico, Cuba occupied a central place in this extended South.[15] As African American intellectual W.E.B. DuBois explains in *Black Reconstruction*, "shut out from the United States territories by the Free Soil movement, the South determined upon secession with the distinct idea of eventually expanding into the Caribbean."[16] It is not surprising, then, that "Cuba and its accompanying slave system played such a prominent role for the Confederacy that it was included in the Union blockade of New Orleans."[17] These circumstances have led some scholars to consider the War between the States and the subsequent movement for Cuban independence as two "American civil wars that share a genealogy" – what

Deborah Cohn and John Smith understand as two "Northern" occupations of racialized "Southern" societies.[18]

Given the imbrication between the U.S. South and Cuba in the nineteenth-century North American imaginary, it is worth asking to what extent

> the timeline of [Cuba's] Ten Years War, 1868–78, add[s] another dimension to what is widely considered in nineteenth-century American literature a milestone and dividing line: 1865 [the end of the U.S. Civil War]. How does the ongoing U.S. intervention in the Caribbean after the Civil War complicate the nationalist racial frame of "Reconstruction"?[19]

After all, the Spanish-Cuban-American War "took place during the same period that 'Jim Crow,' or legal segregation, was being established throughout the South."[20] This historical coincidence of internal colonialism in the U.S. South and formal empire in the Caribbean forces us to ask how ideologies from the post-Reconstruction era influenced U.S. interpretations of Cuba's anticolonial war – in which slave emancipation clearly played a role – in propaganda such as the Evangelina texts.

Sexual violence and racial ascendency in Wilmington and Havana

Known as "Reconstruction," "the violent, dramatic, and still controversial era that followed the Civil War" was marked by Northern occupation of the South in an effort to oversee emancipation and black enfranchisement.[21] The process of reintegrating the region into the nation formally ended in 1877. This so-called "Redemption" of the South was marked by the election of anti-Reconstructionist white supremacists, such as Dixon, to state governments.[22] This return of the Old Guard was followed by the gradual institution of formal segregation under state governments and racialized terror at the hands of the Ku Klux Klan.

The reconstituted white supremacist regime would seek to justify itself through the gendered language of sexual violence, which appeared in North American discourse on both the U.S. South and Cuba in the 1890s. These attitudes manifest themselves in Dixon's *The Leopard's Spots* when a character inveighs against "everything that the soul of the South loathes and that the Republican party has tried to ram down our throats – Negro supremacy in politics and Negro equality in society."[23] In his references to emancipation and African American suffrage as an act of blacks "ramming" themselves, Dixon alludes to the Reconstruction-era myth of the black rapist of white women. Interracial rape served the late-nineteenth century South as a metaphor for the supposed post-War racial dispossession of whites, as "an exercise of power by a [black] man over [a white] man, because the woman in question was assumed to be a dependent wife or daughter within a household headed by a white propertied man."[24] Cultural studies scholar Sandra Gunning explains that "what might have begun in the late 1860s and 1870s as a political struggle was increasingly characterized by the 1890s as [...] an encroachment on the sacred Anglo-Saxon male right to everything in American society and civilization." In the metaphor of "social rape" that developed from this situation, "American society and civilization came increasingly to be figured as the white female body: silent, helpless, in immediate need of protection from the black beast"– an allegory that would come to structure the discourse of Anglo-Saxon supremacy at home and abroad.[25]

The Redemptionist reassertion of white dominance over African Americans would be achieved in 1898, while Anglo-Saxon forces were securing their own dominion over heavily black Cuba and the New York presses were publishing *The Story of Evangelina Cisneros*. On 10 November 1898, white Southern elites would overthrow the freely elected, racially integrated, government of Wilmington, North Carolina, killing as many as 300 people in what is considered to be the only successful *coup d'état* in U.S. history. Viewed by some as "the culmination of the post-Reconstruction struggle against black franchise," the impact of the events at Wilmington helped to consolidate the Southern racial regime of the proceeding seven decades by establishing a state of exception that would uphold the principles of white supremacy in the United States and its imperial sphere of influence.[26]

The ostensible catalyst of the violence was an 18 August 1898 article by African American journalist Alexander Manly refuting a pro-lynching speech made a year earlier by Rebecca Latimer Felton (later the first female U.S. senator). Echoing arguments first articulated by Ida B. Wells in 1892, Manly argued – contrary to a belief that had been slowly gaining currency for the last three decades – that many victims of lynching had not engaged in rape, but in consensual relations. Viewed as an affront to the traditional racial order, Manly's comments were met with an anti-black campaign in the white press, in which "editors focused on the supposed interest of black men in white women, perhaps the most sensitive subject in Southern race relations."[27] Filling the pages of papers across North Carolina, the discourse of the black rapist soon crept into whites' subconscious understanding of race relations as "the myth of 'negro domination' over white womanhood became the powerful tool that white supremacists used throughout their campaign to dismantle African Americans' political and economic power" in the South and to justify racial-imperial projects in Cuba.[28] A poem published in the 8 November 1898 edition of the *Wilmington Messenger*, for example, reads:

Proud Caucasians one and all;
Be not deaf to Love's appealing
Hear your wives and daughters call,
See their blanched and anxious faces,
Note their frail, but lovely forms;
Rise, defend their spotless virtue
With your strong and manly arms.[29]

In this poem, "proud Caucasian" men are entreated upon to "defend" the "spotless virtue" of "blanched" white women from an evil so obvious that it apparently need not be named. This sort of anti-black propaganda would set off a wave of lynchings and racial violence culminating in the 10 November 1898 Wilmington massacre, carried out just two days after the poem was published.[30]

Considered the "literary figure most closely associated with the stereotype of the black rapist," Dixon was particularly fascinated with the idea of white women "as the victim[s] of an 'alien' rapist" and, in his oeuvre, presented "the rise and fall of Reconstruction in North Carolina as a struggle between a besieged but chivalrous white South and a rampaging black (male) population that equates freedom with access to white women."[31] Both *The Leopard's Spots* and *The Clansman* feature extended representations of freedmen committing acts of sexual violence against white women. The following passage from *The Clansman* represents a particularly vicious mobilization of the black rapist trope:

> Gus stepped closer, with an ugly leer, his flat nose dilated, his sinister bead-eyes wide apart gleaming ape-like, as he laughed:
>
> "We ain't atter money!"
>
> The girl uttered a cry, long, tremulous, heart-rending, piteous.
>
> A single tiger-spring, and the black claws of the beast sank into the soft white throat and she was still.[32]

Invoking the racist trope of Afro-descendants as "apes," employing an especially condescending and distorted literary rendering of African American Vernacular English, stressing Gus's supposed animality through the references to "tiger-springs" and "claws," and juxtaposing the blackness of those claws with the victim's "soft white throat," Dixon presents the reader with a strikingly racist metaphor of emancipation and black suffrage as a "violation" of the white supremacist order.[33]

Sharing the same space on the pages of 1890s newspapers, the Redemptionist myth of the black rapist would become discursively imbricated with Spanish atrocities in Cuba, the U.S. war effort, and its aftermath – a discourse in which the Evangelina Cisneros affair played a significant part. Even before the events in Wilmington, African American activist Ida B. Wells in a 21 March 1898 address had connected Southern Redemption to the Caribbean conflict by comparing "lynching crimes" to "Cuban outrages."[34] Occurring within a discussion of rape accusations, Wells's use of the word "outrage" – a euphemism for sexual violence – cannot be considered casual. Rather, it points to how gendered racial discourses on the South and on Cuba were becoming intertwined during the 1890s.

It is not surprising, then, that the polysemous word should appear multiple times in *The Story*. A chapter entitled "Protests and Petitions" opens with a reference to the "burnings, murder, and other outrages" committed by the Spanish army in Cuba.[35] Invoking the same discourse of defense of "blanched [...] wives and daughters" as the *Wilmington Messenger*, Julia Ward Howe appeals "to every brother who would defend a sister from outrage" to rescue Cisneros from her colonial captors.[36] Evangelina herself, in her narrative, asks President McKinley to save "the mothers and daughters of Cuba [...] from further outrage."[37] Echoing Redeemer black rapist discourse through the reiterated references to "outrage," *The Story* "paint[s] the situation in Cuba," like that supposedly existing in the U.S. South, "as especially pernicious for white women, who might be forced to suffer the worst of indignities."[38]

Not coincidentally, the trope of interracial rape is noticeably present in U.S. political cartoons on Cuba during the period. Even as Cuban nationalist texts such as Cirilo Villaverde's 1882 *Cecilia Valdés* used *mulataje* as a metaphor for anti-colonial *cubanía* –positing a mixed-race nation against a white Peninsular and criollo colonial apparatus – the U.S. press of the pre-War period tended to represent the island as a white damsel in distress.[39] Hearst even went so far as to portray Spanish General Valeriano Weyler as a "rapist of women."[40] Almost as an extension of the Redeemer discourse that framed racial violence as white men defending "their" women from supposed black animality, 1898 drawings such as "Uncle Sam – I'll Take Care of This Lady Now" and "Don't Cry Little Girl. Uncle Sam is going to take you home with him. After that I'll tend to you, young man," appearing in *The Baltimore Morning Herald* and *The Indianapolis News*, respectively, would portray Anglo-Saxon men protecting white Cuban women from strikingly dark-skinned Spaniards.[41] An 1898 image by artist Grant Hamilton entitled "The Spanish Brute" takes the racist trope further, representing the Iberian metropolis as a violent gorilla in a clear precursor to the discourse of bestiality that Dixon later would deploy in *The Clansman*.[42] On the one hand, the cartoon draws on then-popular associations of blackness with Spanishness, a topic that has been explored in recent years by literary scholars such as Barbara Fuchs, María de Guzmán, and John C. Havard.[43] On the other, it reflects "intermittent rumors of an armed uprising by blacks in support of Spain against their American oppressors," a discursive development that collapses African Americans and Spaniards into one other as common enemies of Anglo-Saxon neocolonial policy in the South and imperial designs on Cuba.[44] Like Wells' comments on Spanish "outrages," the evidence that I describe here points to the development of a single tropological network in which Redeemers and jingoes both participated as they discussed post-Emancipation political realities in the South and in the Caribbean.

Participating in this transnational racial-gender discourse, *The Story* figures "swaggering, leering Spanish soldiers" as black rapists.[45] For example, Berriz, a "short, ugly, dark little man with bushy hair and black whiskers on his cheeks," is blackened discursively in Cisneros' description of him.[46] Importantly, the Lieutenant Colonel presents sexual relations with him as an alternative to Evangelina's father being sent to to an African penal colony: "if your father should be sent to Ceuta or to the Chaferinas [*sic*], you would be to blame. You cannot expect to have all favors and give nothing in return."[47] Later, he tells Evangelina that, "If I send him to Cueta [*sic*] or the Chaferinas, it is your fault – yours alone."[48] By suggesting, through their interchangeability, that the coerced rendering of "favors" to the racialized Berriz and imprisonment in "Africa" are equivalent undesirable fates, the text metaphorically transforms Berriz into a black rapist of Redemptionist mythology. In this world of "black" Spanish predators, it seems that "a meaningful part of what" Decker, like the "proud Caucasian" men of Wilmington, "was rescuing was [Evangelina's] whiteness."[49]

As Berriz's discursive blackening makes clear, the specter of racialized sexual violence haunts the Cisneros texts, qualifying and containing the interracial reality of a separatist Cuba that, recently having abolished slavery, soon would contemplate black suffrage. A 28 August 1897 *New York Journal* article entitled "Truth Too Black to Be Hidden" reports that "an accused but unconvicted girl of good character, education, and refinement has been kept in the Casa de Recogidas [...] for upwards of a year [...] [I]t was the intention to send her to Cueta [*sic*], the most loathsome of penal colonies, for twenty years."[50] Here, the "girl of good character, education, and refinement" on her way to face a "black" truth in Africa parallels Dixon's Southern civilization, down whose "throat" "Negro supremacy in politics and Negro equality in society" supposedly are being "rammed."[51] Similarly, one of the authors of *The Story of Evangelina Cisneros* worries that, following her trial, the white Cuban woman will be banished to "Africa, where she would be at the absolute mercy of Spain's worst criminals."[52] The text ominously invites the reader to consider "what the fate [of African imprisonment] meant to a pure young girl who had been all her life tenderly guarded and cared for."[53] Not unlike the "spotless" maids and matrons of Wilmington in the "manly arms" of their fathers and husbands, Evangelina, according to the writer, has "absolutely no experience – child that she was," a detail that underscores the sexual nature of the ills that await her in Ceuta.[54] Least there be any doubt about the threat of racialized rape, *The Story* glosses Ceuta as an "African penal settlement" or "African penal colony" at least twice, placing the modifier "African" before another adjective that too easily can be interpreted as a phallic pun.[55]

A letter from Julia Ward Howe to Pope Leo XIII reprinted in *The Story* is more explicit, as she asks the Pontiff to plead Evangelina's case to Spanish Queen Regent María Cristina de Habsburgo. In her letter, the writer expresses her fear that the white Evangelina "is in danger of suffering a sentence more cruel than death – that of twenty years of exile and imprisonment in the Spanish penal colony of Ceuta, in Africa, where no woman has ever before been sent" – again, as punishment for her participation in a process deeply tied to abolition and black political mobilization.[56] She uses similar language ("torment worse than death") in an editorial later published in *The Story*, while a letter by Vania Davis speaks of Evangelina's "fate worse than death."[57] Invoking the common nineteenth-century phrase "worse than death" to refer to potential rape in Africa, the imperial propaganda text mobilizes the same myth of the black rapist as is found in Southern Redeemer writings – Dixon, for example, alludes to the euphemism three times in two pages in *The Leopard's Spots*.[58] This equivalence between post-Emancipation Cuban and Southern societies that the North American jingoist press draws through the trope of the black rapist works to incorporate the Caribbean island discursively into the United States by presenting the two areas as under a common racial "threat." If, as Gilmore argues, Southern white men were moved to violence in order to protect their "blanched wives and daughters" from the supposed threat of black assailants, by inscribing Evangelina's story into the racist national mythology of the black rapist, Howe, Davis, and others incorporate the Cuban woman – and, by extension, the country that she represents – into the U.S. national family. This assimilation is reinforced by her receipt of "immediate U.S. citizenship" in the closing pages of *The Story*.[59]

Evangelina, 1898, and the U.S. family reunion

As a new member, Evangelina would enlarge the U.S. national family imperially while altering domestic dynamics between North and South. *The Story of Evangelina Cisneros* prominently features the family of Colonel Fitzhugh Lee, consul general of the United States in Havana. As his surname would indicate, Lee was the nephew of Robert E. Lee, commander of the Confederate forces during the Civil War.[60] In her narrative of the events, Evangelina stresses that Lee's solicitous wife visited her in prison and "spoke to me as she might to her own daughter."[61] That the white Cuban has been "adopted" by the ex-Confederate family becomes evident at the end of the narrative, when Evangelina's suitor Carlos Carbonell appears at the Lees' home in Richmond, former capital of the Confederacy, to ask for her hand in marriage. The act situates the Cuban woman under the patriarchal tutelage of Consul Lee, represented simultaneously as a U.S. imperialist and an heir to the Confederacy. Similarly, Karl Decker, who led the *Journal*'s mission to rescue Evangelina from her Havana jail, was "the son of a Confederate colonel."[62] It is important to note that Lee and Decker are representatives of the post-War generation, scions of Southern families that have "risen again" after losing the Cause. As with the mythical black rapist that reappears in the Evangelina texts, then, Lee's and Decker's Southern genealogies serve to inscribe the Cisneros affair within the metanarrative of Southern Redemption.

Importantly, this family attitude towards Evangelina is not the particular prerogative of the Confederates, and, when the *criolla* is presented to President McKinley at the White House, she is accompanied by the widow of Northern General John Logan, who appears to fill in for the girl's dead mother.[63] What emerges here, then, is not the traditional rivalry between North and South, but the union (or reunion) of Logan's North – presented not as a military champion, but as a maternal chaperone – and a South "redeemed" in the benevolently paternalist forms of Lee and Decker. Related through their new "daughter," whom they – like the white men of Wilmington – have saved from "African" domination, the two sides of the U.S. national family are reconciled through their mutual, white supremacist, interest in the white Cuban woman's wellbeing in the face of the black social and political advances occurring throughout the extended South at the time. Connecting white neocolonialism in the South with U.S. imperialism in the Caribbean, Evangelina's rescue from African rape by Anglo-Saxon saviors serves to tie Southern Redemption to the rise of the United States as a global power.

As it features collaboration from both sides of the U.S. national family, the letter-writing campaign discussed at the beginning of *The Story* exemplifies the text's use of adoption as a metaphor for national reconciliation through imperial gazing. Tellingly, the widows of both Confederate president Jefferson Davis and Union general Ulysses S. Grant took part in this effort to "cut through the animosities between North and South that festered after the Civil War and unite the women of the United States in a common cause."[64] Upon signing the petition to María Cristina, Nancy McKinley, mother of then-President McKinley, exclaimed that

> the women of America can accomplish a great deal sometimes, and I can assure them they have my hearty endorsement and prayers for success. I hope the Queen Regent will listen to the voices of the American women and her own conscience, and set the Cuban child free,

positing the group of U.S. women as moral guides to the Spanish Regent.[65] Given her relation to the president, Nancy McKinley's quote serves to frame the petition to María Cristina de Habsburgo within the same family allegory that Evangelina's adoption by the Logans and the Lees represents. This can be seen when soon-to-be adoptive mother Mrs. Logan, who drafted the missive, suggests to the Spanish Regent that Evangelina's case "must appeal to your mother's heart" and insists that the ruler take action.[66] In this way, the Northern and Southern signatories not only perform the reunification of the national family by adopting Evangelina, they also, through this maternal act of protecting the Cuban when the Spanish Regent has abandoned her, show themselves to be the "true" mothers of the young colonial when the representative of the "mother country" fails to shield her from racialized rapists.[67] The campaign thus evidences the ability of the post-Reconstruction era North American national family to put aside their regional differences in order to save the white Cuba(n) from a fate "worse than death" at "African" hands, in contrast with Mother Spain's apparent inability to do the same and resolve her own racialized conflict on the Empire's Southern periphery. Even as it complicates the gender binary upon which the black rapist mythology rests by granting greater agency to white women (while resisting interrogation of the construct's underlying racist assumptions), like

Decker's rescue and the Logan's and the Lee's metaphorical adoption, the signatories' maternal gesture serves to justify the U.S. intervention in the island's independence movement that would occur a short year later.

Thus, as the bi-regional rallying around the Cuban captive's cause makes clear, the U.S. military intervention on the island represented "the first time since the Civil War that the North and South had united in a common goal, which built badly needed unity" and paved the way for expansion into the moribund Spanish Empire.[68] This is also reflected in a chapter of *The Leopard's Spots* entitled "The New America," in which Dixon presents Northern withdrawal from the former Confederate States of America at the end of Reconstruction as though it were a consequence of the national unity forged in the conflict with Spain, explaining that, after the war:

> Negro refugees and their associates once more filled the ear of the national government with clamour for the return of the army to the South to uphold Negro power, but for the first time since 1867 it fell on deaf ears. The Anglo-Saxon race had been reunited. The Negro was no longer the ward of the republic. Henceforth, he must stand or fall on his own worth and pass under the law of the survival of the fittest.[69]

In much the same way that the potential annexation of slaveholding Cuba "contributed significantly to the polarization of North and South" before the Civil War, the postbellum invasion of the island functions for Dixon to finally resolve sectional tensions within the United States.[70] As in the Evangelina texts, here, too, the Southern Lost Cause finds itself in U.S. imperialism and "the Anglo-Saxon" nation, newly united, enters "the new century with the imperial crown of the ages on [its] brow and the scepter of the infinite in [its] hands."[71]

It is important to note that, despite what Dixon describes, Reconstruction did not end in 1898, but in 1877. However, as mentioned previously, in addition to the beginning of formal empire in the Caribbean, 1898 was also a key year for U.S. race relations, as it marks the date of another historical event: the Wilmington insurrection (to which Dixon alludes elsewhere in his novel), in which the gains of Reconstruction were definitively reversed by the interlocking forces of racial terror and gender policing – ideologies that also would create the conditions of possibility for Evangelina's imperial adoption by the re-United States. This relationship between Cuba and North Carolina would have been apparent to readers at the time. "On November 12, 1898, the *New York Herald* ran stories about the U.S. presence in Cuba, the 'race riot' in Phoenix, South Carolina, and the massacre of Black people in Wilmington, North Carolina."[72] Similarly, the front page of the *New York Journal and Advertiser* (the *New York Journal*'s new name) from the day after the massacre features stories about both the events in Wilmington and Theodore Roosevelt, who had been elected governor of New York after his successful campaign in the Caribbean. While the articles about Roosevelt appear on the left-hand side of the paper and those about Wilmington on the right, the columns are not even, and the two stories collide on the page, making it difficult for the reader to determine where one starts and the other stops. The rest of the issue is filled with news from occupied Cuba. The two racialized conflicts thus become entangled with one another on the *Journal*'s pages, tying "the racial question at home to America's world mission abroad" through the myth of the back rapist and suggesting that "the South's regional redemption from an imperialist North lays the foundation for national imperialism at the turn of the century."[73]

Conclusion

A reconsideration of the well-known place of yellow journalism in the Spanish-Cuban-American War in the frame of the "extended South" or "American Mediterranean" allows us to think about the transnational dimensions of postslavery, a historical moment frequently examined from the national perspective.[74] By focusing on the intertwining of white Redeemer neocolonial and Anglo-Saxon imperial discourses through the black rapist trope, we add a new layer of nuance to our understanding of the U.S. invasion and occupation of Cuba. After all, the U.S. intervention into the island's affairs represented a military and political domination justified in part by a desire to "redeem" the post-abolition former Spanish colony from the racialized debasement of the Spanish colonial world and the more egalitarian iterations of the separatist project. The United States' unsuccessful efforts after the Caribbean War to disenfranchise Afro-Cubans, as well as its involvement in the 1912 repression of the Partido Independiente de Color – an event that also responded to rumors of rape – demonstrate the mobility of the Redemptionist racial and gender paradigms popularized by writers such as Dixon in the imperial context of the circum-Caribbean.[75] The discursive domestication of Evangelina and Cuba within the extended South thus illuminates a transnational racial-imperial ideological-tropological network that would develop in the early-twentieth century Americas and influence race politics in the two Souths.

Notes

1. González and Quintan, *Evangelina Cossío Cisneros y William Randolph Hearst*, 13–14.
2. Ibid., 7–8.
3. Albert, *The Rescue of Evangelina Cisneros*, 132.
4. For histories of the war, see Foner, *Spanish-Cuban-American War*, and Pérez, *Cuba between Empires*. For a discussion of historiographic representations of the war, see Pérez, *The War of 1898*.
5. Martínez-Echazábal, "Mestizaje," 32.
6. Ferrer, *Insurgent Cuba*.
7. Martí, "Nuestra América" and Dixon, *The Clansman*, 46.
8. Qtd. in *The Story*, 41. Though an abolitionist, Howe infamously puts her racist views on Afro-descendants on display in her travel narrative *A Trip to Cuba*.
9. Dixon, *The Leopard's Spots*, 90.
10. Roggenkamp, *Narrating the News*, 16.
11. Ibid., 18. Though, as Helg shows, the black rapist trope certainly exists in Cuban discourse from the period, as well, canonical Cuban texts by Gertrudis Gómez de Avellaneda and Anselmo Súarez y Romero, for example, display (perhaps insincerely) much more positive attitudes towards black male sexuality. North American writing on Evangelina Cisneros seems not to have dialogued with this Cuban race discourse. For a comparison of the Cisneros affair in U.S., Cuban, and Spanish periodicals, see Wilcox. For a general discussion of race and gender in the nineteenth-century exile press, see Lazo, *Writing to Cuba*. For a reading of Cisneros in the context of U.S. Latino literature, see Torres-Salliant.
12. Iglesias Utset, *Las metáforas del cambio*, 15.
13. Guterl, *American Mediterranean*.
14. Bone, "The (Extended) South"; Wallerstein, *Capitalist World Economy*.
15. Gruesz, "The Gulf of Mexico System."
16. DuBois, *Black Reconstruction*, 42.

17. Alemán, "From Union Officers," 91. On Cuban contributions to the Union and Confederate armies, see Tucker, ed. *Cubans in the Confederacy*; Alemán, "From Union Officers to Cuban Rebels"; and Lazo, "Confederates in the Hispanic Attic."
18. Ibid., 105.
19. Lazo, "Introduction," 16.
20. Russell, *African Americans*, 1.
21. Foner, *Reconstruction*, xvii.
22. Clark, "Introduction," xii.
23. Dixon, *The Leopard's Spots*, 196.
24. Edwards, *Gendered Confusion and Strife*, 8.
25. Gunning, *Rape, Race, and Lynching*, 7. For a black feminist critique of the myth of the black rapist, see Davis, *Women, Race, and Class*, 172–201.
26. Gillman, *Blood Talk*, 97.
27. Prather, "We Have Taken," 30.
28. Kirshenbaum, "The Vampire," 9.
29. Qtd. in Gilmore, "Murder, Memory, and the Flight of the Incubus," 75.
30. It is important to point out the largely fictitious nature of this discourse, which rarely included testimony from the alleged victims themselves. Gilmore has shown that there was, in fact, no statistical increase in the incidence of rape in North Carolina between 1897 and 1898 (76).
31. Gunning, *Rape, Race, and Lynching*, 28; Durham, *White Rage*, 84; Leiter, "Thomas Dixon, Jr," n. p. For an overview of race and gender in Dixon's oeuvre, see Lyerly, "Gender and Race."
32. Dixon, *The Clansman*, 304.
33. Kim Magowan, for her part, deconstructs the "black beast" trope to show how white men also are depicted as animalistic in Dixon's novels. For a biographically based, psychoanalytic explanation of the black rapist myth in Dixon's oeuvre, see Williamson, *Crucible of Race*, 141–175. For a queer reading of the subject, see Stokes, *Color of Sex*, 133–157.
34. Wells, "Remarks," 862. For more on comparisons between Spanish violence and U.S. lynching in the U.S. African American press, see Russell, *African Americans*, 44–48.
35. Cisneros, *The Story*, 31.
36. Qtd. in ibid., 41.
37. Ibid., 221.
38. Fountain, "Questions of Race and Gender," 39.
39. Pérez, *Cuba in the American Imagination* and Roggenkamp, *Narrating the News*, 106.
40. Sánchez Pupo, *La prensa*, 52. Pérez notes that U.S. discourse from the occupation period, conversely, normally allegorized Cuba as a black child. See *Cuba in the American Imagination*, 95–174. On Africanity as an anti-colonial metaphor, see Williams, *The Crucible of Race*. Sartorius, for his part, recently has problematized the widely accepted dichotomy between white loyalists and Afro-Cuban sepratists. See *Ever Faithful*.
41. Qtd. in Pérez, *Cuba in the American Imagination*, 75 and 83.
42. Qtd. in Charonon-Duetsch, "Cartoons," 13.
43. Fuchs, *Exotic Nations*; de Guzmán, *Spain's Long Shadow*; Havard, *Hispanism*. Even Cuban nationalists at the time looked doubtfully on Spanish claims to whiteness, such as when Villaverde writes: "*Es que tu padre, por ser español, no está exento de la sospecha de tener sangre mezclada, pues supongo que es andaluz, y de Sevilla vinieron a América los primeros esclavos negros. Tampoco los árabes, que dominaron en Andalucía más que en otras partes de España, fueron de raza pura caucásica, sino africana*" (Just because your father is Spanish doesn't mean he's exempt from the suspicion of having mixed blood. I suppose he's Andalusian, and the first black slaves came to América from Seville. And the Arabs, who were more dominant in Andalusia than in other parts of Spain, weren't of pure Caucasian race, either. They were African). *Cecilia Valdés*, 135.
44. Gillman, *Blood Talk*, 91. On African American participation in the war against Spain, see Kaplan, "Black and Blue" and Russell, *African Americans*.
45. Cisneros, *The Story*, 141.

46. Ibid., 157.
47. Ibid., 170.
48. Ibid., 171.
49. Torres-Saillant, "Recovering," 442.
50. Qtd. in Albert, *The Rescue of Evangelina Cisneros*, 82.
51. Dixon, *The Leopard's Spots*, 196.
52. Cisneros, *The Story*, 36.
53. Ibid., 35. For a study of the figure of the Cuban woman – particularly the Afro-Cuban woman – in nationalist discourse, see Kutzinski, *Sugar's Secrets*. For a historical study of the role of Cuban women in the independence movement, see Prados-Torreira, *Mambisas*.
54. Cisneros, *The Story*, 36.
55. Ibid., 32 and 61.
56. Howe, qtd. in Cisneros, *The Story*, 39.
57. Ibid., 41; Davis, qtd. in ibid., 38.
58. Dixon, *The Leopard's Spots*, 126–127.
59. Roggenkamp, *Narrating the News*, 112.
60. Campbell, *The Year that Defined American Journalism*.
61. Cisneros, *The Story*, 189.
62. Albert, *Rescue*, 121.
63. Cisneros, *The Story*, 222.
64. Albert, *Rescue*, 58.
65. Qtd. in Cisneros, *The Story*, 46–47.
66. Qtd. in Ibid., 43–44.
67. Widow of the late Spanish king Alfonso XII, María Cristina de Habsburgo was of Austrian, not Spanish, birth. This fact seems not to have impacted how the Anglo-American women discussed here saw her.
68. Albert, *The Rescue of Evangelina Cisneros*, 22.
69. Dixon, *The Leopard's Spots*, 418.
70. Tucker, *Cubans in the Confederacy*, 4.
71. Dixon, *The Leopard's Spots*, 439.
72. Davis, *Women, Race, and Class*, 117.
73. Rogin, "The Sword," 153; Thomas, "*The Clansman's*," 321. The details of Dixon's views on U.S. imperialism remain a subject of scholarly debate. Williamson and Thomas argue that Dixon's faith in U.S. empire gradually increased during the war years and their aftermath, while Michaels contends that the author's racism prevented him from endorsing U.S. Anglo-Saxon entanglements with non-white peoples abroad.
74. For a notable exception, see Scott, *Degrees of Freedom*.
75. Helg, *Our Rightful Share*, 169–176, 197–198, 211, and 216. For more on the impact of U.S. imperialism on race structures in early-republican Cuba, see de la Fuente, *A Nation for All*, and Ferrer, *Insurgent Cuba*.

Acknowledgements

This work was supported by the University of Minnesota Morris Faculty Research Enhancement Fund.

Disclosure statement

No potential conflict of interest was reported by the author(s).

ORCID

Thomas Genova http://orcid.org/0000-0002-9444-8679

References

Albert, Kyle Hunter. "The Rescue of Evangelina Cisneros: 'While Others Talk the Journal Acts.'" Master's thesis, University of Montana, 1984.

Alemán, Jesse. "From Union Officers to Cuban Rebels: The Story of the Brothers Cavada and Their American Civil Wars." In *The Latino Nineteenth Century*, edited by Jesse Aleman and Rodrigo Lazo, 89–109. New York: New York University Press, 2016.

Bone, Martyn. "The (Extended) South of Black Folk: Intraregional and Transnational Migrant Labor in *Jonah's Gourd Vine* and *Their Eyes Were Watching God*." *American Literature* 79 (December 2007): 753–779.

Campbell, W. Joseph. *The Year That Defined American Journalism: 1897 and the Clash of Paradigms*. New York: Routledge, 2006.

Charonon-Deutsch, Lou. "Cartoons and the Politics of Masculinity in the Spanish and American Press During the War of 1898." *Prismasocial* 13 (December 2014–May 2015): 109–148.

Cisneros, Evangelina. *The Story of Evangelina Cisneros*. New York: Continental Publishing, 1898.

Clark, Thomas D. "Introduction." In *The Clansman: An Historical Romance of The Ku Klux Klan*, edited by Thomas Dixon Jr., v–xvii. Lexington: University Press of Kentucky, 1970.

Davis, Angela Y. *Women, Race, and Class*. New York: Vintage, 1983.

De la Fuente, Alejandro. *A Nation for All: Race, Inequality, and Politics in Twentieth-Century Cuba*. Chapel Hill: University of North Carolina Press, 2001.

Dixon, Thomas. *The Clansman: An Historical Romance of the Ku Klux Klan*. (1904). Lexington: University Press of Kentucky, 1970.

Dixon, Thomas. *The Leopard's Spots: A Romance of the White Man's Burden, 1865–1900* (1902). Ridgewood, NJ: Gregg Press, 1967.

Dixon, Thomas. *The Traitor: A Story of the Fall of the Invisible Empire*. New York: Doubleday, 1907.

DuBois, W.E.B. 1935. *Black Reconstruction in America*. Edited by Herbert Aptheker. Millwood, NY: Kraus-Thomson, 1976.

Durham, Martin. *White Rage: The Extreme Right and American Politics*. London: Routledge, 2007.

Edwards, Laura F. *Gendered Confusion and Strife: The Political Culture of Reconstruction*. Urbana: University of Illinois Press, 1997.

Ferrer, Ada. *Insurgent Cuba: Race, Nation, and Revolution, 1868–1898*. Chapel Hill: University of North Carolina Press, 1999.

Foner, Eric. *Reconstruction: America's Unfinished Revolution, 1863–1877*. New York: Perennial Classics, 1988.

Foner, Phillip S. *The Spanish-Cuban-American War and the Birth of American Imperialism*. 2 vols. New York: Monthly Review Press, 1972.

Fountain, Anne. "Questions of Race and Gender: Evangelina Cisneros and the Spanish-Cuban-American War." *SECOLAS Annals* 39, no.1 (March 1999): 36–43.

Fuchs, Barbara. *Exotic Nation: Maurophilia and the Construction of Early Modern Spain*. Philadelphia: University of Pennsylvania Press, 2009.

Gillespie, Michele K., and Randal L. Hall. *Thomas Dixon Jr. and the Birth of Modern America*. Baton Rouge: Louisiana State University Press, 2006.

Gillespie, Michele K., and Randal L. Hall. "Introduction." In *Thomas Dixon Jr. and the Birth of Modern America*, 1–22. Baton Rouge: Louisiana State University Press.

Gillman, Susan. *Blood Talk: American Race Melodrama and the Culture of the Occult*. Chicago: University of Chicago Press, 2003.

Gilmore, Glenda E. "Murder, Memory, and the Flight of the Incubus." In *Democracy Betrayed: The Wilmington Riot of 1898 and Its Legacy*, edited by Timothy B. Tyson and David S. Cecelski, 74–91. Chapel Hill: University of North Carolina Press, 1998.

Gómez de Avellaneda, Gertrudis. *Sab*. 1841. Ed. José Servera. Cátedra: Madrid, 2003.

González González, Oscar, and José Antonio Quintan Veiga. *Evangelina Cossío Cisneros y William Randolph Hearst: dos figuras en la historia*. Nueva Gerona: El Abra, 2002.

Griffith, D.W., dir. *The Birth of a Nation*. USA: D. W. Griffith Corp., 1915.

Gruesz, Kirsten Silva. "The Gulf of Mexico System and the "Latinness" of New Orleans." *American Literary History* 18 (Autumn 2006): 468–495.

Gunning, Sandra. *Rape, Race, and Lynching*. New York: Oxford University Press, 1996.

Guterl, Mathew. *American Mediterranean: Southern Slaveholders in the Age of Emancipation*. Cambridge, MA: Harvard University Press, 2008.

Guzmán, María de. *Spain's Long Shadow: The Black Legend, Off-Whiteness, and Anglo-American Empire*. Minneapolis: University of Minnesota Press, 2005.

Havard, John C. *Hispanism and Early US Literature*. Tuscaloosa: University of Alabama Press, 2018.

Helg, Aline. *Our Rightful Share: The Afro-Cuban Struggle for Equality, 1886–1912*. Chapel Hill: University of North Carolina Press, 1995.

Hoganson, Kristin L. *Fighting for American Manhood: How Gender Politics Provoked the Spanish-American and Philippine-American Wars*. New Haven, CT: Yale University Press, 1998.

Howe, Julia Ward. *A Trip to Cuba*. Accessed 22 April 2020. https://americanliterature.com/author/julia-ward-howe/book/a-trip-to-cuba/summary, 1860.

Iglesias Utset, Marial. *Las metáforas del cambio en la vida cotidiana: Cuba 1898–1902*. Havana: Unión, 2003.

Kaplan, Amy. "Black and Blue on San Juan Hill." In *Cultures of United States Imperialism*, edited by Amy Kaplan and Donald Pease, 219–236. Durham, NC: Duke University Press, 1993.

Kaplan, Amy, and Donald E. Pease, eds. *Cultures of United States Imperialism*. Durham, NC: Duke University Press, 1993.

Kirshenbaum, Andrea Meryl. "'The Vampire That Hovers Over North Carolina': Gender, White Supremacy, and the Wilmington Race Riot of 1898." *Southern Cultures* 4, no. 3 (Fall 1998): 6–30.

Kutzinksi, Vera. *Sugar's Secrets: Race and the Erotics of Cuban Nationalism*. Charlottesville: University of Virginia Press, 1993.

Lazo, Rodrigo. "Confederates in the Hispanic Attic: The Archive Against Itself." In *Unsettled States: Nineteenth-Century American Literary Studies*, edited by Dana Luciano and Ivy Wilson, 31–54. New York: New York University Press, 2014.

Lazo, Rodrigo. "Introduction." In *The Latino Nineteenth Century*, edited by Jesse Aleman and Rodrigo Lazo, 1–19. New York: New York University Press, 2016.

Lazo, Rodrigo. *Writing to Cuba: Filibustering and Cuban Exiles in the United States*. Chapel Hill: University of North Carolina Press, 2005.

Lazo, Rodrigo, and Jesse Alemán, eds. *The Latino Nineteenth Century*. New York: New York University Press, 2016.

Leiter, Andrew. "Thomas Dixon, Jr.: Conflicts in Literature and History." Accessed 22 April 2020. https://docsouth.unc.edu/southlit/dixon_intro.html.

Lyerly, Cynthia Lynn. "Gender and Race in Dixon's Religious Ideology." In *Thomas Dixon Jr. and the Birth of Modern America*, edited by Michele K Gillespie and Randal L. Hall, 80–104. Baton Rouge: Louisiana State University Press, 2006.

Magowan, Kim. "Coming between the 'Black Beast' and White Virgin: The Pressures of Liminality in Thomas Dixon." *Studies in American Fiction* 27, no. 1 (Spring 1999): 77–102.

Martí, José. "Nuestra América." *Revista Ilustrada de Nueva York*. Accessed 22 April 2020. http://bibliotecavirtual.clacso.org.ar/ar/libros/osal/osal27/14Marti.pdf, 1891.

Martínez-Echazábal, Lourdes. "Mestizaje and the Discourse of National/Cultural Identity in Latin America, 1845–1959." *Latin American Perspectives* 25, no. 3 (May 1998): 21–42.

Michaels, Walter Benn. "Anti-Imperial Imperialism." In *Cultures of United States Imperialism*, edited by Amy Kaplan and Donald Pease, 365–392. Durham, NC: Duke University Press, 1993.

New York Journal and Adviser. 18 August 1898. Accessed 22 April 2020. https://chroniclingamerica.loc.gov/.

Pérez Jr., Louis A. *Cuba between Empires, 1878–1902*. Pittsburgh: University of Pittsburgh Press, 1983.

Pérez Jr., Louis A. *Cuba in the American Imagination: Metaphor and the Imperial Ethos*. Chapel Hill: University of North Carolina Press, 2008.

Pérez Jr., Louis A. *The War of 1898: The United States and Cuba in History and Historiography*. Chapel Hill: University of North Carolina Press, 1998.

Pérez Cisneros, Enrique. *En torno al '98 cubano*. Madrid: Verbum, 1997.

Prados-Torreira, Teresa. *Mambisas: Rebel Women in Nineteenth-Century Cuba*. Gainsville: University Press of Florida, 2005.

Prather, Sr., H. Leon. "We Have Taken a City: A Centennial Essay." In *Democracy Betrayed: The Wilmington Riot of 1898 and Its Legacy*, edited Timothy B. Tryson and David S. Cecelski, 25–48. Chapel Hill: University of North Carolina Press, 1998.

Roggenkamp, Karen. *Narrating the News: New Journalism and Literary Genre in Late Nineteenth-Century American Newspapers and Journals*. Kent, OH: Kent State University Press, 2005.

Rogin, Michael. "'The Sword Became a Flashing Vision': D.W. Griffith's *The Birth of a Nation*." *Representations* 9 (Winter 1985): 150–195.

Romine, Scott. "Thomas Dixon and the Literary Production of Whiteness." In *Thomas Dixon Jr. and the Birth of Modern America*, edited by Michele K Gillespie and Randal L. Hall, 124–150. Baton Rouge: Louisiana State University Press, 2006.

Russell, Timothy Dale. "African Americans and the Spanish-American War and Philippine Insurrection: Military Participation, Recognition, and Memory, 1898–1904." Ph.D. diss, University of California, Riverside, 2013.

Sánchez Pupo, Miralys. *La prensa norteamericana llama a la guerra, 1898*. Havana: Ciencias Sociales, 1998.

Sartorius, David. *Ever Faithful: Race, Loyalty, and the Ends of Empire in Spanish Cuba*. Durham, NC: Duke University Press, 2014.

Scott, Rebecca J. *Degrees of Freedom: Louisiana and Cuba after Slavery*. Cambridge, MA: Harvard University Press, 2005.

Scott, Rebecca J. *Slave Emancipation in Cuba: The Transition to Free Labor, 1860–1899*. Pittsburgh: University of Pittsburgh Press, 1985.

Slide, Anthony. *American Racist: The Life and Films of Thomas Dixon*. Lexington: University of Kentucky Press, 2004.

Smith, Jon, and Deborah Cohn. *Look Away! The U.S. South in New World Studies*. Durham, NC: Duke University Press, 2004.

Stokes, Mason. *The Color of Sex: Whiteness, Heterosexuality, and the Fiction of White Supremacy*. Durham, NC: Duke University Press, 2001.

Suárez y Romero, Anselmo. *Francisco. El ingenio, o las delicias del campo*. 1880. Edited by Mario Cabrera Caqui. Havana: Ministerio de Educación. Dirección de Cultura, 1947.

Thomas, Brook. "'The Clansman's Race-based Anti-imperialist Imperialism." *The Mississippi Quarterly* 62, no. 2 (Spring 2009): 303–333.

Torres-Saillant, Silvo. "Recovering US Cuban Texts." *Latino Studies* 3, no. 3 (November 2005): 432–442.

Tucker, Philip Thomas, ed. *Cubans in the Confederacy: José Agustin Quintero, Ambrosio José Gonzalez, and Loreta Janeta Velazquez*. Jefferson, NC: McFarland, 2002.

Tyson, Timothy B., and David S. Cecelski, eds. *Democracy Betrayed: The Wilmington Riot of 1898 and Its Legacy*. Chapel Hill: University of North Carolina Press, 1998.

Villaverde, Cirilo. *Cecilia Valdés, o La Loma del Ángel*. 1882. Edited by Jean Lamore. Madrid: Cátedra, 1992.

Wallerstein, Immanuel. *The Capitalist World Economy*. Cambridge: Cambridge University Press, 1979.

Wells, Ida B. *Lynch Law in Georgia*. Chicago, 1899. Accessed 22 April 2020. https://archive.org/stream/lynchlawingeorgi00well/lynchlawingeorgi00well_djvu.txt.

Wells, Ida B. 1898. "Remarks to President McKinley." In *Lift Every Voice: African American Oratory 1787–1900*, edited by Phillip Sheldon Foner and Robert J. Branham, 861–862. Tuscaloosa: University of Alabama Press, 1998.

Wells, Ida B. *Southern Horrors: Lynch Law in All Its Phases*, 1892. Accessed 22 April 2020. https://archive.org/stream/southernhorrors14975gut/14975.txt.

Wilcox, Carol. "Cuba's 'Hot Little Rebel' and Spain's 'Criminal Fugitive': The Prison Escape of Evangelina Cisneros in 1897." In *Sensationalism: Murder, Mayhem, Mudslinging, Scandals, and Disasters in 19th-Century Reporting*, edited by David B. Sachsman and David W. Bulla, 155–170. New York: Routledge, 2017.

Williamson, Joel. *The Crucible of Race: Black-White Relations in the American South Since Emancipation*. New York: Oxford University Press, 1985.

The journey of Víctor Lucumí Chappotín from Saint-Domingue to Cuba: Slavery, autonomy, and property, 1797–1841

Aisnara Perera Díaz and María de los Ángeles Meriño Fuentes

ABSTRACT
When considering cases such as Víctor Lucumí Chappotín's, a slave of the Lucumí nation who owned slaves in Cuba during the 1830s (a period when the illegal slave trade was blooming), scholars have tended to ask certain types of questions: Did the law recognize such forms of ownership? Were slaves allowed to acquire other slaves for their own benefit? In this essay, we aim to go beyond the strictly juridical terrain to reflect on the conditions that allowed for this singular situation and evaluate the degree of autonomy implied in the ability to own individuals with whom the slave shared a social and juridical condition. To do so, we examine the goals and motivations of those who consented this usufruct and those who held it.

On 15 February 1840, the *moreno* (black man) Víctor Lucumí Chappotín passed from this life into the next. He had been sick in bed for weeks. On 26 January of the same year, having called the captain of the district of Puerto de la Güira – in the jurisdiction of Havana, approximately 65 kilometers southwest of the Cuban capital – he had dictated a detailed will to him. They met in the *bohío* (hut) that served as his quarters on the La Mariana coffee plantation to attest to the veracity of the story of success and improvement that the Lucumí elder was recounting. Perhaps those present already knew the most notable events of his life. The gravity of the moment demanded clarification and a few omissions rather than picturesque details. The will attests to a quite typical trajectory. In terms of social mobility, Víctor's life was comparable to that of other Africans liberated in Spanish or Portuguese America. In terms of his traditions, it was similar to those of the people living in the Bight of Benin, in West Africa, where he was probably from.

The document shows that Víctor was romantically involved with several women, that he had three children and two grandchildren, and that he ended up marrying a companion from his time in captivity, with whom he had no descendants. Regarding his property, he said that it had been acquired "with our own work" and that he possessed five slaves, a house in the town of Guanajay, and sums of money lent to various people.[1] We also know that he was generous with one of his female slaves, granting her manumission at no charge. Finally, he named his surviving children and grandchildren as sole heirs – but these heirs, it should be noted, were enslaved by the very same individuals he appointed as executors of the will.[2] To fully understand this picture, we should add one important detail: Víctor had obtained his slaves while he was still in captivity. In other words, he was a *"esclavo señor"* (slave/owner), a term first used in 2010 by the Brazilian historian Carlos Eugênio Libano Soarez and then in 2016 by João José Reis.[3] His freedom became official on 27 January 1838, one year after the death of his master.

To date, there are very few references to similar cases of slaves owning slaves in plantation-era Cuba. According to Alejandro de la Fuente, some 15 percent of the slaves who purchased manumission in Havana between 1601 and 1610 did so by paying with "another slave of their property," a method known as "manumission by substitution."[4] This method was also used in the Brazilian city of Salvador da Bahia from the end of the eighteenth century until the abolition of slavery in 1888.[5] After recognizing the exceptional nature of his finding, De la Fuente attributes it to the flexibility of the social class structure in Havana at the time and to the economic context, which was marked by the commercial boom produced by the stationing of the Fleet of the Indies in its port. He does not analyze factors such as the sex, age, color, and ethnic origin of the people manumitted in this fashion in further detail, so we are unsure if the substitution was done, as in the case of Brazil, with captives of the same sex, age group, status, and place of origin. In her study of the communities of slaves of the Crown in the mining town of El Cobre, in the Eastern part of Cuba, the North American historian María Elena Díaz mentions that, in the first half of the eighteenth century, some of them declared other slaves among their property.[6] As she observes, captives were transferred through inheritance. Most times, a family member who been manumitted earlier received them, and heirs shared the usufruct derived from the captives. Díaz also points out that, by the 1770s, there seemed to have been either "harsher restrictions on royal slaves' customary entitlement to own slaves" or "a greater propensity of the Cobreros to invest in self-manumission rather than in slaves."[7] According to Díaz, purchase (rather than inheritance) was sometimes the means by which the Cobreros increased the number of their slaves. The local slave market – characterized, above all, by clandestine arrivals from the Caribbean region – was sufficiently dynamic to make this possible. Díaz observes that the so-called "slaves of the King"[8] could own and inherit property, including slaves. Precisely because they were "slaves of the King," they enjoyed certain privileges. Now, whether the Crown granted them especial privileges or not, the consent of their master was also necessary.

The *Leyes de Partidas* of King Alfonso X, the basis for the Indian slave legislation, held that "everything a slave earns, in whatever manner he earns it, must belong to his master."[9] In theory, the slave had no right to acquire any movable or immovable property. In practice, even tribunals treated people in captivity as active agents in the acquisition and holding of goods. In Spanish and Portuguese America, masters often allowed enslaved persons to keep the money or peculium that they earned.[10] As Spanish historian Manuel Lucena has rightly pointed out, "the peculium totally contradicted the fundamental principle that the slave was dominated by his master and had no right to possess anything."[11] He offers an explanation by establishing a close link between the right to manumission and self-purchase as the most frequent way to obtain it.[12] At any rate, evidence suggests that this generic and sometimes vague practice included not only cash earmarked for purchasing freedom, but also, for example, the money invested in 1819 by the African slave Juana María de la Candelaria, born in Senegal, to buy two slaves in Gorea. Juana later used one of these slaves to pay for the trip that brought her back to Havana, where she visited the tribunals to petition for her freedom and that of her husband, who had been kidnapped.[13] Similarly, money was used in this way between 1831 and 1840, when Víctor bought four slaves; in 1849 and 1850, in the city of Bejucal, when the Lucumí slaves Pedro, Manuel, and Buenaventura Acosta bought small houses; and in 1848, when the *pardo* (mulatto) slave Cirilo Recio partnered with two free *pardos* to create a funeral service association in the city of Puerto Príncipe (currently Camagüey).[14]

Our main focus in this essay is the slave/owner Víctor Lucumí Chappotín. Generally, in cases such as his, researchers have raised basic juridical questions such as the following: Did the law recognize and/or permit such possession? Did slaves have the legal capacity to acquire and/or enjoy it for their own benefit? We propose to go beyond legal considerations and instead reflect upon the conditions that led his owner to allow Víctor to become a slave/owner, as well as upon the reasons that led Víctor to invest in slaves rather than using his money in a different way, such as paying for his own freedom or that of his children or grandchildren. Attending to the experiences and sociocultural background of both owners and captives, we also consider the motivations and final goals of those who consented to this exceptional usufruct and those who enjoyed it. We should recall that in Dahomey and Yoruba states "[s]ome slaves who attained military and government positions accumulated slaves of their own, but they acquired these slaves as dependants themselves. These elevated slaves almost formed a caste of high-ranking slave officials in some places."[15] Could Víctor have been the slave of a slave/owner in Yoruba territory? Or maybe he was simply familiar with the practice and tried to experiment with it as part of his Atlantic journey? Finally, we will show how changes in economic conditions could ruin any plan of social mobility. When owners faced difficult circumstances, the written laws that clearly privileged owners were put in practice, curtailing the initiatives of enslaved persons such as Víctor.

Víctor Lucumí Chappotín's Caribbean journey

Starting in the 1760s, at an unprecedented rate, warships and small ships used by civilians to flee warlike conditions created by European colonial powers joined the Caribbean commercial routes normally traveled by boats loaded with captives, flour, salted meats, drinks, precious metals, draft animals, and all kinds of merchandise. But even this upsurge in Caribbean travel was no match for the human movement that began in August 1791, caused by a slave uprising in the French colony of Saint-Domingue. Between this event and the proclamation of the Republic of Haiti in 1804, an estimated thirty thousand people left what was then the richest Antillean colony.[16]

Like thousands of other Africans, Víctor Lucumí found himself at the center of things from the beginning. His participation, however, was not a traditional heroic struggle against an oppressive system. He and a small group of fellow slaves – Nicolás and Alejo Congo, Bárbara Lucumí, Dolores Mina, and several creoles – stayed with their owner, a white Creole of French Spanish origin named Don Francisco Chappotín Guzmán, while others, with liberating fury and a thirst for vengeance, broke the chains of slavery. According to Laurent Dubois,

> During the first eight days of the insurrection they [the slaves] destroyed 184 plantations; by late September over 200 had been attacked, and "all of the plantations within fifty miles of either side of le Cap had been reduced to ashes and smoke." In addition, almost 1,200 coffee plantations in the mountains surrounding the plain had been sacked. According to

> one observer, "one can count as many rebel camps as there were plantations." Estimates of the numbers of insurgents varied widely, but by the end of September there were at least 20,000, and by some estimates up to 80,000, in the insurgent camps.
>
> "They are spurred on by the desire of plunder, carnage, and conflagration, and not by the spirit of liberty, as some folks pretend," one white merchant wrote of the insurgents. But plundering masters' homes, destroying the infrastructure of the plantations on which they were enslaved, and killing those who had enslaved them were powerful ways to pursue liberty. Indeed, they were the only ways available to most of the slaves.[17]

A few weeks after the first uprising in the north of the colony, the "mulattos" who claimed their right to equality proclaimed by the French National Assembly reached an agreement with the whites who opposed it.[18] This took place in Croix de Bouquets, a southern parish where the Chappotín Guzmán's properties were located, not far from Port-au-Prince. After the pact was signed in an effort to establish unity, approximately twenty-five thousand insurgents from the parish returned to their "habitations" – the name that the French gave to plantations. The peace would not last long.[19] We know, however, that in the confusing political panorama of the moment, Don Francisco and his brother Mariano quickly took sides with the Royalist camp supported by Spain – hence, their reputation as Hispanophiles – that had declared war against the French Republic in March of 1793.

The Chappotín Guzmáns – closely connected to the Creole nobility of the colony[20] – might have been among the many landowners who armed their slaves, having them fight the so-called "free coloreds," whom they believed responsible for inciting "the *ateliers* (enslaved workers) of the plantations" to rebel.[21] If that was the case, Víctor and the other captives who accompanied Don Francisco had to fight against the forces organized by the Republic's commissioners who, facing English and Spanish threats of invasion and the resistance of the Royalist colonists, opted to declare the abolition of slavery in the southern departments in August 1793, a measure taken for the east of the colony in October of that year.[22]

The historian John K. Thornton was the first to observe the importance of the warfare experience of Africans living in Saint-Domingue. Such experience explains the military effectiveness that they showed since the initial organization of the uprising to the final victory. Relativizing his own thesis, the author also observes that

> in the struggle between mulattoes and various white factions in the South and West, both of these elite groups armed their slaves, formed them into military units and used them to reach their slaves, formed them into military units and used them to reach their own goals. The military experience of these slaves might have been important, but perhaps not decisive, since most of the organizational skills and even the tactical programmes came from the European background of these who organized the slaves.[23]

But why allow some to be active agents and others only executors of the plans made by leaders of European origin? We rather believe that military experience would have also played an important role in cases like the one we are studying and that both Alejo Congo and Víctor Lucumí probably had more knowledge of warfare than landowners such as the Chappotín Guzmán brothers – civilians who learned how to fight pressed by the circumstances.

Of course, it is possible that many of those who stayed at their master's side, whether as soldiers or not, did so under coercion, with the promise of freedom, or from an instinct for survival. We think that the loyalty of these slaves towards their owners – such as the one shown by Víctor – was likely the result of a political calculation. In Africa, "[d]eliberately or not, the employment of slaves in the army prevented the consolidation of slave consciousness, while continued military action made flight more difficult by reducing the areas where it was safe to be."[24] Besides, what had freedom meant to Víctor until that moment? Maybe his captivity and his journey across the ocean were the product of a war, and he therefore knew about the risks of falling in the hands of an enemy. Did he necessarily think that freedom was more than seeing the place where his daughter Luisa had been born burn down? Could anybody deny the dangers of emancipation? These are questions that only Víctor could have answered. Being just one more of the 54,000 Yoruba speakers brought to Saint-Domingue between 1776 and 1800,[25] he chose to defend his owner, his family, his fellow captives, and his own life – maybe with the skills of those warriors who moved around the upper valley of the Ogun river protecting the trade routes of the Oyó kingdom.[26]

This heterogeneous group of Africans and creoles fought along the southern border. After resisting the "pillage of negroes" for months, in April 1795 Don Francisco Chappotín received the rank of Lieutenant-Colonel.[27] He commanded and financed a militia integrated by white people of the Grandbois. At the same time, he formed a company of hussars with free *pardos*. With this separation, he intended to avoid the misgivings and rivalries caused, in his own words, by "color."[28] He heard about his new rank when Toussaint Louverture had already defeated the Hispanophile party and the troops sent from Cuba (the Infantry Regiment and the Havana Free *Moreno* Battalion.)[29] For the second time in less than four years he traveled to Spanish soil. At the village of Neyba, on his way to the city of Santo Domingo, he heard the news of the Peace of Basel, signed in July 1795. The terms of the treaty included ceding the colony to the French, thereby requiring religious and military officials to evacuate within twelve months. In December of the same year, following "the fate of the Spanish," Don Francisco, his brother, five officials from the now-defunct legion, and a group of slaves embarked for Havana.[30]

They arrived in January 1796 and did not receive a warm reception. The Captain-General of Cuba prevented them from disembarking because there were nineteen individuals in their entourage who "were of color," the majority of them minors and children of the Africans Víctor and Alejo, as well as of the *pardo* Nicolás.[31] Such a measure responded to the tensions surrounding the arrival of the so-called auxiliary troops, integrated by the "black French" loyal to Charles IV. Considering this unexpected situation, Don Francisco opted to stay with those he called "servants" in the Cabaña fortress at the mouth of the bay,

> where said General allowed [me] to keep them until His Majesty's resolution, to whom under my word of honor I can assure that they have behaved with the greatest loyalty and that, on different occasions, they have saved my life, and that lately they have given the most sincere testimony of their good behavior, because, having been able to stay with the Republicans or the English, they preferred to be vassals of His Majesty.[32]

Despite the prestige they had earned with their service to the Spanish flag in September, they were kept in the military fortress. They asked for and received permission to travel to Trinidad de Barlovento. Trinidad was a small island that belonged to the Captaincy-General of Venezuela and had been transformed – at least, that was the general impression – into an oasis in the middle of a Caribbean set ablaze by slave uprisings, with a sudden rise in sugar and coffee plantations founded by emigrants from Saint-Domingue.[33] The order included a provision allowing the Chappotín brothers to take their slaves with them. Their stay there would end on 16 February 1797, in the middle of a new war, when the English took the island. The terms of surrender allowed the Chappotíns and their servants to return to the city of Havana as evacuees.[34] This time Don Francisco was permitted to disembark with all of his companions, not so much because the prohibition of entry to "blacks contaminated by the revolution" had been rendered ineffective, but rather because of the actions taken by their former comrades from "the past war with the French" to help them.[35]

Havana may have reminded Víctor of his arrival in Port-au-Prince as a black *bozal* (a slave newly imported from Africa) some ten years earlier. Very close to the mouth of the bay, and in sight of the ships entering its port, there was the slave market: long and rustic buildings called barracks, that according to some witnesses were similar to the ones on the African coast, distinguishable as the only structures in an otherwise uninhabited area. Behind him, he left the emerging freedom of hundreds of thousands of future Haitian citizens. Ahead of him lay Cuba's thriving slave society.

Land of opportunity: The Cuban west and the French émigrés (1791–1809)

There is no consensus as to the number of French refugees that arrived in Cuba between 1791 and 1809, years that mark the first arrival at the port of Baracoa and the decree ordering all those who had not naturalized to depart, issued in reaction to the invasion of Spain by Napoleon Bonaparte's armies. The figures range from 15,000, as proposed by the demographer Juan Pérez de la Riva, to 25,000, reported by the historian Ramiro Guerra y Sánchez.[36] Regarding the refugees' geographic distribution, the census data of 1808 confirms that the eastern part of the island, where 9,236 individuals were located, was their principal destination, with the other 1,128 spread across the center and the west. There are two reasons for this imbalance: the first has to do with the proximity of the eastern ports to Saint-Domingue; the second with the colonial government's favorable disposition to the arrivals, due to its interest in using them to develop a region that had been left on the margin of the economic boom experienced in the west.

Despite the attraction that the Cuban southeast undoubtedly held for many emigrants, notably that the price of virgin soil was much lower than that offered on the west of the island, there was no shortage of official efforts to direct them to the latter. The Chappotín brothers and their slaves were still on their journey when the members of the *Junta Directiva del Real Consulado de Agricultura y Comercio* (Board of Directors of the Royal Consulate of Agriculture and Commerce) in Havana did everything possible to stimulate coffee production, with the support of the Crown, seeking the experience of the first French émigrés who settled in the jurisdiction of Havana. As the degree of success of these émigrés would determine whether others, Creole or Spanish, followed in their footsteps, the Consulate was willing to grant a loan equivalent to "the value of ten negroes to the subject who has the best cultivated coffee plantation and is the best suited to serve as a model for other coffee cultivators."[37] Of the five plantations evaluated, those named Limones, owned by Don Santiago Bellaume, and Las Virtudes, owned by Don Antonio Morejón Gato, were in the jurisdiction of Guanajay, the entrance to the western region – the San

Marcos Plain, Cayajabos, Cuzco, Aguacate, and the Sierra del Rosario – where the majority of French coffee planters (55) settled around 1809. Over the first decades of the nineteenth century, between gullies and little valleys, coffee plantations were established in what were once pastures and cattle ranches, taking advantage of the fertile soil.[38]

The records indicate that Don Mariano Chappotín was the first of the brothers to settle in the region, founding a coffee plantation named La Mariana.[39] After having tried his hand at other ventures,[40] Don Francisco – who in 1807 was father to three children with a woman named María Micaela Seydel Tabares, daughter of a Spanish soldier whom he had married in the cathedral of Havana in April 1798[41] – followed in his brother's footsteps. His status as a naturalized Spaniard and his experience in matters of war would later help in his being appointed as Captain of the district of Puerta de la Güira (created in 1818). He was one of the founders of the town of the same name and the region's military governor.[42]

Don Francisco, it must be said, had better luck as a coffee planter than as a soldier. Of course, the high price of beans helped him as much as his managerial skills.[43] In 1827, when his wife died, there were three coffee plantations – La Gloria, El Salvador, and La Ascensión – among the conjugal partnership's assets. La Ascensión was the most valuable, estimated – with 158 slaves (106 men and fifty-two women), 337,000 coffee trees, and machines for processing grain – to be worth 271,524 pesos.[44] Appearing in their inventory were: Víctor; his children Luisa, José María, and Juana; his grandchildren, Pablo and María Antonia; the creoles of Saint-Domingue, Sansón, Alejo, and Miguel, the first two of whom were *contramayorales* (slave drivers); and the *pardo* Nicolás, who was already free and owned two slaves and a little mason house in the town of Artemisa.[45]

Everything seems to indicate that Víctor followed the path of his old friend Nicolás rather than that of the rebellious maroons that Don Francisco helped to repress.[46] Taking advantage of the place he had earned among the more than two hundred slaves who worked on his master's coffee plantations, he acquired property – a plan favored by his ability to move between the towns of Puerto de la Güira, Artemisa, and Guanajay.[47] The first village was the center of the richest and most populated district in Vuelta Abajo, where there were small shops and service establishments, and Artemisa was frequently visited by the owners of the surrounding farms and by the residents of the capital, who chose to visit in December and January due to its pleasant climate.[48] Surely this environment allowed Víctor to offer his expertise in coffee cultivation – skills he had possibly acquired in Yoruba territory, and developed further in Saint-Domingue – to newcomers in exchange of a payment probably similar to the one received by free day laborers. It also allowed him to establish relationships beyond the plantation and to sell the fruits and animals produced there, especially pigs. The pigs raised by blacks on the farms, it was well known, supplied not only "the inhabitants of this district [Puerto de la Güira], but also most of the adjoining ones."[49]

Faithfulness pays off: A captive master of slaves (1831–1837)

On Sunday, 16 January 1831, the priest of the auxiliary church of Puerta de la Güira baptized several African adults – among them, a young Carabalí named Úrsula. The girl, "about twelve years old," was the slave of Víctor Lucumí, who in turn was the slave of Don Francisco Chappotín.[50] So far, the sources that show the presence of slave/owners in the island are parish records (where we might discover more cases in the future) and notarial records (of manumission and sales/purchases).[51] As João Reis observes, in practice in the absence of other documents such as receipts, the birth records "functioned as proof of ownership," even if, in theory, authorities considered them just proof of Christendom. This idea gained much more traction in Cuba after 1820, when the only way to buy slaves firsthand was to go to smugglers who, for obvious reasons, could not publicize their sales before a notary since the legal slave trade had been prohibited.[52] The priest did with Chappotín Guzmán's slave what he had been doing with the rest of his parishioners, be they powerful landowners or humble peasants: assure them, through baptism, a "quiet and peaceful possession," something that Don Francisco had already done by allowing Víctor to use his peculium in such an unusual way.

Víctor also had to make careful calculations in order to choose a slave who was not too expensive, for example, *mulecas*, who were between six and fourteen years old, as he did not have much money to invest in their purchase.[53] He selected a woman, Úrsula, as his first purchased slave not only due to economic considerations but also because a slave womb can produce more slaves. Despite the high risk, slave motherhood was the surest way for small owners to increase the number of their slaves. It was also understandable that Víctor would put Úrsula to work on agricultural tasks rather than domestic duties. Supposing that Víctor did not need an additional slave to help raise his children, and that he was not in an urban environment that would have allowed him to employ her in tasks such as peddling goods or food, Úrsula, like her future fellow slaves Nicolasa and Serafina, could very well be put to work collecting or separating the aromatic beans that would stand before her in piles of varying quality. As an American traveler observed in his 1844 description of a coffee estate, slaves engaged in this activity faced long heaps of berries that they had to separate into several qualities, and "accompanied their work with a low, monotonous song, while a black overseer moved about them, occasionally examining their pickings, and chiding the more careless."[54] Víctor's wife probably had enough experience with such tasks to share with the laboring young women to increase their value. In any case, Úrsula became a source of income via rent, adding to the other sources Víctor already possessed, such as the breeding of animals, farming, and even his willingness to work as an experienced laborer for anyone looking to start cultivating the fields in a region known for its plantations.[55]

Víctor came from an African region where captives were allowed to own certain goods, including other people. This might partly explain his decision to invest his savings in slaves. If, on the contrary, he had been a free man in Africa, he would have been immersed in any of many other forms of dependence: by family lineage, by indentured slavery or temporary service to pay off a debt (*Iwofa*), or by pawnship.[56] Regardless, the evidence suggests that Don Francisco Chappotín encouraged Víctor to become a slave/owner by giving him his first captive, a Carabalí man named Cayetano. Víctor had been Cayetano's *padrino* (godfather) since 1819. This donation was unusual, as the things offered to captives – or those they inherited – tended to be money, animals, dwellings, or items for personal use, but not slaves. It probably happened in 1827, when Don Francisco also granted Nicolás his freedom. With such an incentive, or reward, the landowner not only acknowledged his slave's loyalty but also transformed him in the owner of his *ahijado* (godson), something quite uncommon in plantation Cuba.[57] This, however, takes us back, once again, to the social and cultural patterns of Yoruba territory, where "[s]laves were also seen as kinless dependents who could be incorporated into domestic groups, and they were a valuable asset that could be sold if circumstances warranted such action."[58] Through the baptismal ceremony, Cayetano was incorporated into Víctor's family circle. The bond thus created, a sort of fictive kinship, could in turn help owners: "Kinship terms could be used to govern slave-master relations, but slaves were not kin. Kinship operated to protect the free and to regulate the status of slaves and pawns."[59] The slave/owner thus had a double ascendency over his property: the juridical power granted by the law and the symbolic power derived from his condition of *padrino*.

The events described here are exceptional and likely the result of the master's decision, leading to an unusual expression of supreme dominion accompanied by humble gratitude. However, it is important to consider Víctor's initiative, as he was clearly not content with owning just one slave. Even if we admit the possibility that he received Úrsula through donation, as happened in the case of his fellow slave Nicolás, it is clear that Víctor aspired to own more once his acquisition of Úrsula made it easier for him to earn money. The parish records attest to the realization of that ambition: in February 1834, a certain Martin Lucumí was listed as his property, followed by another adolescent, who would be named Serafina Conga, baptized on 12 October of that year. Úrsula's first daughter, born weeks earlier, was also baptized that day.[60]

There is evidence that Víctor intended to use the money he accumulated to buy more slaves, maybe in an effort to strengthen his status among the other slaves (trade skills and strong leadership were very important as well). Becoming a slave/owner and having dominion over others who benefitted him symbolically and economically would probably produce a dramatic effect, positioning him above his fellow captives. But regardless of his ultimate goal, he seemed paradoxically more interested in investing in slaves than in purchasing his freedom. Why? We believe that his close relationship with his master and the captives who accompanied him since Croix des Bouquets probably made him aware of his owner's will to grant many of them their freedom. If this was the case, why would he pay the 450 pesos that he was worth in 1826 for something that he would get for free as retribution for his loyalty and service? Scholarship on manumission and freedom claims has shown that slaves who were liberated through wills, even those liberated through a verbal promise, almost always knew that their masters intended to do so. Some of them bided their time and conducted themselves properly, others pressed their masters to free them sooner, while still others offered to pay for themselves.[61]

Víctor therefore chose to wait for an opportune moment to complete his purchase. According to the Cuban historian Manuel Moreno Fraginals,

> blacks were abundant and cheap during the period from 1821 to 1837 [...] In summary, one hundred thousand slaves were imported during the period between 1826 and 1835, destined to replace the workers consumed in the expanding coffee economy, which at the time was greater than that of sugar.[62]

Of course, there was a significant difference between Víctor and the other buyers: in his case, master and slaves shared the same legal status.

Víctor Lucumí Chappotín was evidently not the only black man who owned slaves in Puerta de la Güira. There existed a small group of twenty-nine free people of color who owned sixty-one captives (eighteen *bozales,* seventeen *párvulos* [children of slaves] and twenty-seven mothers and fathers) who, between 1816 and 1847, were registered in baptismal ceremonies. The most notable among them was the free *morena* Rosa Mataran, owner of a coffee plantation named Paciencia, whose slaves were baptized between 1841 and 1847. She was the biggest slave owner among those of her class and status. It is also worth mentioning that among these owners there were seven men and women identified as African, who owned 22.2 percent of the *bozales* baptized during the aforementioned period.

Libertos (freed slaves) tended to buy so-called "new" slaves. This was what Víctor did. The same was true of many of the slave/owners in the city of Salvador de Bahia between 1790 and 1850 studied by Reis. Like Víctor, the vast majority of the slave/owners living in the capital of Bahia had been born in Africa. Also, they all waited for good market conditions, for example, the moment when political decisions with regards to the transatlantic slave trade led to lower prices. Lastly, neither Víctor – who owned a captive identified as Lucumí, the thirteen-year old Martín, baptized in 1834 – nor the 56 percent of the Africans manumitted in Salvador refused to become slave/owners of individuals from their own nation.[63]

To enslave men and women of one's same ethnic origin was taboo in certain African regions, but the prohibition could be suspended under exceptional circumstances such as food shortages. Normally, new slaves were generated through wars or kidnapping. In Cuba, as we have observed in our book *El cabildo carabalí viví de Santiago de Cuba,* the practice of enslaving men and women of the same ethno-linguistic group was not uncommon.[64] Reis admits that maybe in Bahia (and in Cuba, we would add)

> enslaving people of the same group happened among slaves (and among freed slaves and slaves) who did not belong to the specific ethnic community from where they were from. In that sense, the Nago from Oyo, for example, would not enslave, in Brazil, the Nago from Oyo; and the Hausa from Katskina would not enslave the Hausa from Katsina,[65]

but he immediately observes that this is not certain. At any rate, we know that Víctor was Lucumí in Cuba and had been Nago in Saint-Domingue, as was his slave Martín – who, we can infer, was one of the hundreds of thousands of victims of the civil wars that led to the fall of the Oyo Kingdom who were sold in the transatlantic slave trade. The main difference between the mature man and the adolescent, who could have been his grandson, resided in the length of their absence from their homeland rather than in a hypothetical geographical distance between the places where they had been born or the existence of ancestral disputes among them. Therefore, rather than ideological or cultural considerations that escape us, Víctor probably considered the low market price as a key factor in his decision to acquire Martín. However, maybe the taboo operated in him as well, as the following detail suggests: his next purchase was a Congo woman. As collective baptism records show, buying Lucumí people was still possible, and Víctor could have easily repeated the experience of enslaving a *pariente* (relative) – as they called themselves in the Americas.

While the Bahia slaves worked in the urban economy, Víctor did so in the countryside. Nevertheless, they all resorted to the same strategy: to employ their human properties in work that they did themselves, or that they knew well from experience. Víctor did not always pocket the money he earned through his slaves, as shown by the fact that when Don Francisco Chappotín died he owed Victor 170 pesos.[66] Maybe this was part of an agreement to free some of his children or grandchildren, or maybe Don Francisco was one of those masters who motivated their captives with promises that they seldom fulfilled. At any rate, being a slave/owner benefitted Víctor. This benefit might have not been in the form of cash as much as in that of social prestige. Thus, in May 1837, when he could still not foresee the freedom included in his master's will, the priest Valdera refers to him as a *moreno libre* (free black) in the baptismal record of Úrsula's second child. The priest had been in charge of that church since its inception in 1818 and knew his flock well. Valdera was wrong about the legal condition of the African man, but not about his social status. His note declared that Víctor was regarded as a free man. Was Don Francisco Chappotín's intention to free him, as written in the clause number sixteen of his will, already known by all parishioners, and even by more people? If this was the case, it probably surprised many. Don Francisco was not among those masters well predisposed to manumit, as suggested by the fact that none of the forty-six *párvulos* who had been born from slaves and baptized as free in Puerta de la Güira between 1818 and 1846 had been born in his coffee plantations. Fifteen of these children, we should note, were born in nine of the fifty coffee plantations that existed in the district in 1846. We believe that this was not due to the fact that parents who were kept as captives by Don Francisco could not invest the twenty-five or fifty pesos (for an unborn or a newborn, respectively) to liberate their children, but rather because the landowner was not inclined to emancipate at the baptismal font – one of the most common gestures of patriarchal generosity.

Difficult times: The weight of the law and the failure of a strategy (1837–1841)

Judging from the export figures from 1827 to 1833, the plans developed since the late-eighteenth century to position Cuba as a large coffee producer were successful. We know that exports reached 25,000 tons in the first year and a record 32,579 tons in 1833. Just a decade later, however, the region experienced a steep decline in international sales. Contributing to this decline was the impossibility of competing with Brazil, the impact of natural phenomena such as hurricanes and droughts on the plantations, and the high cost of labor.[67]

The specter of decadence had been hovering over the plains of Puerta de la Güira since before the death of Don Francisco. Nevertheless, there was a rather optimistic tone in the will that he dictated in December 1836.[68] The document, in which he settled his accounts with his sons Miguel and Antonio,[69] laid out his property, and entrusted his soul to God, was sealed until after his death. But the secrecy must have been relative, as Victor and his wife Dolores, along with nineteen other enslaved people, would probably have known that their master would free them – out of loyalty or as a "duty of conscience."[70] Don Francisco's heirs were very likely surprised by the landowner's generosity and the resulting decrease in their capital, both in money and in labor power, taking into account that ten of the manumitted were youths and children, and only five were adults over sixty years old. A landowner generously granting freedom to more than twenty captives was unusual enough, but the fact that these captives were rural slaves made this even more extraordinary. It would be difficult to find a similar case in nineteenth-century Cuba. In coffee and sugar plantations, freedom was as costly as the high value of skilled workers (carpenters, masons, *maestros de azúcar* [sugarmasters]) who could achieve it. After saving money for years, those captives often had to seek a judge to demand that the master accept losing such a valuable worker.

The family immediately resisted enacting Don Francisco's will through a series of small but significant actions. First, the slaves' formal freedom was delayed by more than five months due to notarial misdeeds. Second, the freed slaves were still listed as slaves in the inventory of La Ascensión, just a few days after they were supposed to have received their freedom papers from a famous Havana notary's office.[71] There was also an attempt to declare Úrsula a "slave of the heirs of Don Francisco Chappotín and the endowment of the La Ascensión plantation in this district" by registering a second baptism on 8 October 1837 under Don Francisco's son Antonio's name, to replace the 15 May 1837 original, in which she appeared as Víctor's slave.[72] In spite of these attempts, in September 1838, the family described the situation of their estate as very desperate:

> the only farm is the La Ascensión plantation, whose harvest is shortened each year as [...] [t]he land gets tired, and as the owners of such plantations have generally known, the prices of the fruits are down and there is no hope of an increase.[73]

Given the circumstances, Víctor believed it prudent to move to the town of Guanajay, where he had "a house of mud, wooden posts, and shingles," but he did not stop acquiring slaves, as evidenced by the mention of a certain Nicolasa Conga among his property.[74] After the division of assets, Víctor moved to the coffee plantation La Mariana, owned by Don Antonio. His son José María and his grandchildren Pablo and María Antonia were also transferred there, while Luisa stayed in the hands of Don Miguel.[75] The separation suffered by the Lucumí family was part of the daily life of slaves. As "people with a price," the enslaved were subject to contracts of all kinds. Settling the assets of a recently diseased owner (in this case, Don Francisco) was a particularly fraught moment for a family.[76]

Maybe such disruption in his family led the now formally free *moreno* Víctor Lucumí Chappotín, "about sixty-five years old,"[77] to reconsider the possibility of redeeming his progeny. It would have been a dream that bordered on the impossible, and a much more complex task than buying *bozales* of a young age at a low cost to profit from their work. Considering the values assigned to Víctor's children and grandchildren – Luisa's was appraised at 450 pesos, José María at 500, Pablo at 550, and María Antonia at 350 – he would have had to collect 1,850 pesos in what remained of his life, and more if we take into account that the price of the youngest would have increased over time.[78] In any case, there are indications that this was his plan because he had given 102 pesos to Don Antonio – something that he admitted after Víctor's death, reintegrating it to his assets.

Whatever Víctor's strategy might have been – for example, to use the wages earned by one of his slaves to manumit the "cheapest" of his descendants, his daughter María Antonia – it failed. Although his last wishes turned his still-enslaved heirs into slave/owners, ostensibly putting them in a position to negotiate a favorable arrangement, the reality was very different. The executors of the will and his widow reached an agreement: to keep and distribute the goods – valued at 1,138 pesos – rather than auctioning them off. The distribution was done as follows: Dolores, his widow, kept the house and Cayetano Carabalí; Luisa, or rather her master Don Miguel, was given 212 pesos in cash; and Don Antonio, in the name of the established heirs, his son and his grandchildren, was also awarded for "two thirds of their appraisal and ten pesos more"[79] the two Conga women Nicolasa and Serafina and the latter's three-year-old daughter. Úrsula was declared free and her value subtracted from the total.

Was Víctor aware of the dangers of designating his captive children as heirs? Could he know that a medieval Roman code would be invoked to deprive them of their inheritance? Probably not. This Castilian law according to which "[...] things that were given in will to the slave can also be demanded by the master as if they had been given to himself,"[80] however, was not always applied. Commonly, freed parents designated legitimate or illegitimate descendants who were living in captivity as heirs and, in general, their will was respected.[81] Many masters demanded that the bequests "to leave slavery" were properly used. In some cases, they gave their captives permission to attend the courts. In others, they went themselves on their behalf. In all cases, a judicial authority approved the use of the bequest to buy freedom.[82]

In this case, however, the law was not interpreted in favor of freedom. Don Francisco's children did not hesitate to use any means to turn everything their slaves had earned into their own property. The law was categorical and clear: they were not obliged to show generosity nor to yield their seigneurial authority and allow their slaves the autonomy necessary to manage the property they had inherited. The events in which Víctor had participated constituted part of a past that, with the death of its protagonists, become blurred. The debt of gratitude that Don Francisco had with those who followed him in his flight from Saint-Domingue had been paid by granting them freedom.

Ultimately, everything indicates that Don Miguel and Don Antonio never intended to improve the fate of the loyal Víctor's descendants. This is further evidenced by the following fact: in November 1842, during the distribution of the inheritance, Serafina gave birth to another son who was baptized in September of the following year, just after Don Antonio was awarded the La Mariana coffee plantation, to which he took her.[83] Another telling detail is that Don Miguel and Don Antonio did not apply the inheritance shares – 212 pesos for each child and 106 for each grandchild – to reduce their respective values and transform them into *coartados* (enslaved persons in the process of paying for their freedom in installments), which was the usual solution when the heirs were captives, as in this case.[84] Of course, inheritance proceedings had to be mediated by the *síndico procurador*, who acted as legal representative of slaves who sued their owners or claimed an inheritance or a lottery prize.[85] While living in the countryside had helped Víctor acquire a *peculium* and invest in slaves, now it turned against his heirs – as they were too far away from any official representative who could advocate for them. Among the 421 captives who filed claims for freedom between 1762 and 1872 in Havana and Santiago de Cuba, only 151 lived in the countryside.

Conclusion

In the first place, it should be noted that the life of the slave/owner Víctor Lucumí Chappotín was exceptional, especially because of the level of autonomy with which he managed the resources that he gained throughout his life, and which he invested in the most precious asset in a slave society: captives. Enslaved persons who acquired property, like Víctor, had no legal right to enjoy it for their own benefit. The slave's ability to manage an estate, regardless of its size or value, required his owner's consent, often with the tacit understanding that manumission by self-purchase was the ultimate goal. Of course, there was a clear difference between owning slaves and keeping small sums of money, animals, or clothing. Víctor never broke the unwritten contract that existed between master and slave, one based on loyalty, good service, and companionship. Such compliance opened the doors to a plan for socioeconomic advancement that respected the norms that guaranteed the stability and preservation of the system. Both master and slave were survivors of a violent revolution in which they had been defeated but from which they probably gained experience and learned to use moderation in the exercise of authority. In that sense, it is worth noticing that some of the most important slave insurrections of the time occurred in coffee plantations like El Salvador, owned by Francisco Santiago Aguirre, and Santa Catalina, owned by the heirs of Catalina de Estrada, which were very close to Don Francisco Chappotín's.[86]

Secondly, given that Víctor's plan took place in a rural area, we can glimpse certain African and Atlantic traits – including forms of agriculture and being a slave/owner, characteristic of the Yoruba people, and his experience growing coffee during his first slavery in Saint-Domingue. He was part of a larger community willing to recreate customs and behaviors in the so-called New World. Some slaves – those who had special skills and were closer to owners and administrators – could participate with a profit margin in the small commercial circuits created among farms, cattle ranches, towns, and stores located at crossroads. They could also benefit from exchanges of services, goods, and favors among slaves of the same plantation. Furthermore, the demand for labor was high in the countryside, especially at the time of harvest. Víctor rented his captives to his own master, having them work in the same property where he did. And given that these captives were not the typical day laborers that abounded in the city – *coartados* who lived away from their owners and who had to give them part of their earnings weekly or at the end of the month – Víctor could keep all of the income that they generated.

Thirdly, the promise of freedom – registered in Don Francisco's 1836 will, when Víctor already owned several slaves – influenced his decision to increase his human properties rather than to buy his freedom or manumit his progeny. For years, Víctor was "*por su cuenta*" (on his own) – a phrase commonly used to describe enslaved people who acted as if they were legally free. Maybe he dreamt of freedom since the day he was first transformed into a commodity. When the Atlantic became the Caribbean and Cuba his destiny, however, this dream was possibly dimmed by the most effective mechanism of seigniorial control: his owner offering him a free manumission. Of course, both master and slave knew that the word "free" was just an adornment. If there was a debtor, it was Don Francisco, who in the distant year of 1797 had confessed that Víctor and his companions had saved his life several times.

Though there are still gaps that need to be filled, the African Víctor Lucumí showed remarkable creativity. He assimilated and reproduced the values of slavers – values that he may have shared from the moment of his African and/or Atlantic enslavement. His heirs, however, had no chance of continuing or imitating his strategy. The new masters had mentalities and needs quite different from the previous one. They assumed command over a world created in the image and likeness of the one that had been erased in Croix de Bouquets by the flames of "the continuous wars of the blacks"[87] – a world that now found itself again in crisis. In order to save it, they needed more disciplinary control and less graciousness toward those who kept it going through their labor.

Notes

1. "Testamentaría del moreno libre Víctor Chappotín," Archivo Nacional de Cuba (hereafter cited as ANC), Escribanía Cabello Ozeguera, leg. 427, n. 9.
2. Ibid.
3. Reis, "De escravo rico," 38.
4. De La Fuente García, "A alforria," 153. Although De La Fuente does not specify the number of slaves who financed their freedom by handing over other slaves, in his article "La esclavitud" he mentions several examples taken from the Havana protocols at the end of the sixteenth century and the beginning of the seventeenth.
5. Nishida, "Manumission and Ethnicity"; Schwartz, "Manumission of Slaves." For now, the most complete study of enslaved people, "gentlemen" as he calls them, in the city of Salvador da Bahía is Reis, "De escravo rico."
6. Díaz, *The Virgin, the King*, 179–198.
7. Ibid., 187.
8. Ibid., 9.
9. Ley 7, Título XXI, Partida 4a; *Los códigos españoles*, 1848, 520.
10. The *peculium* refers to the capital earned by a slave, "derived from gifts, from a portion of the salaries that the slave received for working outside the house, from tips from guests, or from the savings of his rations," Lucena Salmoral, *Leyes para esclavos*, 22–23.
11. Ibid.
12. It was assumed that the *peculium* would be used to finance manumission, hence the provisions of the Slave Regulations promulgated by the Captain General of Cuba Gerónimo Valdés in 1842: "Article 13. On Sundays and holidays, and in the hours of rest on days of labor, slaves will be allowed to be employed within the farm in manufacturing or other occupations that yield their personal benefit and utility, to be able to acquire money and then freedom," *Bando de Gobernación*, 61.
13. Perera and Meriño, *Libertad sin abolición*, 13–14.
14. "Protocolo de José de la Luz Portela," ANC, Protocolo Notarial, folios 167–167 vto., 1845. "Venta real de finca. Protocolo Notarial de Justo Barona," folio 604 vto., 1859. "Expediente promovido por Julián Arias y Pedro Olivera pardos ingenuos de esta vecindad contra Cirilo Recio también vecino sobre disolución de una sociedad constituida en un tren funerario," Archivo Histórico Provincial de Camagüey, Fondo Alcaldías Mayores del partido judicial de Puerto Príncipe, leg. 13, no. 13. 1858.
15. Lovejoy, *Transformations in Slavery*, 167.
16. Von Grafenstein, "El 'autonomismo criollo.'"
17. Dubois, *Avengers*, 113.
18. On the question of race in Saint-Domingue, see Garrigus, "Colour, Class and Identity."
19. Kimou, "La rebelión de Galbaud."
20. Of the three Chappotín Guzmán sisters, one was married to the Marquis of Besné, another to the Marquis of Villimos, and the third to Vicente de Mazadé, governor of the colony between 1787 and 1789, Santa Cruz y Mallén, *Historia de familias cubanas*, 55.
21. Scott and Hébrard, *Freedom Papers*, 30.
22. The invasion took place between September 1793 and June of the following year, when Spanish military forces occupied towns in the north and east, and the English occupied towns in the south and west, see James, *Los jacobinos negros*.
23. Thornton, *African Soldiers*, 63.
24. Lovejoy, *Transformations in Slavery*, 166.
25. Eltis, "A Diáspora dos Falantes," 297.
26. Of course, Víctor could have also been a peaceful inhabitant, one of the many who suffered the voracious pull of the Atlantic slave market. As Lovejoy observes, "After the middle of the eighteenth century, the origins of slaves exports changed. While Aja and Yoruba still predominated, reflecting the same likelihood as in the earlier period that Aja, Yoruba, and imported slaves who were at least partially acculturated were the majority of exports, now

slaves from further north appear regularly in the registers of slave ships. [...] The frontier of enslavement had moved inland, therefore. This expansion of the catchment area was a logical feature of the large-scale, sustained export of slaves," *Transformations in Slavery*, 83.

27. "Nombramiento de teniente coronel para Francisco Chappotín, francés emigrado de la isla y su pase a Trinidad junto con los esclavos que le han sido fieles," Archivo General de Simancas (hereafter cited as AGS), GM, leg. 7161, f. 238.
28. Ibid.
29. We refer to the excellent analysis done by historian Ada Ferrer on the military forces sent from Cuba to intervene in the war being waged in Saint-Domingue, bearing in mind that this was the context in which the Chappotín brothers and their slaves were involved, see Ferrer, *Freedom's Mirror*, 83–145.
30. "Nombramiento de teniente coronel para Francisco Chappotín," AGS, GM, 7161, f. 238.
31. Victoria Ojeda, "Tensión en el Caribe hispano."
32. "Nombramiento de teniente coronel para Francisco Chappotín," AGS, GM, 7161, f. 211.
33. Zaragoza, *Las insurrecciones en Cuba*, 57.
34. "Carta n° 33 del Gobernador de Santo Domingo D. Joaquín García, al Príncipe de la Paz, remite con informe favorable sendos memoriales del Teniente Coronel, D. Francisco Chappotín, D. Felipe Tirado, D. Felipe Carvajal, Dª María Blasina Muñoz, madre del cabo Francisco Sánchez, y D. José Mª Salazar, que elevan a S.M. con motivo de la evacuación de la isla," AGI, Estado, 5B, no. 90, f. 1.
35. "Don Francisco de Chappotín sobre acreditar la edad que tiene y su cristiandad," ANC, Escribanía de Gobierno, leg. 243, no. 6. f. 1, 1798.
36. Pérez De La Riva, *El Barracón*; Guerra y Sánchez, *Manual de historia*.
37. Five plantations competed, three of them managed by French émigrés. However, the prize went to a Spaniard, Don Antonio Robredo, as recommended by Francisco de Arango, trustee of the Royal Consulate, and José Agustín Caballero, in his capacity as director and secretary of the Royal Patriotic Society, respectively. "Expediente instruido con el objeto de fomentar en esta isla el plantío, cultivo y beneficio del café," ANC, Junta de Fomento, leg. 92, no. 3929, f. 9, 1796–1803.
38. Ramírez Pérez and Paredes Pupo, *Francia en Cuba*, 30.
39. Ibid., 59.
40. "Cristóbal Arozarena y Ca. contra el Teniente Coronel Francisco Chappotín sobre procedentes y contrato mercantil," ANC, Tribunal de Comercio, leg. 3, no. 1, 1801.
41. The marriage was celebrated in the cathedral of Havana in April of 1798. In February of that year a notice announced his intentions to acquire a home. "Decent house desired for rental by Lieutenant Colonel Don Francisco Chappotín and gratitude to whomever provides it," *Papel Periódico de la Havana*, Thursday, 15 February 1798.
42. De La Torre and Noda, "Marien: Noticias históricas," 237.
43. We have data on the sales of the San Salvador coffee plantation from 1818 to 1823 that show the quantitative jump from the 2,207 pesos obtained from the harvest in the first year to the 12,860 pesos of the last one. "Incidente a la testamentaría del Sr Coronel Francisco Chappotín promovido por el Pbro. Domingo Aguirre y remuneración de servicios (1837–1838)," ANC, Escribanía de Guerra, leg. 827, no. 12482.
44. The value of the 158 slaves was calculated at 44,650 pesos, or 16.4 percent of the total value of the plantation.
45. Without a doubt, Nicolás was seen as a model worthy of imitation, even though not everybody was willing to do so. Those who transgressed the rules by escaping or through other acts of resistance were punished with mahogany clamps and imprisoned with metal shackles, correctional devices that were used in all three plantations, according to their inventories. "Intestado de Micaela Seydel y Tabares," ANC, Escribanía de Guerra, leg. 927, no. 13880, 1827.
46. Chappotín served as a coordinator for slave-catcher parties that moved around the área, see "Solicitud del Sr. Francisco Chappotín de que se le entreguen 1.000 pesos para gastos de la cuadrilla perseguidora de palenques en la Vuelta de Abajo," Junta de Fomento, ANC, leg. 29, no. 1451, 1826.

47. As evidence of the master's confidence in Víctor we may refer to his role as godfather to *bozales*, as in August 1819 he accompanied twenty-nine adult men to the baptismal font. Among them was Cayetano Carabalí, his future slave. "Libro quinto de bautismos de pardos y morenos de la iglesia de Puerta de la Güira, da principio el día 5 de abril de 1819 y concluye el 29 de julio de 1820," Instituto de Historia de Cuba (hereafter cited as INC).
48. Vives, *Cuadro estadístico*, 22 and 50.
49. De La Torre and Noda, "Marien: Noticias históricas," 236.
50. "Libro noveno de bautismos de pardos y morenos de la iglesia de Puerta de la Güira, da principio en diciembre de 1827 y concluye en enero de 1831," IHC, ff. 166 vto. 167, entries 822 and 823.
51. "Escritura de compra de la esclava María de Jesús, carabalí, coartada en 250 pesos, por José Francisco y María Gertrudis Cabrera, morenos esclavos de D. Lorenzo de Cabrera, 26 de agosto de 1796," ANC, Protocolo de José Salinas.
52. In writing their records, the parish priests used the data provided by slave-owners, the parents or godparents of the baptized, and their own knowledge of the parishioners. "Minuta de oficio remitiendo ejemplares de la Real Cédula de 26 de noviembre de 1814 relativa a que informen las autoridades sobre las clases de libros que usan para sentar las partidas de bautismos y matrimonios," AGI, Indiferente 1534. In the case of African slaves acquired through the illegal slave trade, it is likely that the owner's word was sufficient, or that he showed them the records provided to them by smugglers, which were written more or less like the following note: "We have received, from Doña Antonia Serrano, three hundred pesos, on behalf of her son Don Zenon Carbo, relating to a package we sold to him. Santiago de Cuba, 30 November 1938, Anglada y Carreras." In this case, the slave was a *bozal* who was baptized under the name Pedro. "Incidente al concurso de D. Mariano Carbó promovido por D. José Ramón Serrano como curador de D. Zenón Carbó para calificar el dominio que le asiste en el negro Pedro," Archivo Histórico Provincial de Santiago de Cuba (AHPSC), *Juzgado de Primera Instancia*, leg. 389, no. 7, 1850.
53. Even though the Cuban slave market has been studied, the statistical figures offered by the authors do not distinguish between the price of newly imported bozales and the slaves that already circulated in the market, when it is evident that such a distinction always existed (Bergad, Iglesias García, and Barcia, *Cuban Slave Market*). Hence, in order to offer these figures, we compare the slaves born in Africa and those born in the New World in the indicated age range, using the Diario de la Habana, second quarter of 1830, as a source.
54. Wurdemann, *Notes on Cuba*, 105.
55. For a description of the various plantations in the area of San Marcos and the mountains of El Salvador in 1828, see the correspondence of the American pastor (Abbot, *Cartas*).
56. Johnson, *The History of the Yorubas*, 123–130. Falola and Lovejoy, "Pawnship in historical perspective," 1–26.
57. See Reveca Figueredo Valdés, *Bautismo y compadrazgo.*
58. Lovejoy, *Transformations in Slavery*, 120.
59. Ibid., 167.
60. "Libro décimo de bautismos de pardos y morenos de la iglesia de Puerta de la Güira da principio en abril de 1831 y concluye en enero de 1837," IHC, ff. 115 and 146, partidas 608 and 768.
61. Perera and Meriño, *Para librarse de brazos*, 229–236; Chira, "Affective Debts."
62. Moreno Fraginals, *El Ingenio,* 272, T.I.
63. Reis. "Escravos donos de escravos," 59.
64. Perera and Meriño, *El cabildo carabalí*, 219–235.
65. Reis, "De escravo rico," 16.
66. ANC. Escribanía de Guerra. Legajo 752. No. 11.321. Testamentaría de D Francisco Chappotín. 1837, f. 142.
67. García Álvarez, "El café."
68. He had given his youngest son, Miguel, four *caballerías* (536,808 square meters) of land and helped him develop a coffee plantation in them, a project that his son would quickly abandon.
69. Don Francisco's oldest child died in 1827.

70. This euphemism was often used to explain the freedom granted to certain slaves who were usually the result of romantic relationships with enslaved women. In this case we suspect that several of the manumitted, described as Creole *pardos* and named María Paula, Coleta, and Lorenzo were, in fact, Don Francisco's children.
71. All the freedom papers were registered between 22 and 29 January 1838, at the office of Don Cayetano Pontón. Protocolo Notarial de Pontón, T. I., 1838, f. 60 to 110, ANC.
72. "Libro undécimo de bautismos de pardos y morenos de la iglesia de Puerta de la Güira da principio el 29 de enero de 1837 y concluye el 30 de agosto de 1838," IHC. ff. 115 and 146, partidas 61 and 108.
73. "Incidente a la testamentaría del Sr. Coronel Francisco Chappotín promovido por el Pbro. Domingo Aguirre y remuneración de servicios (1837–1838)," ANC, Escribanía de Guerra, leg. 827, no. 12482, f. 104.
74. "Testamentaría del moreno libre Víctor Chappotín," ANC, Escribanía Cabello Ozeguera, leg. 427, n. 9, f. 3 vto.
75. "Escritura de adjudicación de bienes del 18 de marzo de 1839," ANC, Protocolo Notarial de Pontón. Vol. I, 1839, f. 254.
76. For a case study on slave families on coffee plantations, see Meriño and Perera, *Un café.*
77. It was the age calculated in 1838, in his savings account. His age was not indicated in the two inventories where he appears as a slave.
78. Plantation inventories did not register the age of slaves.
79. "Testamentaría del moreno libre Víctor Chappotín," ANC, Escribanía Cabello Ozeguera, leg. 427, n. 9, f. 33 vto.
80. *Los Códigos españoles,* 1848, 520.
81. Among the 184 wills dictated by *morenos* and *pardos* in the city of Santiago de Cuba between 1853 and 1855, there are fourteen by African freedmen who had enslaved children and name them their heirs. We thank Adriana Chira for this information, gathered from the Archivo Histórico Provincial de Santiago de Cuba.
82. "D. Carlos Serrano le reclama a Inés Palacios, como albacea y heredera de Antonio Solórzano, la libertad de su esclavo Pablo José Ferrer," ANC, Audiencia de Santiago de Cuba, leg. 691, no. 15632, 1838. "Diligencias promovidas por Margarita López, esclava de D. Manuel de igual apellido en reclamo de lo que le dejara su madrina Basilia Echavarría por su fallecimiento," leg. 322, no. 7711, 1849.
83. "Libro doce de bautismos de pardos y morenos de la iglesia de Puerta de la Güira da principio el 14 de febrero de 1841 y concluye el 22 de junio de 1845," IHC, f. 114, partida 491.
84. On the practice of *coartación* in Cuba, see de la Fuente, "Slaves and the Creation."
85. Perera and Meriño, *Estrategias de libertad*, 137–180. In Brazil, the equivalent of the *síndico* was the curator, see Grinberg, *Liberata*, 35–40. For a case in which coffee plantation slaves were represented by the mayor of the municipality of Havana, see "Incidentes a los que sigue la sucesión de D. Juan David contra los herederos de D. Nicolás Mendive sobre la entrega de un cafetal seguida por la representación del caballero síndico sobre la libertad de varios esclavos (1826–28)," ANC, Escribanía de Daumy, leg. 442, no. 3.
86. For an analysis of insurrections in this region, see Barcia, *Seeds of Insurrection*.
87. "Don Francisco de Chappotín sobre acreditar la edad que tiene y su cristiandad," ANC, Escribanía de Gobierno, leg. 243, no. 6. f. 3, 1798.

Acknowledgements

The authors would like to thank Professor João J. Reis for calling our attention to the question of slaves owned by slaves in Cuba, as well as for his valuable observations and comments on the text that we presented in an early version at the annual meeting of the Tepoztlán Institute for the Transnational History of the Americas, held 19–26 July 2017. We also express our gratitude to the meeting organizers for the opportunity to share those intense days, as well as to the discussants and the rest of the participants. We are also thankful to the project Diáspora Negra, directed by the Institute of Cuban History (IHC) of Havana, and to the photographer Lourdes Ortega, in charge of reproducing the series preserved in the churches of the old bishopric of Havana, whose work allowed us to consult the parish records of Puerta de la Güira and Guanajay. Also, thanks to the Cuban historian David Domínguez for sending us the documents held at the Spanish archives, and to Víctor Goldgel Carballo for his efforts in having this essay see the light of day in English, but most of all for giving us courage when the water seemed to have surrounded us from all sides. Lastly, we would like to thank the two anonymous reviewers for *Atlantic Studies*. Their comments, suggestions, and criticism made the text get closer to what we had envisioned since we first found the documents that serve as the basis of this essay. An earlier version of this research appeared in Freire and Secreto, *Formas de Liberdade*, 17–42.

This article was translated into English by Joshua Doyle-Raso.

Disclosure statement

No potential conflict of interest was reported by the author(s).

References

Abbot, Abiel. *Cartas*. La Habana: Ediciones del Consejo Nacional de Cultura, 1965.

Alberto, L. Paulina. "Liberta by Trade: Negotiating the Terms of Unfree Labor in Gradual Abolition Buenos Aires (1820s–30s)." *Journal of Social History* 52, no. 3 (Spring 2019): 619–651.

Bando de gobernación y policía de la isla de Cuba, expedido por el Escmo. Sr. Don Gerónimo Valdés, Presidente, Gobernador y Capitán General. La Habana: Imprenta de Gobierno y Capitanía General, 1842.

Barcia, Manuel. *Seeds of Insurrection: Domination and Resistance on Western Cuban Plantations, 1808–1848*. Baton Rouge: Louisiana State University Press, 2008.

Bergad, Laird W., Fe Iglesias García, and María del Carmen Barcia. *The Cuban Slave Market, 1790–1880*. Cambridge: Cambridge University Press, 1995.

Chira, Adriana. "Affective Debts: Manumission by Grace and the Making of Gradual Emancipation Laws in Cuba, 1817–68." *Law and History Review* 36, no. 1 (2018): 1–33.

De La Fuente García, Alejandro. "A alforria de escravos em Havana, 1601–1610: Primeira conclusões." *Revista de Estudos Económicos* 20, no. 1 (1990): 139–159.

De La Fuente García, Alejandro. "La esclavitud, la ley y la reclamación de derechos en Cuba: repensando el debate de Tannenbaum." *Debates y Perspectivas* 4 (2004): 37–68.

De La Fuente García, Alejandro. "Slaves and the Creation of Legal Rights in Cuba: *Coartación* and *Papel*." *Hispanic American Historical Review* 87, no. 4 (2007): 659–692.

De La Torre, José Maria, and Tranquilino Sandalio Noda. "Marien: Noticias históricas, geográficas y estadísticas de esta jurisdicción." *Memorias de la Real Sociedad Económica de La Habana*, no. 4, 2nd series, 226–241. La Habana: Imprenta del Faro Industrial, 1847.

Díaz, María Elena. *The Virgin, the King, and the Royal Slaves of El Cobre: Negotiating Freedom in Colonial Cuba, 1670–1780*. Stanford, CA: Stanford University Press, 2000.

Díaz Espinoza, Raúl Esteban. "La invisibilización de la Revolución de Haití y sus posibles resistencias decoloniales desde la negritud." *Relaciones Internacionales* 25 (2014): 11–33.

Dubois, Laurent. *Avengers of the New World: The Story of the Haitian Revolution*. Cambridge, MA: Harvard University Press, 2004.

Eltis, David. "A Diáspora dos Falantes de Iorubá, 1650–1865: Dimensões e Implicações." *TOPOI* 7, no. 13 (2006): 271–299.

Falola, Toyin, and Paul E. Lovejoy. "Pawnship in Historical Perspective." In *Pawnship, Slavery, and Colonialism in Africa*, edited by Paul E. Lovejoy, and Toyin Falola, 1–26. Trenton, NJ: Africa World Press, 2003.

Ferrer, Ada. *Freedom's Mirror: Cuba and Haiti in the Age of Revolution*. New York: Cambridge University Press, 2014.

Figueredo Váldez, Reveca. *Bautismo y compadrazgo en la feligresía de San Hilarión de Guanajay, 1773–1845*. La Habana: Editorial de Ciencias Sociales, 2019.

Freire, Jonis, and Maria Verónica Secreto, eds. *Formas de Liberdade: Gratidão, condicionalidade e incertezas no mundo escravista nas Américas*. Rio de Janeiro: Manu Editora, 2019.

García Álvarez, Alejandro. "El café y su relación con otros cultivos tropicales en la Cuba colonial." *Catauro* 18 (2008): 5–26.

Garrigus, John D. "Colour, class and identity on the eve of the Haitian revolution: Saint-Domingue's free coloured elite as *colons américains*." *Slavery & Abolition* 17, no. 1 (April 1996): 20–43.

Grinberg, Keila. *Liberata: a lei da ambigüidade as ações de liberdade da Corte de Apelação do Rio de Janeiro no século XIX*. Rio de Janeiro: Centro Edelstein de Pesquisas Sociais, 2008.

Guerra y Sánchez, Ramiro. *Manual de historia de Cuba: desde su descubrimiento hasta 1868*. La Habana: Editorial de Ciencias Sociales, 1971.

James, C. L. R. *Los jacobinos negros: Toussaint L'Ouverture y la revolución de Saint-Domingue*. Translated by Ramón Garcia. La Habana: Fondo Editorial Casa de las Américas, 2010.

Johnson, Samuel. *The History of the Yorubas: From the Earliest Times to the Beginning of the British Protectorate*. Lagos: C.M.S. (Nigeria) Bookshops, 1956.

Kimou, Atsè Alexis-Camille. "La rebelión de Galbaud y la libertad general de los esclavos de Saint-Domingue (1793–1794)." *Nuevo Mundo Mundos Nuevos* (2014). Accessed 17 November 2017. doi:10.4000/nuevomundo.66356.

La Rosa, Gabino, and Mirtha T. González. *Cazadores de esclavos: diarios*. La Habana: Fundación Fernando Ortiz, 2004.

Lovejoy, Paul E. *Transformations in Slavery: A History of Slavery in Africa*. Cambridge: Cambridge University Press, 1983.

Lucena Salmoral, Manuel. *Leyes para esclavos: el ordenamiento jurídico sobre la condición, tratamiento, defensa y represión de los esclavos en las colonias de la América española*. Madrid: Fundación Ignacio Larramendi, 2005.

Meriño Fuentes, María de los Ángeles, and Aisnara Perera Díaz. *Contrabando de bozales en Cuba: perseguir el tráfico y mantener la esclavitud (1845–1866)*. San José de las Lajas: Ediciones Montecallado, 2015.

Meriño Fuentes, María de los Ángeles, and Aisnara Perera Díaz. *Familias, agregados y esclavos: los padrones de vecinos de Santiago de Cuba (1778–1861)*. Santiago de Cuba: Editorial Oriente, 2011.

Meriño Fuentes, María de los Ángeles, and Aisnara Perera Díaz. *Un café para la microhistoria: estructura de posesión de esclavos y ciclo de vida en la llanura habanera*. La Habana: Ciencias Sociales, 2008.

Moreno Fraginals, Manuel. *El Ingenio: el complejo económico social cubano del azúcar*. La Habana: Ciencias Sociales, 1978.

Nishida, Mieko. "Manumission and Ethnicity in Urban Slavery: Salvador, Brazil, 1808–1888." *Hispanic American Historical Review* 73, no. 3 (August 1993): 361–391.

Perera Díaz, Aisnara, and María de los Ángeles Meriño Fuentes. *Para librarse de lazos antes buena familia que buenos brazos. Apuntes sobre la manumisión en Cuba*. Santiago de Cuba: Editorial Oriente, 2009.

Perera Díaz, Aisnara, and María de los Ángeles Meriño Fuentes. *El cabildo carabalí viví de Santiago de Cuba: familia, cultura y sociedad (1797–1909)*. Santiago de Cuba: Editorial Oriente, 2013.

Perera Díaz, Aisnara, and María de los Ángeles Meriño Fuentes. *Estrategias de libertad: un acercamiento a las acciones legales de los esclavos en Cuba (1762–1872)*. La Habana: Editorial de Ciencias Sociales, 2015.

Perera Díaz, Aisnara, and María de los Ángeles Meriño Fuentes. *Libertad sin abolición: la dimensión política de los conflictos entre africanos y traficantes en los tribunales cubanos. La Habana 1795–1844*. Matanzas: Editorial Vigía, 2016.

Pérez de la Riva, Juan. *El barracón y otros ensayos*. La Habana: Editorial de Ciencias Sociales, 1975.

Ramírez Pérez, Jorge Freddy, and Fernando Antonio Paredes Pupo. *Francia en Cuba: los cafetales de la Sierra del Rosario (1790–1850)*. La Habana: Ediciones Unión, 2004.

Reis, João José. "De escravo rico a liberto: a história do africano Manoel Joaquim Ricardo na Bahia oitocentista." *Revista de História* 174 (2016): 15–68.

Reis, João José. "Escravos donos de escravos na Bahia oitocentista." Unpublished.

Santa Cruz y Mallén, Francisco Xavier de. *Historia de familias cubanas*, vol. 2. La Habana: Editorial Hércules, 1940.

Schwartz, Stuart B. "The Manumission of Slaves in Colonial Brazil: Bahia, 1684–1745." *Hispanic American Historical Review* 54, no. 4 (November 1974): 603–635.

Scott, Rebecca J., and Jean M. Hébrard. *Freedom Papers: An Atlantic Odyssey in the Age of Emancipation*. Cambridge, MA: Harvard University Press, 2012.

Thornton, John K. "African Soldiers in the Haitian Revolution." *Journal of Caribbean History* 25, no. 1&2 (1991): 50–80.

Victoria Ojeda, Jorge. "Tensión en el Caribe hispano. Los negros ladinos de La Española en La Habana." In *La excepción americana. Cuba en el ocaso del imperio continental*, edited by Imilcy Balboa, and José A. Piqueras, 105–130. Valencia: Fundación Instituto de Historia Social, 2006.

Vives, Francisco Dionisio. *Cuadro estadístico de la Siempre fiel Isla de Cuba, correspondiente al año 1827*. La Habana: Establecimiento de las Viudas de Arazoza y Soler, 1829.

Von Grafenstein, Johanna. "El 'autonomismo criollo' en Saint-Domingue en vísperas de la revolución haitiana de 1791." In *Las Antillas en la era de las Luces y la Revolución*, edited by José A. Piqueras, 27–41. Madrid: Siglo XXI, 2005.

Wurdemann, John G. *Notes on Cuba, Containing an Account of Its Discovery and Early History*. Boston: James Munroe, 1844.

Zaragoza, Justo. *Las insurrecciones en Cuba: apuntes para la historia política de esta isla en el presente siglo*. Madrid: Imprenta de Manuel G. Hernández, 1872–1873.

Getting locked up to get free in colonial Cuba

Rachel Price

ABSTRACT

This essay examines the histories of two enslaved Africans living in Cuba and sent to prison in the mid-nineteenth century, to consider the ways in which prison represented a path to freedom within and beyond slave societies. Formerly enslaved people in Cuba and Puerto Rico, released from bondage upon entering the carceral system, were often resold into slavery upon completion of their prison sentences – but not always. The essay focuses first on the case of Gregorio Lucumí, imprisoned in Cuba, whose civil status post-sentence was debated by authorities seeking to discourage crime as a means to secure prison sentences that might yield freedom from slavery. It then turns to the lengthier case of Isidoro Gangá, sent to prison in Melilla, North Africa, and who, post-sentence, appealed for freedom via free soil principles.

In 1846 Gregorio Lucumí, an African-born man enslaved in Cuba, commenced a prison sentence in Havana for allegedly having killed his godson Martín Congo on 17 June 1844 in a pasture belonging to Florentino Amenteros.[1] There had been no witnesses, but authorities found Congo with his throat slit, cuts to his lateral right jugular vein and to the first vertebrae in his neck, and evidence of two traumas. Lucumí, who almost certainly had been forcibly taken to Cuba and enslaved at some point in his youth – he had "country marks" or scarifications on his face, and, given his last name, was likely Yoruba[2] – confessed that he had hit Congo with a stick, but denied that he had inflicted any wounds with a sharp instrument. Still, a judge in Villa Clara sentenced Lucumí to ten years in prison.

When Lucumí successfully completed his sentence in 1856, however, his civil status was pondered by legal authorities. Following Roman law and according to Chapter 23 of the 1784 *Código Negro Carolino* (Code of Legislation for the Moral, Political, and Economic Governance of Blacks on the Island of Hispaniola), designed to apply to Spain's American colonies, when an enslaved person committed a crime that resulted in damages, his or her master could decide whether to assume responsibility to the third party, or formally end any possessive relation with the enslaved person, so avoiding possible indemnification.[3] Although the *Código Negro Carolino* was not ultimately approved by the Spanish government, many of its laws drew on prior established ordinances and suggested the basis for processing slaves accused of crimes; it furthermore informed the subsequent 1789

Instrucción sobre educación, tratamiento y ocupaciones de los esclavos (Instruction on education, treatment and occupations of slaves).[4]

When Lucumí was sentenced to prison, his owner had apparently chosen to renounce rights and responsibilities over him. Thus the question remained whether Lucumí, once released from prison, was now to be a free man, or to be reenslaved.[5] The question would take on greater importance in subsequent similar cases, where non-Caribbean, non-slaveholding prison locations would be decisive. But already the mere fact of Lucumí's having done time in prison raised the question for authorities about his possible freedom post-incarceration.

Recent scholarship has emphasized the many ways that enslaved people in the Americas sought and achieved freedom not only through marronage and rebellion, but often through legal means, in so doing shaping the very laws defining enslavement.[6] Throughout colonial histories and across varying slave regimes in the Atlantic world, what it meant to be enslaved or free, and the division between enslavement and freedom, was more variegated and shifting than the terms suggest. Individual cases mattered greatly.

In nineteenth-century Cuba, a large class of free people of color existed, comprised of people born free as well as the more recently emancipated.[7] Various established avenues allowed for enslaved people to gain freedom papers. The clearest and most frequently employed method in the Spanish-speaking Caribbean was *coartación*, or self-purchase. Yet there also existed myriad paths for authorities and slaveowners to reenslave free people.[8] What is more, the post-Haitian Revolution Atlantic world produced simultaneous and differing degrees of abolition; as people of color circulated throughout the region, they often were forced to prove their free status. As Rebecca Scott and others have argued, "the existence of a set of laws declaring that persons could be owned as property did not, even in the nineteenth century, answer by itself the question of whether a given person was a slave."[9]

Scott has documented, for instance, claims to "freedom by prescription": that is, having lived openly as free for sufficient time, a category already specified in the *Siete Partidas de Alfonso X*, the medieval legal codes that still determined much of Iberian slave law in the nineteenth century.[10] Adriana Chira has also described a variety of freedom suits through which enslaved people sought and received manumission, from "manumission by grace," to prescription, to claims which monetized affective labor.[11] Aisnara Perera Díaz and María de los Ángeles Meriño Fuentes have exhaustively catalogued additional avenues to freedom in colonial Cuba (including being prostituted by a master, and refugees' conversion to Catholicism). As Alejandro de la Fuente notes, from the earliest colonial period slaves in the Americas not only sought freedom, but indeed through their exploitation of the legal system transformed "what the law had envisioned as masters' obligations into slaves' rights."[12] That is, they worked with existing slave laws to turn them to their favor.

The laws were often complicated. As Chira notes, several legal systems regulating enslavement coexisted in nineteenth-century Cuba. The *Siete Partidas* had long before enumerated several routes to manumission, including good conduct – "by which the authors referred to the provision of incriminating information regarding the behavior of counterfeiters, possible political traitors, or eloping virgins" – injury at the hands of abusive owners, "marriage to a free woman in the presence of the owner," religious ordination, and prescription.[13] To these medieval allowances additional modern avenues accrued.

This study examines one possible and somewhat paradoxical route to freedom – that of serving prison time. It is this possibility that was raised in the post-carceral legal meditations on Lucumí's fate. His case is followed by another involving Isidoro Gangá, this latter case noteworthy insofar as it appears to have prompted specific legislation, examined below in detail. This study limits its analysis to these two cases from Spain's *Archivo Histórico de la Nación*: many more cases may well exist in additional Spanish and Caribbean archives, such as Cuba's *Archivo Nacional*. Indeed, in a legal deliberation examined below about whether prison time sufficed to ensure freedom for a formerly enslaved convict, authorities reference "similar" earlier cases in which convicts were reenslaved upon completion of prison time, suggesting a broader tradition of decisions concerning ex-slaves' post-carceral status.

Lucumí's case history is brief and inconclusive. A note from the director of the prison where he served out his sentence stated that the prisoner's conduct was exemplary, observed that Lucumí had satisfactorily performed hard labor, manifesting "a laudable conformity and an unequivocal remorse for his guilt," and added that the convicted man "does not doubt that returning to society he will conduct himself with more consideration and prudence."[14] In light of these considerations, and arguing that the penalty ought not be perpetual, the *fiscal* (prosecutor) believed that the case should be judged favorably for Lucumí, according to the former slave's sentence. This is a confusing phrase, since Lucumí's original sentence included being resold to pay off the costs of his case, whereas "favorable" to the formerly enslaved man would, presumably, mean to live as a free person.

Slaves who had completed prison time were regularly sold back into slavery upon their release to pay for the costs of their legal cases, as Havana's Audiencia Pretorial itself admitted when debating Lucumí's case. First the Audiencia noted that the case was "similar to others before it" for which it was customary to sell slaves at auction in order to pay off the owner's legal fees in the case brought against them.[15] Crucially, the text announced, this practice was designed "so that the crime may never serve as a means for the acquisition of freedom" lest "such examples serve as a pernicious stimulant and encourage crimes."[16] The Prosecutor then went on to emphasize that despite meditating on how to avoid such encouragement and "the danger to which society could be exposed if the natural desire that one must assume in slaves to achieve their emancipation were to lead to the incentive in such cases," the report should respond favorably to Gregorio Lucumí's request to lift his retention clause.[17]

Most striking about these passages is the Audiencia's explicit warning against the calculated use of incarceration as a conduit to freedom. What space might these literal prisons have opened up in what was effectively the giant prison of a slave-holding island? Was it possible that an incarcerated enslaved person might have viewed prison as a space and time that allowed for some degree of freedom? In a slave society in which harsh punishment and death were sanctioned treatments, might prison have offered a space of protection or abatement? While the case invites such philosophical questions about what freedom and incarceration meant, the Audiencia was aware of far more practical allures of prison for the enslaved.

The Audiencia's warning serves as an important prelude to a more elaborate legal case brought a decade later that would test the idea that prison might be used by formerly enslaved people as a route towards freedom – if not as a deliberate, *a priori* strategy (although implicitly this too), at least an avenue seized upon and used to advantage. In 1866, as the "illegal" slave trade to Cuba wound down, and in the immediate wake of the United States' abolition of slavery and conclusion of its Civil War, Spanish authorities would decide that formerly enslaved prisoners could *not* be reenslaved as part of their sentence, if they had lawfully been liberated via free soil laws. But they also suggested that henceforth overseas prisons, located on free soil, ought not be the destination for enslaved prisoners from the Caribbean.

Slave law in mid-nineteenth-century Cuba

Specific laws governed the lives of the enslaved in the Americas since the earliest colonial times. After widespread abolition of slavery in the early nineteenth century by the newly independent nations of Latin América, slave laws continued to be honed and issued for Spain's remaining Caribbean colonies. Although the *Siete Partidas* were applied throughout the Americas, a number of royal documents and slave codes also specified aspects of manumission, treatment, and other aspects of negotiating the nature of bondage. In 1768 a *Real Cédula* specified and enshrined as juridical referent certain conditions for manumission.[18] In 1789 the Crown drafted the *Instrucción sobre educación, tratamiento y ocupaciones de los esclavos*, used "in spirit" even though not approved, Manuel Lucena Salmoral writes, as a concession to protesting Latin American slaveowners.[19] Addressing "excessive" abuse and establishing general treatment for slaves, the *Instrucción* did not specifically address manumission. It did, however, clarify the role of the *procurador síndico* (syndic procurador) as that of protector of slaves: the *procurador* would provide legal representation in lieu of what a free person could expect, and would also determine punishments for slaves' crimes.[20] Lucena Salmoral notes that the *Instrucción* would later be the model for slave laws specific to Cuba and Puerto Rico.[21]

In 1825 Spain established a *Comisión Militar Ejecutiva y Permanente* (Permanent Executive Military Commission) in Cuba to hear cases in which both free and enslaved people were to be tried and sentenced for common and political crimes, with little due process.[22] Then, in 1826, a new slave code was written for Puerto Rico that was adapted and implemented in Cuba in 1842.[23] This would be the most important code for determining treatment of, and legal possibilities for, the enslaved in the moment of Cuba's greatest intensification of "second slavery": that period following the abolition of the trade, but which saw the inauguration of massive "illegal" importation as well as greater plantations.[24] After 1827, the *síndicos procuradores* were allowed to wholly defend slaves who had committed a crime, rather than collaborate with and defer to the relevant slaveowners; the *procurador* was now a "*defensor de oficio*," a kind of pro bono defender.[25]

Spain instituted free soil principles for the Peninsula in a Royal Order issued on 29 March 1836, but the Crown maintained the legality of slavery in Cuba and Puerto Rico.[26] The 1836 Royal Order specified that enslaved peoples traveling with their owners to Spain could immediately declare themselves to be free once arrived (or after their visit). The legislation was amply exploited by enslaved men and women accompanying slaveholders from the Caribbean to Spain. But it was also loosely or not at all enforced, making it far from an automatic path to freedom.[27] In reality, as Aurelia Martín Casares and Margarita García Barranco argue, courts regularly ignored these petitions or sided with slaveowners. That the petitions had to be registered, rather than the freedom granted immediately, reveals that the law had to be fought for actively and sometimes unsuccessfully by enslaved people.[28]

Penal laws differed between Spain and the Caribbean colonies, and they differed within Cuba with respect to free people and the enslaved. Spain's 1837 Constituent Courts – revising the liberalism aspired to in Spain's 1812 Constitution – voted that Spain and its overseas territories should be governed by separate laws. As José Antonio Piqueras explicates, citing from the 1837 *Diario de Diputado de Cortes Constituyentes* (Journal of Constitutive Court Representatives), Spain and America allegedly needed different civil codes – that code "which determines the relations between people and things" – and different penal codes, "because otherwise," as *Diputado* (representative) Vicente Sancho argued, "how would the slave, on plantations of some 400 or 500, serve 'his master voluntarily'"?[29] What's more, Piqueras details, the 1837 Constitution and electoral laws specified that just as Spain and Cuba were to have different laws, *within* Cuba there ought to exist different laws according to skin color.[30] This was the same moment in which African-descended people, both enslaved and free, were excluded from the census, helping to justify the expulsion from the Courts of *diputados* from Cuba and other overseas territories (*ultramar*).[31]

1844 saw a series of coordinated insurgencies that made up a vast anti-slavery conspiracy in Cuba known as *La Escalera* (the Ladder Conspiracy). The aftermath was characterized by an infamous crackdown on anyone accused of participation in the conspiracy.[32] As Michelle Reid-Vazquez has explored, what followed from that terrible "year of the lash" were punitive measures that were principally, though not exclusively, levied against free people of color (enslaved people of color and whites were also targets, however). These measures included executions, arrests, torture, exile, dismantling of militias of color, restrictions of black social organizations, and the passage of legislation restricting job opportunities, social activities, and prohibiting specific behavior towards whites.[33] Reid-Vazquez notes that between 1844 and 1845, moreover, the Cuban administration shipped away from the island hundreds of free black people, some to be "imprisoned overseas in Spain or Spanish North Africa."[34] Cuba's colonial regime was dedicated to removing from the island those people it imagined to pose a threat to plantation society.[35] Spain's overseas prisons particularly received political prisoners or those seen as putting in peril the colonial order. Gregorio Lucumí is alleged to have committed his apparently non-political murder in 1844; the apolitical nature of the crime may well have accounted for his incarceration in Cuba.

Even as the immediate aftermath of the Escalera Conspiracy saw a backlash against free people of color, the enslaved continued to seek avenues to freedom in a wider Atlantic context that was shifting in the 1850s and particularly the 1860s, as abolition was pronounced in the United States and a more liberal Spanish monarchy perceived the institution to be imperiled.[36] The pursuit of freedom was nothing new of course, and took many forms.[37] De la Fuente has focused in particular on the history of *coartación.* Gloria García Rodriguez reprinted dozens of cases in which enslaved people petitioned for changes of owners, freedom, recompense, restitution; García Rodriguez argues that "the strict observation of the existing legislation by the enslaved work force illustrates the extent to which rural slaves had an exact knowledge of the norms that affected them."[38] Perera Díaz and Meriño Fuentes have documented a broad range of strategies for achieving freedom. Keila Grinberg and Sue Peabody, meanwhile, have explored how free soil legislation was regularly exploited by enslaved Africans and African-descended people in the Americas who traveled to Spain or other places in which a free soil principle had been established, such as Trinidad, Haiti, and European nations.[39]

In addition to being only erratically honored, the 1836 Royal Order establishing free soil in the Peninsula was ambiguous with respect to how and to whom the law should be applied. As Casares and García Barranco note, the original Order had declared that "only as free persons, and in no other way, could slaves be brought to Spain, expressly warning those owners who wished to bring back slaves that they were obliged to free them as soon as they reached the Peninsula."[40] This left the status of enslaved prisoners brought to Spain under other conditions ambiguous. The fate of those enslaved people brought to Spanish enclaves in North Africa (rather than to the Peninsula itself) might have equally remained vague. A Royal Order of 2 August 1861, reaffirming free soil principles, mentioned that those slaves from Cuba and Puerto Rico "who come to Spain [*España*] with their owners" should consider themselves emancipated.[41] By specifying Spain and not the Peninsula, the North African fortresses *may* have been included; a subsequent 1862 Royal Order expanded this edict and used the language of *Península*.[42]

Thus while Spain's free soil laws specifically imagined their application to the enslaved people living with slaveowners in Spanish colonies in the Caribbean, the awkwardness of the division between Spanish law on the Peninsula and that in the Americas forced numerous clarifications by Spanish authorities of the reach and applicability of free soil principles. As pressure for the abolition of slavery continued from agents both within and beyond the Spanish empire, a series of laws and orders evolved to address mounting free soil claims.

What laws applied to prisoners, and specifically to imprisoned slaves? It is difficult to disentangle which penal codes and slave codes determined the status of formerly incarcerated, formerly enslaved people in Cuba and Puerto Rico. It also remains difficult to ascertain to what extent the enslaved were aware of and taking advantage of the laws' discrepancies. Bianca Premo has pointed to such bottom-up shaping of Spanish modern law by enslaved and other subaltern people in the viceroyalties of Mexico and Peru a century earlier; as she writes, in freedom suits "slaves brought to life the modern conception of freedom as the objective of human action."[43] The cases examined here invite further research in the context of Spain's prison laws and free soil legislation as applied to its Caribbean colonies.

Casares and García Barranco explore in detail one 1858 case (decided in 1861) that successfully challenged the illegal reenslavement of a 10-year old Cuban boy named Rufino following his transit through Spain – a case that became, the authors write, "a fundamental pillar of abolitionist legislation."[44] This important 1861 ruling reaffirming the power of free soil principles was then referenced in an 1864 case brought by a man formerly enslaved in Cuba named Isidoro Gangá, which stretched the application of the decision on the relatively simple case of Rufino.[45]

Gangá's case also raised once again the question that had been posed in the case of Gregorio Lucumí seven years prior: namely, what should be the status of ex-convicts who had been slaves at the time of their prison sentence, upon the sentence's successful completion? In Lucumí's case the mere fact of having successfully served out his time in prison seemed possibly – though not conclusively – enough to change his legal status from that of slave to that of a free man. In the subsequent case, however, Gangá appealed for his freedom specifically because of free soil principles triggered by his moving through Spain's global penal system. Gangá's crime of murdering his *mayoral* (overseer) was, in the eyes of the Cuban authorities, more threatening to the colonial slave and sugar regime than Lucumí's murder of another enslaved man over personal disagreements. Gangá was sent from Havana to Málaga en route to prison in a North African Spanish enclave. His prison term completed, Gangá then went to Cádiz to appeal the final portion of his sentence: reenslavement in Cuba.

Isidoro Gangá

Isidoro Gangá was born in "Guinea," a term that often referred to Upper Guinea, though occasionally it also extended to greater Senegambia and to the West African coast more generally (what was called the Gangá or Kanga nation in slave trade discourse was largely located in what is now Sierra Leone).[46] Gangá's parents are listed as unknown, and given his documented age of 25 at the time of the crime (1852), he may well have been young when taken from his homeland, enslaved, and eventually sold to Miguel Delgado in Havana, Cuba.[47]

Gangá was accused of having murdered his overseer in coordination with several other men. He would be more fortunate than his coconspirators in his sentencing: although José Criollo received the lightest sentence (two years of labor in shackles on his owner's farm), "the Chinese Longino and the black Alejandro Criollo" were sentenced to death by *garrote* (strangulation), while Damián, José, and Isidoro Gangá received 10 years in overseas prisons, "*con prohibición de volver a la Isla cumplida que sea su condena*" (with the prohibition against returning to the Island upon completion of their prison term).[48] The men were also forced to pay the fees for the case brought against them, divided between the soon-to-be executed Longino and Alejandro, and the others.

Upon sentencing in 1853, Gangá was transferred from Havana to Melilla, then to Málaga, and then to Chafarinas, off the coast of Morocco.[49] It was this transfer through the Iberian Peninsula that presumably first established Gangá's status as a free man, albeit an imprisoned one, in his own reckoning. In 1855 he was transferred again to Melilla, a Spanish enclave known for its fortress and which had been established in 1497 in Moroccan territory. In 1864, having completed his ten-year prison sentence, Gangá requested that he not be sent back to Cuba to be sold at public auction to underwrite the costs of the legal case that led to his incarceration, a stipulation that had initially been included in his sentence.

Gangá is but one of many people charged with crimes in Cuba and sent to prisons located in Spanish territories in North or West Africa: Ceuta, Melilla, or Fernando Poo. Spain favored such penal colonies for those people from the Caribbean whom it felt threatened the "peace" of the islands, a peace and tranquility insisted upon time and again in anxiously assured letters from Puerto Rico's and Cuba's Captain Generals to Spain despite all evidence to the contrary, as restive populations of enslaved people and anti-colonial thinkers rebelled continuously against the colonial slaveholding regime.

Problematic figures sent to such prisons included anti-colonial agents, free people of color after 1844, enslaved people fighting for their freedom, among others. Christian De Vito writes that from the 1830s up to the outbreak of Cuba's Ten Year's War in 1868, "punitive flows" of prisoners from Cuba to Puerto Rico, Santo Domingo, and Ceuta were designed to remove conflictive persons from sugar plantations to protect the lucrative industry.[50] Fernando Poo (now Bioko), Ceuta, and the Philippines were favored destinations for convicts and deportees classified as "abolitionist agents from the surrounding British colonies, as well as those viewed as 'internal enemies.' These included 'incorrigible' vagrants and lumpen proletarians, and members of the Abakuá mutual aid societies" (an Afro-Cuban secret society derived from the Ekpé leopard society from Calabar.)[51] Susan Martin-Márquez has argued that these Spanish penal colonies were used to "prolong the large-scale regimes of slavery" in Cuba and Puerto Rico, and that deportations of black Cubans were also part of "ongoing whitening campaigns" (during and after the Ten Years War many separatists and insurgents were also sent to the overseas prisons).[52] And in 1860 hundreds of *emancipados*, Africans aboard intercepted illegal slave ships carrying them to enslavement in the Caribbean, were sent to Fernando Poo to carry out infrastructural work.[53]

One group of deportees in particular left its mark on these prison enclaves and their surroundings: as the ethnomusicologist Isabela de Aranzadi has studied extensively, a cultural legacy continues into the present in Ecuatorial Guinea from nineteenth-century deported members of Abakuá, sometimes referred to by the name for a ritual dancer, *ñáñigo*. These deportees were sent from Cuba to Fernando Poo between 1862 and the end of the century.[54] Ritual dances termed *Ñánkué* are still practiced in Bioko, passed down from the Cuban *ñáñigo* deportees. De Vito claims that these deportations of *ñáñigos* to Fernando Poo brought deportees "in close proximity to their homelands in Old Calabar," but he offers no evidence that any of the deported *ñáñigos* had further contact with, or travel to, Calabar after imprisonment.[55] De Vito alleges (based on claims by the *fin-de-siglo* Spanish criminologist Rafael Salillas) that those sent to Ceuta, in North Africa likewise "kept their rituals alive during their captivity."[56]

Since much separates North and Sub Saharan Africa geographically, linguistically, and culturally, the mere return to the African continent need not have signaled a return at all for people forced as children to migrate initially west as captives from African slave ports sent to the Caribbean, and then years later eastward again as prisoners. Still, the implications of the eastward migration are intriguing. What proportion of West Africans might Gangá have encountered in Melilla? Was the carceral space more or less propitious for fostering alliances and links than the many flourishing West African communities in Cuba itself (of which numerous *cabildos* – mutual aid societies, often organized around and named for African ethnicities or "nations" – are but one example)?[57] Given that Gangá had already allegedly collaborated across "ethnic" and linguistic lines to do away with his Spanish overseer (he conspired in the alleged murder with a "criollo," or Cuban-born black man, and a "Chinese"), was ethnic affiliation even relevant for him?

The "return" to the African continent as prisoners might, however, have introduced for some enslaved West- and West Central Africans the potential for layers of collaboration, and for geopolitical and even religious conflict. For instance, given that a number of West African-born slaves like Gangá were sent from the Caribbean to North African prisons, it seems possible that some men who had been raised as Muslims before their capture and enslavement in the Americas might have ended up later conscripted into Catholic Spain's ongoing battles against Muslim Moroccans. Indeed, as North African resistance to the Spanish enclave of Melilla spurred a series of skirmishes and wars with

Spain, Gangá and other prisoners were drafted into defending the fortress against attacks from the local populations.

On 22 September 1855 Gangá and others "of his class" were armed and dispatched from the prison into "*campo infiel*" (enemy territory) to (successfully) defuse a heavy caliber cannon that "the Moors" had directed towards the Spanish.[58] Three weeks later, by royal order, Gangá was awarded a year reduction in his prison sentence for his valiant participation in the rebuff. In November he again dismantled parapets and repulsed attacks, and in January his sentence was reduced another three months for his performance, then another seven months more. From his original sentence of ten years, four months, and eight days a total of some twenty months were ultimately commuted, thanks to Gangá's participation in fighting off the North Africans who contested Spanish presence in the region.

In 1864, almost ten years after these initial conscripted battles and with the prison sentence successfully served, authorities turned to rulings issuing from the Rufino case to consider Gangá's ultimate fate. The 2 August 1861 Royal Order that the Queen determined after evaluating Rufino's case stated that even in cases in which formerly enslaved people liberated by Spain's 1836 free soil laws returned to a country where slavery remained extant, they would remain free; enslaved people emancipated by coming to the Peninsula could not be reenslaved.[59]

Gangá's case was slightly different than Rufino's, however. Gangá had not come to Spain with a slaveowner. Instead he had been sent as a convicted criminal to a Spanish fortress in North Africa. The courts were primed to look particularly favorably on Gangá, as his participation in anti-Morrocan battles was consistently evoked in documents in his case file as evidence of good conduct.[60] But Gangá based his own case for freedom strictly on the free soil principle: he argued that while being transferred from Havana to Málaga, en route to Chafarinas, Ceuta, he stepped foot in "the Metropole," thereby securing his liberty.[61] Gangá appealed to the regional Council in Cádiz; a majority found he should not be sent back to Cuba to be sold and reenslaved, while a minority advocated for maintaining the final portion of his sentence.[62]

An 1864 decision by the Governor of Cádiz on whether Isidoro Gangá should be sent back to Havana argued that Gangá, having arrived in Cádiz to plead his case, was "to be transferred as decided by the Audiencia Pretorial of Havana, with the object that he complete the last part of his sentence which is that of being sold at public auction to satisfy with his sale the expenses of his case." [63] As the Governor weighed the case, he noted that Gangá referred to the Queen's 1861 ruling on Rufino: "The unfortunate black man interpreting in his favor the extant legislation considers himself to be free and in possession of his civil state of free man since the moment that he stepped foot in the Metropole, and elevated to this Government an instance seeking the grace that derives from the Royal Order of August 2 1861."[64]

It is unknown how a prisoner in Melilla such as Gangá may have gained knowledge of the ruling on Rufino. Did Gangá arrive in Spanish overseas territories already aware, from years of life in Cuba, of other former slaves' use of the 1836 free soil laws? Were ports such as Cádiz abuzz with discussions of free soil? Casares and García Barranco argue that the 1857 Dred Scott case in the United States, in which an enslaved man brought by owners to free soil sued unsuccessfully for his freedom upon return to a slave-holding state, would have been known to Cubans adjudicating free soil cases in the Iberian world.[65] Piqueras also stresses the degree to which the United States, with its structural paradoxes of an avowed constitutional liberalism that nonetheless enshrined in its laws slavery and limited democracy to a wealthy elite, served as a reference, justification or background for Cuban legal theorists accommodating slavery.[66] In Gangá's dossier, an 1865 letter drafted by the Ultramar section of the Council of State alludes both to strong anti-slavery movements in Europe and to "recently transpired events" in the United States as context for Gangá's case.[67]

On 13 May 1864 the governor of Cádiz opined that to send Isidoro back to Cuba to be sold at public auction would "violate the treaties that prevent the sale of blacks," and noted again that "Isidoro considered himself free from the mere fact of having come to Spain."[68] A letter to the Minister of Government followed, in which Gangá's attorneys, including one Francisco Millan,[69] wrote that the case, "despite its minor volume, offers extraordinary importance and gravity given the question to which it refers and the singularity of the case."[70] Millan alternated between a Christian and nationalist rhetoric critiquing slavery and a dry parsing of precedent. Thus he objected to the idea that "a national being, having received baptism, redeemed by the blood of the Savior, might be sold in public for money and by auctioneering, as if a piece of furniture, or a beast, not even to satisfy a debt of his own, nor for the damage caused by him, but to pay the costs for lawyers and procurators, scriveners and sheriffs."[71] Here, national personality and Christian baptism (rather than sheer humanity) separate an enslaved person from a mere thing or animal.

A majority, but not all, of the Council found Gangá's case compelling. The Council did not find "perfectly applicable" the Royal Order of 2 August 1861, which dealt with only "slaves that come with their owners to the Peninsula, not those that, like Isidoro Gangá, come, not in their owner's confidence, but probably even against their [owner's] will, and, what's more, not to live in the [Peninsula] as free men but to serve out a sentence."[72] One dissenter from the Council's decision in favor of Gangá's freedom declined to take into consideration the question of slavery, "whether good or bad," writ large.[73] He argued, against the attorneys' language, that Gangá's proposed resale into slavery to pay off the costs of his case was neither surprising nor "barbarous."[74] The debate continued: to send Gangá back to be sold violated Spain's 1835 treaty with England terminating the slave trade, but to free him encouraged crime as a pathway to freedom.[75]

In January 1864 the Comandante General Gobernador Civil de Ceuta weighed in, granting "absolute license" to Isidoro Gangá for his exit from the prison in Melilla "and his transfer to the town [*pueblo*] that he prefers, after requesting the corresponding passport."[76] What happened in the coming two years is obscure. Gangá clearly did not go to the *pueblo* of his choice, but neither was he sent to Cuba. For on 16 October 1866, Isidoro was again in court, still battling for his freedom.[77] The case would prove important for considerations of the fate of formerly enslaved prisoners in Spanish territory, in the waning years of Cuba's second slavery.

While we do not know what transpired in those two years, a few clues exist as to how the government was responding to cases like Gangá's, and eventually to Gangá himself. On 12 July 1865 another Royal Order directed to the Gobernador Superior Civil de Cuba was established "declaring free a fugitive slave from Cuba from the moment that he steps foot on the Peninsula."[78] The enslaved person occasioning this additional Order, Valentín Colón, was a prisoner in the jail of Ourense, Galicia, and the Governor of the

Province requested that Colón be considered free, "as he has been residing in the Peninsula"; his case was submitted along with that of another man, Francisco Ruiz, who claimed freedom after having been brought by his owner to the "United States of the North."[79] Gangá knew of the precedent, as a document in his case file affirms; it is possible too that his attorney informed him.[80] The *de oficio* attorneys representing formerly enslaved prisoners prepared cases as requested by a judge. Whether these lawyers were also activists, abolitionists, or merely dutiful professionals depended upon the luck of the draw, as they were assigned turns as pro bono lawyers annually at the law schools. It is unlikely, though not impossible, that any one such lawyer was specifically invested in anti-slavery causes.[81]

On 30 January 1865 Gangá's delay was again presented to the Director General of Penal Establishments. The Director answered on 17 February that the case file about Isidoro Gangá's freedom or transport to Havana was pending a report by the Provincial Council of Cádiz, requested by Royal Order the prior 2 June 1865.[82] At this point Gangá had been in a jail, post-prison sentence, for over two years.[83] In 1866 a letter was sent to the Minister of Ultramar Alejandro Castro asking whether Gangá should be immediately set free "as a consequence of that which had been laid out in a Royal Decree of September 29, 1866."[84] The author wrote that in light of Gangá's lifted retention and the reasoning presented, "the Government in my charge did not carry out transfer to America, issuing the case file in consultation with the Ministry of Governance 13 May of said year 1864."[85] Gangá had not been sent back to Cuba.

The Minister of Ultramar was then consulted by Cádiz in relation to an important ruling from October 1866. The author of the letter referenced "the publication of 29 of last month inserted into the *Gaceta* of the second of this month," which "resolves the question fully in the interest of humanity" and notes that "instructions will still be circulated for the execution of the cited Decree."[86] The publication referenced is the Royal Order of 29 September 1866, which declared free "all slaves that pass to a country where servitude does not exist, and prohibiting sentencing them to overseas prisons."[87] This order was designed, it would appear, to address the apparent loophole by which an enslaved prisoner might become free through free soil litigation. The first article of the order specified that:

> any individual of color, man woman or child that finds him or herself in servitude in our provinces of Puerto-Rico or Cuba, will determine him or herself to be emancipated and free upon touching the territory of the Peninsula and its adjacent islands, or upon arriving at the maritime jurisdiction and zones of the same, whatever may be the cause by which is verified the fact of disembarking in said territory or of finding themselves in the waters of its maritime jurisdiction [...][88]

The Royal Order thus includes islands beyond the Peninsula in the free soil ambit (Balearic, surely, but possibly also Fernando Poo). Subsequent articles 2, 3, and 4 specified that henceforth prisoners could not be sentenced to overseas prisons in order to underwrite damages incurred by a slave; that criminals who were also slaves would serve out their sentences in prisons situated in Cuba and Puerto Rico; that the indemnification for slaves from the Caribbean liberated by Spanish free soil laws was to be satisfied by "special dispositions" and was to be no greater than the value likely to be fetched at slave auctions; and that when enslaved people were sold to pay off the damages they had wrought (known as *noxa*), public defenders would determine such prices, and the emancipated former slave, now carrying out his sentence in the Peninsula, would be a free man, but required to indemnify the purported damages.[89]

These articles are a study in the ambivalence that fundamentally characterized Spain's free soil laws and which eschewed full abolition in the Empire's territories. The Order allows for free soil principles to stand but obliges formerly enslaved former prisoners to pay off the court fees for their initial sentencing. It states that enslaved people convicted of crimes and sent to overseas prisons could not be forced to be sold back into slavery but also appears to seek to head off future cases in which damages occasioned by a slave – *noxa* – might result in the convicted criminal's deportation to specifically *overseas* prisons. This provision was presumably designed to prevent stints in overseas prisons from becoming routes to freedom, already feared in Lucumí's case. Given the dates and its referencing in Gangá's case file, the order seems to have been based on his history and used to settle his case.

In 1866 the Council of State also opined that Gangá should be *"puesto en libertad"* (made free). The Council reiterated that henceforth enslaved people convicted of crimes should not be sent to overseas prisons, to avoid additional such situations. It argued that "crime should in no case benefit the delinquent" and warned against "the great danger of seeking emancipation through a forbidden path [...] Freedom cannot be the result of an illicit act."[90] It suggested that the Government, on behalf of Gangá, would pay Havana's Audiencia Pretorial for the costs of the court case (not in excess of whatever price Gangá would have garnered at public auction), rather than return him to Cuba to be sold in order to underwrite such costs.[91]

Spain's Archivo Histórico Nacional, which houses the case, summarizes its outcome as follows: "case file instructed in the Ministry of Governance with the aim of said Gangá having solicited the freedom that was granted him by Royal Order December 16 1866, in virtue of the Royal Decree of the prior September 29 which declares free those slaves that enter into places where there is no slavery."[92] Yet Gangá's file leaves his ultimate destination unstated.

Scholars such as Saidiya Hartman, Marisa Fuentes, Jennifer Morgan and others have meditated profoundly upon the promises and limits of archival work on enslaved people.[93] Like the people at the heart of their research, Lucumí's and Gangá's cases promise, but frustrate, the desire for further knowledge about the two men. In what villages or empires were they born? In what years did they arrive in Cuba, at what age, and how and when did they learn Spanish sufficiently to plead their cases? How did Gangá learn of the free soil laws of 1836 and 1861? How, after ten years in Melilla, did he travel to Cádiz to plead his case, and how did he secure the services of his lawyer (a public defender very likely assigned to him)? Were Lucumí and Gangá ultimately "set free"? If so, where did Gangá go once his free status was determined: to Cádiz or another town in Southern Spain? To North or West Africa? Back to Cuba as a free man? What links were established in the prisons of Melilla, Ceuta, and Fernando Poo among enslaved West Africans, and did any facilitate paths back to prior homelands – or did these men now consider themselves more at home in the vast reach of the Spanish Empire? Did they make alliances with some of the "Chinese slaves" and Caribbean-born black men also sent to these prisons?[94]

While these questions remain unanswered, the histories are significant for what information they do provide. Taken together, the two cases – possibly among many more – offer insight into the strategies that formerly enslaved people sought to gain freedom, including incarceration. Prison itself, which may have leveled the statuses of formerly enslaved and formerly free men and women, here surfaces as an unlikely, and forcibly suppressed, conduit to potential liberty.

Further research into other cases – the "earlier such cases" that the Audiencia refers to in Lucumí's case – that debate the civil status of formerly enslaved prisoners, in both Caribbean and Spanish prisons, would help elucidate the extent of the legal debate, should such cases be documented. The two cases examined here stand out for the West African provenance of their litigants, though this was hardly uncommon. Similar debates might well lurk within case files of other formerly enslaved prisoners in Melilla originally from "Ultramar" (the Caribbean or the Philippines) soliciting the lifting of retention clauses.[95] Lucumí's case is noteworthy for the Audiencia's explicit stating that prison should not be used by slaves as a vehicle for freedom; Gangá's, identified as "exceptional" and "singular" in documents in his case file, is important for the extensive debates about non-Caribbean prisons as spaces of free soil and for the articles about incarceration and freedom (from slavery) that it provoked.[96] But how exceptional were these two cases? The allusion to cases similar to and preceding Lucumí's suggest they may not have been so unique, and that a class of formerly enslaved incarcerated people pushed Spanish law to meditate on these questions.

Prisons throughout the former slave-holding Atlantic today, from the United States to Brazil, are filled with disproportionate numbers of African-descended inmates. They are manifestations of anti-black racism and repression, the afterlife of racialized slavery. These two cases also reveal, however, how, in the most sadistic and intense moment of Latin America's second slavery, a repressive feature of judicial systems could be exploited as a path to a more enduring liberation. Life in prison may have been a space of some kind of freedom in a landscape of terror. And incarceration could be a route, in at least a few instances, to liberation from bondage.

Notes

1. Archivo Historico Nacional (A.H.N.) of Madrid, Spain. Ultramar Leg. 4649/60, *Expediente ... G. Lucumí.*
2. Lucumí's case file notes that in addition to facial scarification he also had scarring on his back; the latter may have been from an overseer's abuse.
3. del Vas Mingo, "El derecho del patronato," 178; Lucena Salmoral, *Leyes para esclavos*, 325, 332–333.
4. Lucena Salmoral, *Leyes para esclavos*, 318.
5. Another similarly summarized case from the A.H.N. includes Ultramar Leg. 4672/36, *Lorenzo Lucumí confinado.*
6. De la Fuente, "Slaves and the Creation"; Cowling, *Conceiving Freedom;* García Rodríguez, "In Search of their Rights."
7. By the early nineteenth century free people of color made up almost 17% of the population of the island, and nearly a third of those of African descent in Cuba, see Reid-Vazquez, *The Year of the Lash*, 25, 17; by the 1860s the number had grown but the percentage of the population remained roughly the same, see Scott, *Slave Emancipation*, 6–7.

8. Chaloub, "The Precariousness of Freedom"; Perera Díaz and Meriño Fuentes, *Estrategías de la libertad.*
9. Scott, "Social Facts, Legal Fictions," 10; Scott, *Degrees of Freedom*; Scott and Hébrard, *Freedom Papers.*
10. Scott, "Social Facts, Legal Fictions," 10.
11. Chira, "Affective Debts," 2.
12. De la Fuente, "Slaves and the Creation," 672.
13. Chira, "Affective Debts,"12.
14. Ultramar Leg. 4649/60 No. 1, *Expediente ... G. Lucumí.*
15. Ultramar Leg. 4649/60 No. 9, *Expediente ... G. Lucumí.*
16. Ibid. This and all subsequent citations from Spanish are my translation.
17. Ibid. The clotted legalese faintly echoes the *Siete Partidas*'s note that if "All the creatures of the world love and desire liberty naturally, how much more so men, who have understanding over all the others, and especially those with a noble heart." Yet it proceeds from the cynical reason that brutally enslaved men and women would "naturally" seek an emancipation that must be prevented at any cost, to facilitate the island's great slave-produced wealth (*Las siete partidas,* Vol. 3, Titulo XXII "De la Libertad," 121).
18. Perera Díaz and Merino Fuentes, *Estrategias* 1: 20.
19. Lucena Salmoral, *Leyes para esclavos*, 8; *Royal decree and instructional circular for the Indies on the education, treatment, and work regimen of slaves*, 31 May 1789, in García Rodríguez, *Voices of the Enslaved*, 47–54.
20. Perera Díaz and Merino Fuentes, *Estrategias* 2: 217.
21. Lucena Salmoral, *Leyes para esclavos*, 8.
22. Perera Díaz and Merino Fuentes, *Estrategias* 1:168.
23. Lucena Salmoral, *Leyes para esclavos*, 432.
24. Tomich, *Through the Prism of* Slavery; Zeuske, *Out of the Americas.*
25. Perera Díaz and Merino Fuentes, *Estrategias* 1:168.
26. "Real órden declarando libres á los esclavos que se conduzcan á la Península," 13–14.
27. Casares and García Barranco, "Legislation on Free Soil," 472.
28. See, for instance, Ultramar Leg. 4759/25, *Expediente de declaración de libertad de la morena María de Jesús.*
29. Piqueras, "El gobierno de la población," 35.
30. Ibid., 27.
31. Ghorbal, "Medir y utilizar la heterogeneidad," 72.
32. Paquette, *Sugar is Made with Blood*; Reid-Vazquez, *The Year of the Lash*; Finch, *Rethinking Slave Rebellion in Cuba.*
33. Reid-Vazquez, *The Year of the Lash*, 13.
34. Ibid., 13–14.
35. De Vito, "Punitive Entanglements," 171.
36. Casares and García Barranco argue this in "Legislation on Free Soil." See also Chira on the circulation in Santiago de Cuba of news about abolition of slavery in the United States (29). In 1866 there were also contested claims that formerly enslaved people from the United States were being smuggled into Cuba to be reenslaved (Ultramar Leg. 4701/61, *Expediente sobre comercio de esclavos*).
37. García Rodríguez, "In Search of Their Rights." Alejandro de la Fuente notes that "the most recent scholarship concentrates on the slaves themselves and on their attempts to find cracks within the Spanish normative system" to be exploited in pursuit of freedom (666).
38. García Rodríguez, "Slaves and the Law," 61.
39. García Rodríguez, *La esclavitud desde la esclavitud.*
40. Casares and García Barranco, 462.
41. "Real Orden declarando que deben considerarse emancipados los esclavos," 39. Cubans were aware of many foreign legal contests concerning free soil: it seems likely, as Casares and García Barranco claim, that they would have learned of the 6 March 1857 decision regarding Dred Scott in the United States – "but willfully and explicitly sought to prevent the legal recognition

of this principle when slaves returned from Cuba from jurisdictions where slavery had been abolished" (467).

42. "Real Orden declarando que los beneficios concedidos," 41.
43. Premo, *The Enlightenment on Trial*, 192.
44. Casares and Barranco, "Legislation on Free Soil," 461.
45. Ultramar Leg. 4700/10 no. 18, *Expediente ... Isidoro Gangá.*
46. Midlo Hall, *Slavery and African Ethnicities,* 80–81, 35.
47. Ultramar Leg. 4700/10 no. 4, *Expediente ... Isidoro Gangá.* Gangá's summary of his case history indicates that he was twenty-five in 1852 when he was convicted of murdering his mayoral.
48. Ultramar Leg. 4700/10 no. 7, *Expediente ... Isidoro Gangá.*
49. Ibid.
50. De Vito, "Punitive Entanglements," 171.
51. Ibid., 172.
52. Martin Márquez, "Transported Identities," 1–30, 2, 21.
53. Lucena Salmoral, *Leyes para esclavos*, 452. See also a request to send *ñáñigos* to the Canary Islands, Ultramar Leg. 4740/62, *Detención de individuos pertenecientes.*
54. de Aranzadi, "Cuban Heritage in Africa." For more on Abakuá and ñáñigos see Quiñones, *Ecorie Abakuá*; Sosa, *Los ñáñigos*; Miller, *Voice of the Leopard*; Brown, *The Light Inside.*
55. De Vito, "Punitive Entanglements," 184.
56. Ibid.
57. Howard, *Changing History*; Perera Díaz and Meriño Fuentes, *El cabildo carabalí*; Barcia Zequeira, Rodríguez Reyes, Niebla Delgado, *Del cabildo de "nación"*; Pérez, *El Cabildo Carabalí Isuama.*
58. Ultramar Leg. 4700/10 no. 7, *Expediente ... Isidoro Gangá.*
59. Perera Díaz and Meriño Fuentes, *Estrategias*, 2:161.
60. Ultramar Leg. 4700/10 no. 13, *Expediente ... Isidoro Gangá.*
61. Ultramar Leg. 4700/10 no. 15, *Expediente ... Isidoro Gangá.*
62. Ultramar Leg. 4700/10 no. 21, *Expediente ... Isidoro Gangá.*
63. Ultramar Leg. 4700/10 no. 18, *Expediente ... Isidoro Gangá.*
64. Ibid.
65. Casares and Barranco, "Legislation on Free Soil," 467.
66. Piqueras, "El gobierno de la población," 45–52.
67. Ultramar Leg. 4700/10 no. 12, *Expediente ... Isidoro Gangá*; Ultramar Leg. 4700/10 no. 21, *Expediente ... Isidoro Gangá.*
68. Ultramar Leg. 4700/10. no. 12, *Expediente ... Isidoro Gangá.*
69. A second lawyer's signature is illegible. Millan was probably D. Francisco de Paula Millan, "abogado de beneficencia, jefe de la secretaria de la Excma. Diputación provincial y secretarios de su comisión permanente, incorporado en 16 de diciembre de 1846." (*Lista de los abogados*, 8).
70. Ultramar Leg. 4700/10 no. 15, *Expediente ... Isidoro Gangá.*
71. Ibid.
72. Ibid.
73. Ibid.
74. Ibid.
75. Ibid.
76. Ultramar Leg. 4700/10 no. 16, *Expediente ... Isidoro Gangá.*
77. Ultramar Leg. 4700/10 no. 18, *Expediente ... Isidoro Gangá.*
78. "Real órden declarando libre á un esclavo fugado de Cuba," 48.
79. "Real órden aprobando el Reglamento," 46. See also Ultramar Leg. 3551/4, *Expediente general de esclavitud.*
80. Ultramar Leg. 4700/10. no. 12, *Expediente ... Isidoro Gangá.*
81. Alina Castellanos (Personal communication 5 March 2020) notes that "an 'activist' or 'humanist' attitude on the part of such defense attorneys was not frequent or even evident" in nineteenth-century Cuba, which took its protocols for assigning pro bono defenders from Spain.
82. Ultramar Leg. 4700/10 no. 27, *Expediente ... Isidoro Gangá.*

83. Ultramar Leg. 4700/10 no. 24, *Expediente ... Isidoro Gangá.*
84. Ultramar Leg. 4700/10 no. 27, *Expediente ... Isidoro Gangá.*
85. Ibid.
86. Ibid.
87. "Real órden declarando libre á todo esclavo que pase á país donde no exista la servidumbre," 48–50.
88. Ibid.
89. Ibid.
90. Ultramar Leg. 4700/10 no. 1, *Expediente ... Isidoro Gangá.*
91. Ultramar Leg. 4700/10 no. 27, *Expediente ... Isidoro Gangá.*
92. http://pares.mcu.es/ParesBusquedas20/catalogo/description/6044633?nm
93. Hartman, *Wayward Lives*; Fuentes, *Dispossessed Lives*; Morgan, *Laboring Women.*
94. See for instance Ultramar Leg. 4715/17, *Expediente de solicitud ... Nicolás Ramírez*, which reads "La Dirección General de Establecimientos Penales remite al Ministerio de Ultramar, para que informe el tribunal sentenciador en Cuba, una instancia del chino esclavo Nicolás Ramírez Viafanes, confinado en el presidio de Melilla, solicitando el alzamiento de la cláusula de retención que tiene su condena" (The Administrative Center for Penal Establishments contacts the Ministry of Ultramar to inform the sentencing tribunal in Cuba of the instance of a Chinese slave Nicolás Ramírez Viafanes, incarcerated in Melilla prison, who requests the lifting of his sentence's retention clause.)
95. A search of the AHN's Ultramar holdings for cases brought by slaves requests the lifting of retention clauses yields eleven files. Only a few are identified as serving time outside of the Caribbean (in Melilla). See Ultramar Leg. 4684/39, *Expediente de alzamiento ... Miguel Canto*, as well as the case of "el chino esclavo" Nicolás Ramirez, cited above, and Ultramar Leg. 4765/71, *Expediente general de confinados políticos de Cuba*, which elaborates: *Expediente del esclavo confinado del presidio de Melilla, Liberato Colás Colás, reputado como emancipado a tenor de lo dispuesto en el Real Decreto de 29 de septiembre de 1866 sobre indemnización a su dueño Antonio Barrionuevo* (File for the slave imprisoned in Melilla, Liberato Colás Colás, held to be emancipated based on the Royal Decree of 29 September 1866 concerning the indemnification of his owner Antonio Barriounevo).
96. Ultramar Leg. 4700/10 no. 10, *Expediente ... Isidoro Gangá*; Ultramar Leg. 4700/10 no. 15, *Expediente ... Isidoro Gangá.*

Acknowledgements

The author thanks David Sartorius, Anya Zilberstein, Adrián López-Denis, and the anonymous reviewers for their assistance with the research, writing, and revision of this article.

Disclosure statement

No potential conflict of interest was reported by the author(s).

Funding

This work was supported by the Program in Latin American Studies at Princeton University.

References

Zequeira, Barcia, María del Carmen, Andrés Rodríguez Reyes, and Milagros Niebla Delgado. *Del cabildo de "nación" a la casa de santo*. Havana: Fundación Fernando Ortiz, 2012.

Brown, Stephen. *The Light Inside: Abakuá Society Arts and Cuban Cultural History*. Washington, DC: Smithsonian Press, 2003.

Casares, Aurelia Martín, and Margarita García Barranco. "Legislation on Free Soil in Nineteenth-Century Spain: The Case of the Slave Rufino and Its Consequences (1858–1879)." *Slavery & Abolition* 32, no. 3 (September 2011): 461–476.

Chaloub, Sidney. "The Precariousness of Freedom in a Slave Society (Brazil in the Nineteenth Century)." *International Review of Social History* 56, no. 3 (November 2011): 405–439.

Chira, Adriana. "Affective Debts: Manumission by Grace and the Making of Gradual Emancipation Laws in Cuba, 1817–68." *Law and History Review* 36, no. 1 (February 2018): 1–33.

Cowling, Camillia. *Conceiving Freedom: Women of Color, Gender, and the Abolition of Slavery in Havana and Rio de Janeiro*. Chapel Hill: University of North Carolina Press, 2013.

De Aranzadi, Isabel. "Cuban Heritage in Africa: Deported Ñáñigos to Fernando Po in the Nineteenth Century." *African Sociological Review* 18, no. 2 (2014): 2–41.

De la Fuente, Alejandro. "Slaves and the Creation of Legal Rights in Cuba: Coartación and Papel." *Hispanic American Historical Review* 87, no. 4 (November 2007): 659–692.

Detención de individuos pertenecientes a la Sociedad llamada Los Ñáñigos, 1876. Archivo Histórico Nacional de Madrid, Ultramar Leg. 4740/62.

De Vito, Christian. "Punitive Entanglements: Connected Histories of Penal Transportation, Deportation, and Incarceration in the Spanish Empire (1830s–1898)." *International Review of Social History* 63, no. 26 (August 2018): 169–189.

del Vas Mingo, Marta Milagros. "El derecho del patronato en los proyectos abolicionistas cubanos." *Anuario de Estudios Americanos* 43 (January 1986): 171–184.

Expediente de alzamiento de cláusula de retención a G. Lucumí, 1856–1857. Archivo Histórico Nacional de Madrid, Ultramar, Leg. 4649/60.

Expediente de alzamiento de cláusula de retención y libertad del negro esclavo Isidoro Gangá, 1863–1866. Archivo Histórico Nacional de Madrid, Ultramar Leg. 4700/10.

Expediente de alzamiento de la cláusula de retención a Miguel Canto. Archivo Histórico Nacional de Madrid, Ultramar Leg. 4684/39.

Expediente de declaración de libertad de la morena María de Jesús por haber estado en Europa, 1871. Archivo Histórico Nacional de Madrid, Ultramar Leg. 4759/25.

Expediente de solicitud de alzamiento de cláusula de retención de Nicolás Ramírez. Archivo Histórico Nacional de Madrid, Ultramar Leg. 4715/17.

Expediente general de confinados políticos de Cuba por infidencia: Deportación de Liberato Colás Colás. Archivo Histórico Nacional de Madrid, Ultramar Leg. 4765/71.

Expediente general de esclavitud: Sobre libertad de los esclavos que vayan a un país donde no exista esclavitud. Archivo Histórico Nacional de Madrid, Ultramar Leg. 3551/4.

Expediente sobre comercio de esclavos con emancipados de Estados Unidos, 1866. Archivo Histórico Nacional de Madrid, Ultramar Leg. 4701/61.

Finch, Aisha. *Rethinking Slave Rebellion in Cuba: La Escalera and the Insurgencies of 1841–1844*. Chapel Hill: University of North Carolina Press, 2015.

Fuentes, Marisa. *Dispossessed Lives: Enslaved Women, Violence, and the Archive*. Philadelphia: University of Pennsylvania Press, 2016.

Garcia Rodríguez, Gloria. "In Search of their Rights: Slaves and Law." In *Breaking the Chains, Forging the Nation: The Afro-Cuban Fight for Freedom and Equality*, edited by Aisha Finch, and Fannie Rushing, 52–64. Baton Rouge: Louisiana State University Press, 2019.

Garcia Rodríguez, Gloria. In *La esclavitud desde la esclavitud: visión de los siervos*. Havana: Editorial Ciencias Sociales, 2003.

Garcia Rodríguez, Gloria. *Voices of the Enslaved: A Documentary History*. Translated by Nancy L. Westrate. Chapel Hill: University of North Carolina Press, 2011.

Ghorbal, Karim. "Medir y utilizar la heterogeneidad: censos, esclavitud y relación colonial en Cuba." In *Orden político y gobierno de esclavos*, edited by José Antonio Piqueras, 53–77. Valencia, Spain: Centro Francisco Tomás y Valiente, 2016.

Hartman, Saidiya. *Wayward Lives, Beautiful Experiments: Intimate Histories of Social Upheaval*. New York: W.W. Norton, 2019.

Howard, Philip. *Changing History: Afro-Cuban Cabildos and Societies of Color in the Nineteenth Century*. Baton Rouge: Lousiana State University Press, 1998.

Las siete partidas del Rey Don Alfonso el sabio, Cotejadas con Varios Codices Antiguos por la Real Academia de la Historia, 3 vols. Madrid: Real Academia de la Historia, 1807.

"Lista de los abogados del ilustre Colegio de Cádiz en el año económico de 1880 a 1881." Accessed August 15, 2019. https://archive.org/stream/CASGA_380316_005/CASGA_380316_005_djvu.txt.

Lorenzo Lucumí confinado pide que se le alce la cláusula de retención, 1861. Archivo Histórico Nacional de Madrid, Ultramar, Leg. 4672/36.

Lucena Salmoral, Manuel. *Leyes para esclavos El ordenamiento jurídico sobre la condición, tratamiento, defensa y represión de los esclavos en las colonias de la América española*. Madrid: Fundación Ignacio Larramendi, 2000. Accessed September 1, 2019. http://www.larramendi.es/i18n/catalogo_imagenes/imagen_id.do?idImagen=10003761.

Martin Marquez, Susan. "Transported Identities: Global Trafficking and Late Imperial Subjectivity in Cuban Narratives on African Penal Colonies." *Journal of Latin American Studies* 51, no. 1 (February 2019): 1–30.

Midlo Hall, Gwendolyn. *Slavery and African Ethnicities in the Americas: Restoring the Links*. Chapel Hill: University of North Carolina Press, 2007.

Miller, Ivor. *Voice of the Leopard: African Secret Societies and Cuba*. Jackson: University of Mississippi Press, 2009.

Morgan, Jennifer. *Laboring Women: Reproduction and Gender in New World Slavery*. Philadelphia: University of Pennsylvania Press, 2004.

Paquette, Robert. *Sugar is Made with Blood: The Conspiracy of La Escalera and the Conflict Between Empires Over Slavery in Cuba*. Middletown, CT: Wesleyan University Press, 1988.

Perera Díaz, Aisnara, and María de los Angeles Meriño Fuentes. *El cabildo carabalí viví de Santiago de Cuba: familia, cultura y sociedad (1797–1909)*. Santiago de Cuba: Editorial Oriente, 2013.

Perera Díaz, Aisnara, and María de los Angeles Meriño Fuentes. *Estrategias de la libertad. Un acercamiento a las acciones legales de los esclavos de Cuba 1762–1872*. 2 Vols. Havana: Editorial de Ciencias Sociales, 2015.

Pérez, Nancy. *El Cabildo Carabalí Isuama*. Santiago: Editorial Oriente, 1998.

Piqueras, José Antonio. "El gobierno de la población heterogénea en la segunda esclavitud." In *Orden político y gobierno de esclavos*, edited by José Antonio Piqueras, 17–52. Valencia, Spain: Centro Francisco Tomás y Valiente, 2016.

Quiñones, Tato. *Ecorie Abakuá: cuatro ensayos sobre los ñáñigos cubanos*. Havana: Ediciones Unión, 1994.

"Real Órden aprobando el Reglamento de Sindicatura de la Habana 1863." In *El libro de los síndicos de ayuntamiento y de las juntas protectoras de libertos. Recopilación cronológica de las disposiciones legales a que deben sujetarse los actos de unos y otras*, edited by Bienvenido Cano and Federico de Zalba, 46. Havana: Impr. del gobierno y capitanía general por S.M., 1875.

"Real órden declarando libre á todo esclavo que pase á país donde no exista la servidumbre, y prohibiendo condenarlos á presidio ultramarino." In *El libro de los síndicos de ayuntamiento y de las juntas protectoras de libertos. Recopilación cronológica de las disposiciones legales a que deben sujetarse los actos de unos y otras*, edited by Bienvenido Cano and Federico de Zalba, 48–50. Havana: Impr. del gobierno y capitanía general por S.M., 1875.

"Real Órden declarando libres á los esclavos que se conduzcan á la Península, 29 March 1836." In *El libro de los síndicos de ayuntamiento y de las juntas protectoras de libertos. Recopilación cronológica de las disposiciones legales a que deben sujetarse los actos de unos y otras*, edited by Bienvenido Cano and Federico de Zalba, 13–14. Havana: Impr. del gobierno y capitanía general por S.M., 1875.

"Real Órden declarando libre á un esclavo fugado de Cuba desde que pise el territorio de la Penísula." In *El libro de los síndicos de ayuntamiento y de las juntas protectoras de libertos. Recopilación cronológica de las disposiciones legales a que deben sujetarse los actos de unos y otras*, edited by Bienvenido Cano and Federico de Zalba, 48. Havana: Impr. del gobierno y capitanía general por S.M., 1875.

"Real Órden declarando que deben considerarse emancipados los esclavos que de cualquier modo vayan á la Península y aunque regresen á la isla, sean reputados como libres, 2 August 1861." In *El libro de los síndicos de ayuntamiento y de las juntas protectoras de libertos. Recopilación cronológica de las disposiciones legales a que deben sujetarse los actos de unos y otras*, edited by Bienvenido Cano and Federico de Zalba, 39–40. Havana: Impr. del gobierno y capitanía general por S.M., 1875.

"Real Órden declarando que los beneficios concedidos por la de 12 de Agosto de 1861 alcanzan á los esclavos que de Cuba y Puerto-Rico vayan á cualquier país donde no se conozca la esclavitud, 12 December 1862." In *El libro de los síndicos de ayuntamiento y de las juntas protectoras de libertos. Recopilación cronológica de las disposiciones legales a que deben sujetarse los actos de unos y otras*, , edited by Bienvenido Cano and Federico de Zalba, 41–42. Havana: Impr. del gobierno y capitanía general por S.M., 1875.

Reid-Vazquez, Michele. *The Year of the Lash: Free People of Color in Cuba and the Nineteenth-Century Atlantic World*. Athens: University of Georgia Press, 2011.

Scott, Rebecca, and Jean Hébrard. *Freedom Papers: An Atlantic Odyssey in The Age of Emancipation*. Cambridge, MA: Harvard University Press, 2012.

Scott, Rebecca. "Social Facts, Legal Fictions, and the Attribution of Slave Status: The Puzzle of Prescription." *Law and History Review* 35, no. 1 (February 2017): 9–30.

Scott, Rebecca. *Degrees of Freedom: Louisiana and Cuba After Slavery*. Cambridge, MA: Belknap Press of Harvard University Press, 2005.

Sosa, Enrique. *Los ñáñigos*. Havana: Casa Las Américas, 1982.

Traslado a la Habana del confinado en Melilla Antonio Gangá, 1863–1864. Archivo Histórico Nacional de Madrid, Ultramar Leg. 4685/63.

Zeuske, Michael. "Out of the Americas: Slave Traders and the *Hidden Atlantic* in the Nineteenth Century." *Atlantic Studies* 15, no. 1 (2018): 103–135.

Appendix

Real órden declarando libre á un esclavo fugado de Cuba desde que pise el territorio de la Península.

1865.—Julio 12.

Excmo. Sr.: Dada cuenta á la Reina [Q.D.G.] de una exposicion dirigida á este Ministerio por el Gobernador de la provincia de Orense, y en la que el negro esclavo Valentin Colon, preso en la cárcel de aquella capital por haberse fugado de esa isla, solicita la declaracion de persona libre; S.M., conformándose con el dictámen del Consejo de Estado en pleno, ha tenido á bien mandar que se considere libre al expresado Valentin Cólon, toda vez que reside en la Península, donde se pierde, con arreglo á las disposiciones vigentes, la cualidad de esclavo de una manera irrevocable. De Real órden etc.—Madrid 12 de Julio de 1865.—Sr. Gobernador Superior Civil de Cuba.

—

Real órden declarando libre á todo esclavo que pase á país donde no exista la servidumbre, y prohibiendo condenarlos á presidio ultramarino.

1866.—Setiembre 29.

En vista de la razones expuestas por el Ministro de Ultramar, y de conformidad con el Consejo de Ministros, vengo en decretar lo siguiente:

Artículo 1. Desde la publicacion en la Gaceta de Madrid del presente decreto todo individuo de color, hombre, mujer ó niño que se hallase constituido en servidumbre en nuestras provincias de Puerto-Rico ó de Cuba, se reputará emancipado y libre al pisar el territorio de la Península y de sus islas adyacentes, ó al llegar á la jurisdiccion marítima y zonas marítimas del mismo, sea cual fuere la causa por la que se verifique el hecho de desembarcar en dicho territorio ó de encontrarse en las aguas de su jurisdiccion marítima. Tambien disfrutara del beneficio de la emancipacion y libertad todo individuo de color, siendo esclavo, cuando en compañía de sus amos ó enviados por ellos pise el territorio ó entre en la jurisdiccion de cualquier Estado en que la esclavitud no exista.

Art. 2. Se prohibe para lo sucesivo la condena á presidio ultramarino con retencion y venta por razon de noxa contra los individuos de color que se hallen en servidumbre. Los criminales á quienes siendo esclavos se les imponga la pena de presidio con retención y sus acesorios las extinguirán en los presidios de las islas de Cuba y Puerto-Rico.

Art. 3. Si el beneficio de la emancipacion y libertad otorgada por el artículo 1° recayese en individuos que hubiesen venido al territorio de la Península y de sus islas adyacentes en virtud de sentencia de los Tribunales de Cuba y Puerto-Rico, siendo allí esclavos el todo ó la parte de indemnizacion á que hubiera de atender con la venta del esclavo ya emancipado y que se prohíbe, se satisfará del modo que determinen en cada caso disposiciones especiales. Dicha indemnización nunca será mayor de lo que hubiera podido producir por término medio la adjudicacion del esclavo en remate público.

Art. 4. Cuando la venta por razon de noxa tuviera por objeto el pago de las costas procesales, se declararán estas de oficio en todos los casos; el esclavo emancipado al venir á la Península para cumplir su condena quedará sujeto en su condicion de hombre libre á indemnizar los daños y perjuicios á las responsabilidades civiles en los términos que prefijen las leyes.

Art. 5. El Ministro de Ultramar dictará las instrucciones convenientes para la ejecucion del presente decreto y para organizar los establecimientos presidiales en término de poder cumplirse en ellos la sentencia á que se refiere el articulo 2°. -Dado en Palacio á veinte y nueve de Setiembre de mil ochocientos sesenta y seis.—Está rubricado de la Real mano.—El Ministro de Ultramar, Alejando Castro.

—

Royal Order declaring free any slave fleeing Cuba upon setting foot in the territory of the Peninsula.

1865.—July 12.

Most Excellent Sir: Upon the Queen's awareness of an exposition directed to this Ministry by the Governor of the province of Orense, and in which the black slave Valentin Colon, prisoner in the jail of that capital for having fled that island, solicits the declaration of free person; Your Excellency, in conformity with the dictamen of the full Council of State, has seen fit to order that said Valentin Colón be considered free, so long as he resides in the Peninsula, where he loses, per arrangement of the current dispositions, in an irrevocable manner, the quality of slave. By Royal Order etc. Madrid 12 July 1865. Sir Civil Governor Superior of Cuba.

—

Royal Order declaring free any slave that goes to a country where servitude does not exist, and prohibiting their sentencing to overseas prisons.

1866.—September 29.

In light of the reasons put forth by the Minister of Ultramar, and in conformity with the Council of Ministers, I hereby decree the following:

Article 1. Since the publication in the Madrid Gazette of the present decree any individual of color, man woman or child that finds him or herself in servitude in our provinces of Puerto-Rico or Cuba, shall consider him or herself emancipated and free upon setting foot in the territory of the Peninsula and its adjacent islands, or upon arriving at maritime jurisdiction and zones of the same, whatever may be the cause by which is verified the fact of disembarking in said territory or of finding oneself in the waters of its maritime jurisdiction. Any enslaved individual of color will also enjoy the benefit of emancipation and freedom when, in the company of his owners or sent by them, he or she steps upon the territory or enters the jurisdiction of any State in which slavery does not exist.

Art. 2. It is henceforth prohibited to sentence individuals of color who find themselves in servitude to overseas prisons with retention and sale for the reason of noxa [damages by a slave]. Criminals who being slaves receive the punishment of prison with retention will serve out their sentences and accessories in the islands of Cuba and Puerto Rico.

Art. 3. If the benefit of emancipation and freedom granted by Article 1 should fall to individuals who have come to the territory of the Peninsula and its adjacent islands by sentencing from the Cuban and Puerto Rican Tribunals, being slaves there, all or part of the indemnification which attends the prohibited sale of the now emancipated slave, will be satisfied by the manner that special dispositions determine in each case. Said indemnification will never be greater than that which might have been produced on average through the adjudication of the slave at public auction.

Art. 4. When the sale for reason of noxa has as its object the payment of processing costs, these shall be declared born by the state in all cases [ex oficio]; the emancipated slave upon coming to the Peninsula to serve out his sentence will remain subject in his condition of free man to indemnify the damages and prejudices to the civil responsibilities in the terms that the laws have specified.

Art. 5. The Minister of Ultramar will order the instructions appropriate for the execution of the present decree and to organize the carceral establishments in terms of being able to realize in them the sentence referred to in the second article.—Given at the Palace the twenty-ninth of September of eighteen hundred and sixty six.—Signed by the Royal Hand.— Minister of Ultramar, Alejandro Castro (Cano and Zalba, El libro de los Síndicos, 48–50).

Index

Note: Endnotes are indicated by the page number followed by 'n' and the endnote number e.g., 20n1 refers to endnote 1 on page 20.

For Product Safety Concerns and Information please contact our EU representative GPSR@taylorandfrancis.com
Taylor & Francis Verlag GmbH, Kaufingerstraße 24, 80331 München, Germany

www.ingramcontent.com/pod-product-compliance
Lightning Source LLC
Chambersburg PA
CBHW081357090726
47908CB00011B/2712
9781032523408